# Structure for Communicating Effectively

**Revised Edition**

D1411248

Christian Liberty Press   1996   Arlington Heights, Illinois

Originally written by Annie Lee Sloan for Christian Liberty Press
Completely revised and updated by Garry J. Moes

A publication of

# Christian Liberty Press

502 West Euclid Avenue

Arlington Heights, Illinois 60004

Scripture references are conformed to The Holy Bible, New King James Version ©1982, Thomas Nelson, Inc., so that modern readers may gain greater comprehension of the Word of God.

Moes, Garry J.

    APPLICATIONS OF GRAMMAR, BOOK 2

    STRUCTURE FOR COMMUNICATING EFFECTIVELY

    Includes glossary and index

    1. English Language—Grammar

Editing by Edward J. Shewan

Layout and cover design by Eric D. Bristley

Printed in the United States of America

# PREFACE

This book is intended to lay a proper foundation for the student's effectiveness in communicating with the English language. The student will learn the basics of English grammar, including the definition and usage of verbs, nouns, adjectives, adverbs, and other parts of speech. In addition, the student will examine how these are to be properly used in phrases, clauses, sentences, paragraphs, and composition. The *Applications of Grammar* series is designed to develop students' skills in using the rules of grammar to communicate effectively for the glory of God.

While some today would discard the need for grammar, this text affirms that the learning of grammatical rules and their proper usage is foundational to good communication. The distinctions between words, their relation to each other in a sentence, and the rules that govern language are the basic building blocks of writing well.

This text is designed to be read carefully by the student so that he may review the grammar knowledge he has already learned and build upon it with new skills. Each lesson should be read carefully and reviewed as necessary. Some of the words used in the text may be new to the student's vocabulary, and their spelling unfamiliar. Therefore, a glossary and index are located at the back of this volume to provide students and teachers with additional reference material.

Many of the lessons will require use of a dictionary. While an unabridged dictionary would be useful, a standard, full-sized, collegiate-level dictionary will be more useful. Small, pocket-size, or greatly abridged desktop editions will likely not provide the amount of information which the student will need to complete many of the lessons in this book. It would also be helpful if the student had access to a set of encyclopedias or other reference works. These will be useful in the several writing assignments included in this textbook. If your school or home does not have adequate resources of this nature, you should visit your local library.

# THE AUTHOR AND EDITOR

**Garry J. Moes** is a free-lance writer, textbook author, and editorial communications consultant. He earned his B.A. in journalism from Michigan State University, East Lansing Michigan, and did postgraduate research at Scandinavian Christian University's Nordic College of Journalism in Sweden. He was a writer, reporter, and editor for The Associated Press for twenty-one years, and has been an essayist, international correspondent, and executive editor for several Christian periodicals.

**Edward J. Shewan** is an editor and writer for Christian Liberty Press. He graduated from Valparaiso University with a B.S. degree in 1974. After a year of mission work in Africa, he attended the Moody Bible Institute's Advanced Studies Program in 1976. Subsequently, he served in Chicago city churches for ten years. In 1983 he graduated from Trinity Evangelical Divinity School with the M.Div. degree. He has also done free-lance editing for David C. Cook Publishing. Ed is the author of *How to Study: A Practical Guide from a Christian Perspective* and *Writing a Research Paper*, both published by Christian Liberty Press.

## TABLE OF CONTENTS

# Introduction

## THE CHRISTIAN VIEW OF LANGUAGE

Students often wonder why they have to study grammar and composition when they already know how to talk and write. Although basic communication skills may be evident, every student needs to thoroughly learn not only how language works but how to use it accurately. In order to speak and write well, students must acquire a proper understanding of grammatical definitions, functions, structures, and rules so that they may verbalize their thoughts with clarity and precision. Few skills are more important to Christian students than the ability to effectively communicate through the written and spoken word.

The student will be able to study language more purposefully if he begins with an understanding of the Christian view of language. Sadly, some students merely study language and grammar because they have been made to do so. They fail to grasp that, because we are made in God's image, good communication is essential to our service of God. As an image bearer of God, the student should consider how the Bible can direct his study of language. Through faith in Jesus Christ he can be reconciled to God and learn how to use language to the end for which it was created. Because language did not originate with us, we do not have the right to use it any way we wish. We must be guided by the Bible. Language skills are not neutral; they must be oriented toward reading, writing, and speaking the truth in love. Linguistic abilities should be developed as part of the student's chief end to glorify God and enjoy Him forever.

## GOD IS THE ORIGIN OF LANGUAGE

> In the beginning God created the heaven and the earth. And the earth was without form and void; and darkness was upon the face of the deep. And the Spirit of God moved over the face of the waters. And God *said* ... (Genesis 1:1-3).

God is the origin of language, for the three persons of the Trinity spoke to each other before time began. When the Father, the Son, and the Holy Spirit speak to each other eternally, their communication is perfect; there is never one word of misunderstanding! The Son of God is called the *Word* of God and the Holy Spirit searches the mind of God and communicates with spiritual words (1 Corinthians 2:10-13). When God created the heavens and the earth, He spoke it into existence by the Word of His power. When He spoke, He uttered a series of sounds—audible symbols which communicated His meaning and brought the creation into being. When God spoke, His Word conveyed both infinite power and eternal meaning—*infinite power* because He manifested His absolute will, and *eternal meaning* because He expressed His infinite mind. His infinite wisdom is revealed in creation, and the creatures He has made serve the purpose of communicating His glory. Thus the rock, for example, is used as a picture of God's unchanging character. Creation itself was designed to provide the basic terms and environment for language.

# GOD GAVE MAN THE GIFT OF LANGUAGE

When God created man in His own image, He gave him the gift of language—the ability to communicate with words. He gave man the ability, like Himself, to convey meaning with his words, but He did not impart the infinite creative power of His speech. Thus, God's Word is the final authority, and men are to speak in submission to that Word. The language of man is to be subject to God, for man by his speech has no power to create or change what God has made. Yet there is a great power to human speech. It not only sets on fire the course of our lives but the course of history as well (James 3:6).

Because language is a gift of God, it has a purpose. It was given first of all as the means by which God would communicate to man. As such, it has a high and holy place in our lives. From the beginning God chose to communicate with man. The first words spoken to Adam and Eve were His charge, "Be fruitful, and multiply, and replenish the earth..." (Genesis 1:28). God's desire to communicate with Adam and Eve in the Garden of Eden was central to their fellowship. They "heard the voice of the Lord God walking in the cool of the day..." (Genesis 3:8). Secondly, language was given so that man would respond to God. God created mankind to praise His name and answer His call. Thirdly, it was given for men to communicate with each other in subjection to God's word. People were given the ability to talk to one another and thereby develop marriage, the family, and other social relationships. The primary instrument for building these relationships is verbal communication. God's purpose for language should direct our study of it.

# RULES FOR COMMUNICATION

For many students, rules are a burden to be disregarded. But the student who is willing to submit to God's order will seek to develop precision in communicating. Because God is a God of order and truth, He has demonstrated the proper use of language in His speech from the dawn of history. For people to communicate properly and effectively with one another, God not only gave language but with it the basic principles of good communication. This does not mean that we have a divinely revealed set of rules from God, but we can learn from the Bible's use of language and build upon the principles that have been learned in the past. In particular, the Bible and the Christian religion have had a central role in molding the English language.

Consequently, the study of grammar—the body of rules for speaking and writing—should be based on the fact that God is the Creator of language and thereby the originator of its order. Good grammar reflects His logic and manifests the orderly structure of His mind. By learning the rules of proper usage, the student will know how to make his thoughts known and communicate in a compelling manner. His purpose is not simply to be able to communicate, however, but to use language effectively to communicate God's truth.

Language and grammar are not mere human conventions which spring from chance evolution to fill a human need. Language expresses a people's culture, religion, and history. This is why language changes over time. Each language has its own characteristics and rules of usage. But every language displays an underlying unity with other languages. Every language is a verbal system of communication. Each has similar patterns of grammar, though not expressed in exactly the same way. Yet at bottom, the basic principles of grammatical structure are common to every language, which is why writings from one language can be translated into another. While the basic principles of grammar may be adapted in unique ways, these are derived from the original language given by God to man.

## LANGUAGE CORRUPTED BY SIN

After our first parents sinned, the same Voice that spoke the world into existence now stood in judgment over mankind. And the language that had been given as a gift to man by the Father of Truth had now been distorted by the Father of Lies. That which was created to praise and worship God had now been used to rebel against the Author of language. Man's fellowship with the Living God had been broken and he no longer desired to hear Him speak.

In addition, the Bible tells us that after the Great Flood, men united by a common language sought unity apart from God at the Tower of Babel. Seeing this, God confused their one language by dividing it into many, and scattered them over the face of the whole earth. Language was thus changed by God to keep men from disobeying His mandate. Because of these different languages there are now barriers between men when they communicate. And sin has continued to pervert the use of language, making it an instrument of lies and manipulation. Today, there are those who would reject all form and grammar and seek to justify any use of language and any breaking of the rules of grammar. As a result, confusion reigns in many quarters, and many people have great difficulty clearly articulating their thoughts in speech and writing.

## THE RESTORATION OF LANGUAGE IN JESUS CHRIST

God chose to restore language in His Son. Jesus, as the second Adam, was sent into the world to undo the sin of the first Adam and its consequences (Romans 5:19). Jesus, who is the Word, was with God in the creation because He is God (John 1:1-3). Jesus is the *logos* or revelation of God to man, for God has spoken to us in His Son (Hebrews 1:1). There is no other name under heaven given among men, whereby we must be saved (Acts 4:12). God's will to communicate with man was one factor that motivated Him to restore language to its rightful state in Christ Jesus. By His death and resurrection, Christ not only provides forgiveness of sin, but also newness of life to those who receive Him by faith. As the Truth, Christ calls his disciples to speak the oracles of God (1 Peter 4:11), lay aside lies, and speak truth to one another (Ephesians 4:25). Jesus is the true source of the meaning of all things. He declared, "I am the Alpha and Omega, the beginning and the ending, saith the Lord, which is, and which was, and which is to come, the Almighty" (Rev. 1:8). As R. J. Rushdoony states:

> Christ's statement has reshaped Western languages and grammars, and, through Bible translation, is reshaping the languages of peoples all over the world. Bible translation is an exacting task, because it involves in effect the reworking of a language in order to make it carry the meaning of the Bible. This means a new view of the world, of God, time and language…. Our ideas of grammar, of tense,[1] syntax, and structure, of thought and meaning, bear a Christian imprint.

Students who profess the Christian faith should have a unique appreciation of the role of ver-

---

[1].    Rousas J. Rushdoony, *The Philosophy of the Christian Curriculum* (Vallecito, CA: Ross House Books, 1985), p. 49-50.

bal communication. It is the Christian, above all, who should seek to be clear and accurate in his use of the written word. His God-given duty is to use language with integrity and accuracy for the sake of promoting the gospel and Kingdom of Jesus Christ. Noah Webster saw this in his day when he wrote:

> If the language can be improved in regularity, so as to be more easily acquired by our own citizens, and by foreigners, and thus be rendered a more useful instrument for the propagation of science, arts, civilization and Christianity; if it can be rescued from the mischievous influence of ...that dabbling spirit of innovation which is perpetually disturbing its settled usages and filling it with anomalies; if, in short, our vernacular language can be redeemed from corruptions, and...our literature from degradation; it would be a source of great satisfaction to me to be
>
> one among the instruments of promoting these valuable objects. [2]

To show that the Christian has the marvelous opportunity to employ language and its power for the service of the gospel, Gary DeMar asserts:

> Ideas put to paper and acted upon with the highest energy and uncompromising zeal can change the world. Even the worst ideas have been used for this very purpose. If minds are going to be transformed and civilizations changed, then Christians must learn to write and write well. Writing is a sword, mightier than all the weapons of war because writing carries with it ideas that penetrate deeper than any bullet. Writing about the right things in the right way can serve as an antidote to the writings of skepticism and tyranny that have plundered the hearts
>
> and minds of generations of desperate people around the world ... [3]

Language as the gift of God needs to be cultivated for serving God. It will not only help the student in academic studies, but in every area of communication, at home, at church, and on the job. Proper English skills are a great asset in serving Christ effectively in one's calling. The student's skill in using English will make a good first impression when he sits for an interview and as he labors in the workplace. The student should take advantage of the time and opportunity he now has available to develop proficiency in English communication. May God bless you as you seek to glorify Him, not only by learning the proper use of English, but in using God's gift of language to spread His Word to every nation.

---

[2].    Noah Webster, *An American Dictionary of the English Language* (New York, NY: S. Converse, 1828); reprint by (San Francisco, CA: Foundation for American Christian Education, 1987), preface.

[3].    Gary DeMar, *Surviving College Successfully* (Brentwood, TN: Wolgemuth & Hyatt Publishers, Inc., 1988), p.225.

# Unit 1
# Using Words

---

## LESSON 1: PARTS OF SPEECH

> **SPEECH is communication or expression of thoughts in spoken words.**
>
> **PARTS OF SPEECH are the classifications of words, to one of which every word must belong.**
> **[English has eight such classifications: noun, pronoun, verb, adjective, adverb, preposition, conjunction, interjection.]**

Although there are many ways to communicate, such as through pictures, gestures, facial expressions, and physical objects, the primary means of communication is the *word*. Words may be spoken or written. Spoken words are sounds or combinations of sounds which represent ideas. Written words are symbols expressing the sounds of spoken words, and they also represent ideas. In either case, words are used in many different ways. In order that our ideas can be communicated in standard ways that everyone can understand, words have been classified according to their **function** in communication. In English, words fall into eight categories called the **parts of speech**. They are listed in the charts below. Learn the contents of these charts.

| USE | EXPLANATION | EXAMPLES |
|---|---|---|
| **1. NOUNS** | Words that name a person, place, thing, idea, or quality | book, tree, lamp, sister, can, clock, James, Iowa, etc. |
| **2. PRONOUNS** | Words that are used in place of nouns | he, she, us, them, everyone, either, who, which, this, etc. |
| **3. VERBS** | Words that express action or a state of being or that help other verbs complete their meaning | run, eat, sleep, tell, be, see, smell, overcome, pray, etc. |

| USE | EXPLANATION | EXAMPLES |
|---|---|---|
| **4. ADJECTIVES** | Words that modify (describe or limit) nouns or pronouns | **tall, easy, green, happy, scenic, improper, new, etc.** |
| **5. ADVERBS** | Words that modify (describe or limit) verbs, adjectives, or other adverbs | **closely, smoothly, easily, plainly, nicely, soon, etc.** |
| **6. PREPOSITIONS** | Words used to show the relationship of a noun or pronoun to some other word in a sentence | **under, around, above, to, for, of, in, near, over, etc.** |
| **7. CONJUNCTIONS** | Words that connect words or groups of words | **and, or, but, although, because, if, since, that, etc.** |
| **8. INTERJECTIONS** | Words that exclaim or express strong feelings or surprise but have little or no grammatical connection with other words in a sentence | **Oh!, Wow!, Phew!, Hey!, Alas!, Goodness!, etc.** |

## NOUNS AND THEIR USE

Nouns are classified into two groups: ***common*** and ***proper***. Proper nouns name a *particular* person, place, or thing. When written, they begin with a capital letter. Common nouns are *general* in nature, naming no particular person, place, or thing. Here are some examples:

| PROPER | COMMON | PROPER | COMMON |
|---|---|---|---|
| Fred | grandfather | Mr. Robert Rodgers | teacher |
| England | country | Capitol | building |
| Nevada | state | Microsoft | business |
| Tulsa | city | John Adams | president |
| Mrs. Winslow | woman | Christianity | religion |

Nouns are also classified according to their ***use*** in sentences. They may be used in six different ways. These are: ***subjects***, ***direct objects***, ***indirect objects***, ***objects of prepositions***, ***predicate nominatives***, and ***appositives***.

| USE | EXPLANATION | EXAMPLES |
|---|---|---|
| **SUBJECT** | The *subject* of a sentence is the word or group of words about which the sentence makes a statement. | *The **weather*** has been pleasant lately. |
| **DIRECT OBJECT** | A *direct object* is a word or group of words that receives the action of a verb. | He hammered a ***nail*** into the plank. |

| INDIRECT OBJECT | An *indirect object* precedes a direct object and indicates to whom or for whom the action of the verb is done. | She gave her ***mother*** a loving embrace. |
| OBJECT OF A PREPOSITION | An *object of a preposition* is a word or group of words following a preposition. The preposition relates its object to some other word or words in the sentence. | The subject <u>of</u> his ***speech*** has been a matter <u>of</u> ***controversy*** <u>during</u> the past ***week***. |
| PREDICATE NOMINATIVE | A *predicate nominative* is a word or group of words following a linking verb and renaming the subject of a sentence or clause. | The man in the truck is the ***foreman*** of the construction project. |
| APPOSITIVE | An *appositive* is a word that follows a nominative (noun, pronoun, or noun-like group of words) and that renames or identifies the first nominative. | George Washington, the first ***President*** of the United States, was from Virginia. |

## PRONOUNS

**Pronouns** are words that are used in the place of nouns to avoid repeating those nouns unnecessarily. They may be used in the same six ways that nouns can be used: as **subjects, direct objects, indirect objects, objects of prepositions, predicate nominatives,** and **appositives.** The noun a pronoun refers to is called the pronoun's **antecedent.** In the sentence "David straightened his room," *David* is the antecedent of the pronoun *his.*

There are eight different types of pronouns. Each type has a special purpose. Study the following chart to understand the use of each type of pronoun.

| TYPE | USE | EXAMPLES |
|---|---|---|
| PERSONAL | Refers to individuals in the same way that a noun is used | **I, me, we, us, you, he, him, she, her, it, they, them** |
| PERSONAL—POSSESSIVE | Indicates possession; is used in the same way that an adjective is used | **my, mine, your, yours, his, her, hers, its, their, theirs, whose** |
| INDEFINITE | Somewhat less exact in meaning than other pronouns, it is called *indefinite* because it does not refer to any particular *antecedent* (a noun or pronoun to which a pronoun refers). | **anybody, anyone, each, one, many, most, either, neither, nobody, no one, one, none, all, some, any, everybody, someone, few** |

| TYPE | USE | EXAMPLES |
|------|-----|----------|
| RELATIVE | Connects or "relates" adjective clauses to the rest of the sentence | that, which, who, whom, whose, whoever, whomever, whichever, whatever |
| DEMONSTRATIVE | Points out and identifies persons or things | this, that, these, those, such |
| INTERROGATIVE | Introduces a question | who, whom, what, which, whoever, whichever, whatever, whose |
| RECIPROCAL | Indicates an interchange of action suggested by a verb | each other (interchange between two) one another (interchange between three or more) |
| COMPOUND REFLEXIVE & INTENSIVE ("self" pronouns) | **Reflexive:** follows verbs or prepositions and "reflects" back to the subject **Intensive:** is used as an appositive and "intensifies" or emphasizes the noun or pronoun that it follows | myself, ourselves, yourself, yourselves, himself, herself, itself, themselves, oneself |

## VERBS

**Verbs** are words that express action or a state or condition of being, or that help another verb complete its meaning. There are three kinds of verbs to serve these three purposes: *action verbs, linking verbs,* and *helping (auxiliary) verbs*.

*Action verbs* usually involve some kind of physical, mental, or emotional activity. *Linking verbs* express a state of being or condition of existence. They "link" the subject of the sentence to a noun, pronoun, adjective, or group of words following the verb which either rename or describe the subject (predicate nominative or predicate adjective). *Helping verbs* combine with main verbs and assist in completing their meaning. The most common helping verbs are *be, have, do, shall, will, should, would, may, might, can, could, must, ought, let, need, used, dare* and their various forms.

Verbs take many forms to express differences in the *time of the action* (**tense**), to indicate from which *perspective the action is done* (**voice**), to indicate the *nature of the action* (**tone**), and to characterize the *state of mind associated with the verb (***mood***)*. These different forms are all built around FOUR BASIC FORMS, known as the *four principal parts* of verbs.

The four principal parts are called:

- First: *present (infinitive)* — I *climb* out of bed every morning.
- Second: *present participle* — I am *climbing* the ladder.
- Third: *past* — I *climbed* the tree yesterday.
- Fourth: *past participle* — I have *climbed* this mountain before.

Here are a few other examples of each type of verb:

| ACTION VERBS | PRINCIPAL PARTS | LINKING VERBS | PRINCIPAL PARTS | HELPING VERBS | PRINCIPAL PARTS |
|---|---|---|---|---|---|
| to see | see, seeing, saw, seen | to be | be, being, was/were, been | to have | have, having, had, had |
| to run | run, running, ran, run | to seem | seem, seeming, seemed, seemed | to do | do, doing, did, done |
| to pay | pay, paying, paid, paid | to feel | feel, feeling, felt, felt | to be | be, being, was, been |
| to eat | eat, eating, ate, eaten | to sound | sound, sounding, sounded, sounded | can | can, —, could, — |

## ADJECTIVES

**Adjectives** are words that modify nouns or pronouns. To "modify" means "to limit" or "describe." Adjectives modify nouns or pronouns by making their meanings more exact, which adds interest to writing.

Adjectives answer the questions **what kind? which one? how many?** or **how much?** about the nouns or pronouns they modify.

| WHAT KIND? | WHICH ONE(S)? | HOW MANY? | HOW MUCH? |
|---|---|---|---|
| an *easy* assignment | the *only* answer | *thirteen* years | *some* sand |
| a *large* deposit | the *third* member | *two more* attempts | *less* leakage |
| *boiled* eggs | the *oldest* brother | *no* reason | *more* compassion |
| the *white* carnation | *these* books | a *thousand* pardons | a *large* volume |
| the *heavy, iron* gate | the *early* bird | a *few* spectators | the *most* precipitation |
| the *hot, bubbly* mixture | the *worst* illness | *many* explanations | the *least* interest |

## ■ *Adjective Location:*

Usually, an adjective *immediately precedes the noun or pronoun it modifies* (see examples in the chart above). Adjectives may also be placed in the predicate (non-subject) portion of a sentence *following a linking verb*. In such cases, an adjective modifying a subject is called a *predicate adjective*.

☞**EXAMPLE:**

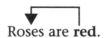

Roses are **red**.

## ■ *Articles:*

The common small words *a, an,* and *the* are called *articles* and they too function as adjectives because they limit (or modify) nouns. (Even though the examples in the chart above are not italicized, they are still considered as adjectives.)

## ADVERBS

**Adverbs** are words that modify verbs, adjectives, or other adverbs. Adverbs usually answer such questions as *how? how much? to what extent? how often? when? where?* or *in which way?* about the words they modify. Here are some examples of adverbs:

| HOW?<br>In Which Way? | HOW MUCH?<br>To What Extent? | WHEN?<br>How Often? | WHERE? | OTHERS |
|---|---|---|---|---|
| warmly, completely, lovingly, slowly, well, happily, timidly, sadly, wrongfully, quietly | only, quite, fully, too, nearly, particularly, so, almost, not, largely, very, more, quite | always, never, annually, once, later, yearly, now, finally, seldom, usually, sometimes, twice, soon | here, there, nowhere, out, somewhere, away, back, around, outside, behind, anywhere, up | yes, no, perhaps, maybe, however, nevertheless, furthermore, moreover |

☞ **EXAMPLES:**

**Adverb modifying a verb:** The rocket rose **quickly** above the clouds.

**Adverb modifying an adjective:** We all had a **rather** tiring day of sightseeing.

**Adverb modifying another adverb:** The mold grew **quite** slowly in the lab dish.

## ■ *Adverb Endings:*

Adverbs have three common endings, *-ly, -wise,* and *-ways,* which may help you identify them. Of course, not all adverbs have these endings. Furthermore, sometimes adjectives end with *-ly*; so you must always check to see which word is being modified before you assume that an *-ly* word is an adverb. But in many cases, adding *-ly* to an adjective will change it into an adverb: *(quiet > quietly, hot > hotly, sudden > suddenly)*. Some nouns can be changed into adverbs by adding *-wise* or *-ways*: *(length > lengthwise, side > sideways)*.

✎ **EXERCISE A** Identify which *part of speech* each of the words in **dark print** is by writing one of the following abbreviations above the word: **N** (noun), **P** (pronoun), **AV** (action verb), **LV** (linking verb), **HV** (helping verb), **ADJ** (adjective), **ADV** (adverb).

    N   LV  N     N

1.  **Music is** a **gift** from **God.**

2.  Everyone loves a **winner**.

3.  The **horse** in the **corral is wild**.

4.  The **baby awoke** when the **door slammed shut**.

5.  **Mary said she had read that book before**.

6.  **I must write** a **letter** to my **grandmother** to thank **her** for the **gift**.

7.  **Check carefully** to see that **you are answering** the **questions correctly**.

8.  **She was happy** to see the **card** she **received** in the **mail**.

9.  **We must hold** to the **faith** of our **fathers**.

10. "The **doctor will be happy** to see **you now**," the **nurse said**.

✎   **EXERCISE B** Identify the *use* of the nouns in **dark print** by writing one of the following abbreviations above them: **S** (subject), **DO** (direct object), **IO** (indirect object), **OP** (object of a preposition), **PN** (predicate nominative), **A** (appositive).

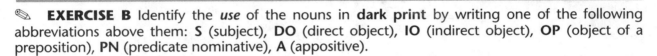

     *S*       *A*                 *OP*            *DO*
1.  **Mike**, the **mechanic** at a nearby **shop**, repaired my **motorbike**.

2.  The **telephone** in the **kitchen** is ringing.

3.  **Mr. Johnson** offered the **boys** a **job** for the **summer**.

4.  **Jesus** is the **Son** of **God**.

5.  **Ronald Reagan**, the 40th **President**, was formerly the **governor** of **California**.

✎   **EXERCISE C** Identify the pronouns in **dark print** by writing one of the following abbreviations above them: **P** (personal), **PP** (personal possessive), **I** (indefinite), **INT** (interrogative), **R** (reciprocal), or **C** (compound). (Consider two-word pronouns to be one word.)

     *P*  *PP*             *I*
1.  **He** is **my** father, as **everyone** knows.

2.  **We** must love **each other** more.

3.  **Everybody** thinks **you** are **her** sister.

4.   **Who** wants to make **himself** a hot dog?

5.   Did **they** hurt **themselves**?

6.   **You** all must forgive **one another**.

# LESSON 2: MORE PARTS OF SPEECH

## *PREPOSITIONS*

A **preposition** is a part of speech that *shows the relationship* of a noun or pronoun (the object of the preposition) to some other word or words in a sentence. In the sentence "The horse trotted **across** the bridge" the preposition *across* relates the verb *trotted* to the noun *bridge*. *Bridge* is the object of the preposition. Very often prepositions show a relationship of direction (to, down), of location (by, in), or of association (with, of). Familiarize yourself with the most common prepositions:

| PREPOSITIONS | | | |
|---|---|---|---|
| aboard | beneath | inside | save |
| about | beside | into | since |
| above | between | like | than |
| across | beyond | near | through |
| after | by | notwithstanding | throughout |
| against | by reason of | of | till |
| along | by way of | off | to |
| alongside | concerning | on | toward |
| amid | contrary to | onto | under |
| amidst | despite | opposite | underneath |
| among | down | out of | until |
| around | due to | outside | unto |
| at | during | over | up |
| atop | ere | past | upon |
| because of | except | per | with |
| before | excepting | pertaining to | within |
| behind | for | regarding | without |
| below | in | regardless of | worth |

## ■ *Prepositional Phrases and Word Order:*

A preposition does not stand alone in a sentence. It must have an object—a noun or pronoun. A preposition and its object, plus any words modifying the object, form a ***prepositional phrase***. Usually, the preposition should be *placed before its object*, although there may be some exceptions. The best rule is this: *if the prepositional phrase can smoothly be written or spoken with the object following the preposition, use that arrangement*. Be especially careful not to end a sentence with a preposition, unless awkwardness or a lack of clarity would result.

# CONJUNCTIONS

A **conjunction** is a part of speech used to *connect* words or groups of words such as phrases, clauses, or (occasionally) sentences. There are two types of conjunctions: *coordinating conjunctions* and *subordinating conjunctions*. *Coordinating conjunctions* connect grammatical elements of *equal* rank. *Subordinating conjunctions* connect grammatical elements of *unequal* rank. The only use of subordinating conjunctions is to join a *dependent clause* to an *independent clause* (see glossary for definitions of these terms).

The following is a chart showing examples of conjunctions.

| COORDINATING CONJUNCTIONS | SUBORDINATING CONJUNCTIONS |
|---|---|
| **SIMPLE:**<br>and, or, but, nor, neither, yet<br><br>**CORRELATIVE:**<br>either...or, neither...nor, not only...but also, both...and | after, although, as, as if, as much as, as long as, as soon as, because, before, if, in order that, lest, since, so that, than, that, though, unless, until, when, whenever, where, wherever, whether, while |
| ☞**EXAMPLES:**<br><br>Jessica **and** Brittany are friends.<br><br>**Either** wash the dishes **or** dust the furniture.<br><br>He is short, **but** he is a good basketball player.<br><br>They were **both** tired **and** hungry. | ☞**EXAMPLES:**<br><br>*If* we can get ready on time, we will be there.<br><br>He always prays **before** he eats.<br><br>She acted **as if** she did not know me.<br><br>The little boy has been lonely **since** his dog ran away.<br><br>I will water your plant **while** you are on vacation.<br><br>We need not fear **as long as** Christ is near us. |

# INTERJECTIONS

The eighth part of speech, the **interjection**, is unique in that it has little or no grammatical relationship to other words in a sentence in which it is found. In fact, in some cases, interjections can stand alone outside of a sentence.

Interjections are words that make a mild or major exclamation. They should be used only sparingly. They are intended to add special emphasis, and if overused, their effect is lost.

The following is a list of the most common interjections of the English language:

| INTERJECTIONS | | | |
|---|---|---|---|
| ah | alas | bah | bravo |
| aha | amen | behold | certainly |
| ahem | attention | boo | eh |
| ahoy | ay | botheration | encore |

| INTERJECTIONS (cont.) | | | |
|---|---|---|---|
| eureka | hooray | O | what |
| excellent | huh | off | why |
| goodbye | hurrah | oh | whoa |
| goodness | hush | ouch | whoopee |
| ha | indeed | pshaw | woe |
| halloo | listen | so | yahoo |
| hello | lo | tush | yea |
| hey | my | tut | yippee |
| ho | nonsense | | |

Certain "swear words" (profanities, blasphemies, and vulgarities) are also considered, grammatically, to be interjections; but Christians must avoid their use since such speech is condemned by God in the Bible *(Ephesians 4:29, Colossians 3:8, Exodus 20:7)*.

## ■ *Punctuating Interjections:*

Interjections are often followed by an exclamation point. However, mild interjections may be followed by a comma or period. A few may be followed by a question mark. If you use an exclamation point or question mark, the next word should be capitalized.

✎ **EXERCISE A** Identify the words in **dark print** by writing one of the following abbreviations above them: **P** (preposition), **C** (conjunction), **I** (interjection).

      *I*       *P*               *C*                       *P*

1.  **Hey**! One **of** you must be wrong, **but** both of you must stop fighting **about** it.

2.  Thirty minutes is a long time to wait **for** a bus, **and** I am growing impatient.

3.  **Both** my brother **and** I are members **of** our church's youth group.

4.  **Amen**! I agree **with** you **on** all **of** your points.

5.  She opened the window **and** shouted, "**Good-bye**!"

6.  Mom **and** Dad wrapped the gifts **while** the children were sleeping **in** their beds.

7.  She was rewarded not **because** she is the "teacher's pet" **but because** she achieved the

    highest grade **in** the class **on** her test.

8.  "**Bah**! **Humbug**!" Scrooge muttered **when** his nephew praised the joys **of** Christmas.

9.  **Contrary to** popular belief, all blondes are not "dumb."

10. We can pass them **to** our children **and** know they are the same **from** year **to** year.

11. The boat pulled **alongside** the dock **and** the passengers disembarked.

12. The bridge **across** the river collapsed **under** the weight of the truck **during** the crossing.

13. You will be punished **unless** you stop doing that immediately.

14. **Although** she was **among** friends, she was nervous **about** her presentation.

---

✎ **EXERCISE B** Underline the prepositional phrases in the following sentences. Double-underline each preposition. Circle the object of the preposition.

1. She walked past the group without notice.

2. The sick youngster fell into a troubled sleep despite his high fever.

3. He wrote to the manufacturer concerning the defects in the product.

4. Inside the box was a tin filled with cookies from his grandmother.

5. The river guide was sprayed with water but kept his wits amidst the swirling waves.

6. She hung the portrait of her grandfather above the fireplace.

7. The soldier with the long, yellow hair was General Custer.

8. The sound of our national anthem at a ball game fills me with patriotic feelings.

9. A group of Christians formed an organization to work for reformation of the Church.

10. The spelling of the man's name was wrong throughout the article.

---

# LESSON 3: DOUBLE-DUTY WORDS

In the first two lessons, we have studied the eight parts of speech. As we noted, all words may be classified as one of these parts of speech. We cannot be too rigid in classifying words, however, because a word may be used as a particular part of speech in one sentence and as a different part of speech in another sentence, depending on how the sentence is constructed. In many cases, therefore, it is not possible to tell which part of speech a word really is when it is *standing alone*. We can identify it only by the way it is used in a sentence.

| Rule 1.1 | A word's use in a sentence determines which part of speech it is. |
|---|---|

☞**EXAMPLES:**

1. She is feeling **well** today. (adjective—modifies "she")

2. The workers dug a **well** on the property. (noun—direct object of "dug")

3. He does **well** at whatever task he tries. (adverb—modifies "does")

4. A good **name** is a valuable asset. (noun—subject of the sentence)

5. What will you **name** your new kitten? (verb)

6. The doctor asked to see his next **patient.** (noun—direct object of "to see")

7. Thank you for your **patient** waiting. (adjective—modifies "waiting")

8. Before I give a speech, I always get a **lump** in my throat. (noun—direct object of "get")

9. We should not **lump** the good with the bad. (verb)

In addition, many words can serve as two parts of speech *at the same time*. Some such words have special names and rules governing their use (such as "demonstrative adjectives" or "conjunctive adverbs"—see below). Others have no special names and follow the normal rules for the part of speech associated with the present use of the word.

## *NOUNS USED AS ADJECTIVES*

**Nouns** are words that name persons, places, things, qualities, or ideas. Normally, they are used as subjects, objects, predicate nominatives, and appositives. But sometimes these naming words may be used as adjectives, as in the examples below.

☞**EXAMPLES:**

1. The milk spilled all over the **kitchen** floor.

2. I like to hear the sound of **tree** spiders on a **summer** evening.

3. A cool **ocean** breeze swept across the beach.

4. I can never seem to find my **letter** opener.

## *POSSESSIVE PRONOUNS USED AS ADJECTIVES*

**Possessive pronouns** are pronouns because they refer to noun or pronoun antecedents. However, they have the character of adjectives because they modify nouns or pronouns.

☞**EXAMPLES:**

1. She stubbed **her** toe. (modifies "toe"—antecedent is "she")

2. Aaron finished **his** breakfast. (modifies "breakfast"—antecedent is "Aaron")

3. I believe that coat is **mine.** (predicate adjective, modifies "coat"—antecedent is "I")

# DEMONSTRATIVE ADJECTIVES

There are five *demonstrative pronouns:* **this, that, these, those,** and **such**. They are pronouns when they are used as substitutes for nouns. However, these same five words are often placed before nouns and modify them as adjectives would. In these cases, they are called *demonstrative adjectives.* (Notice an example in the previous sentence: "these cases.")

☞**EXAMPLES OF DEMONSTRATIVE *PRONOUNS:***

1. **This** is a good book.

2. **These** are good apples.

3. I had hoped our relationship would not come to **that**.

4. Tell **those** who wish to go that they should get on the bus now.

5. **Such** is the fate of the wicked.

☞**EXAMPLES OF DEMONSTRATIVE *ADJECTIVES:***

1. **This** book is very interesting.

2. Where did you get **these** apples?

3. **That** remark was inappropriate.

4. Tell **those** people to get on the bus now.

5. You should not say **such** things.

# CONJUNCTIVE ADVERBS

Another group of double-duty words are **conjunctive adverbs**. These words are adverbs that are *used as coordinating conjunctions* connecting two independent clauses. (An independent clause is a group of words expressing a complete thought, having a subject and a predicate, and forming a part of a sentence.) They may also be used parenthetically as sentence **interrupters** (see those marked with * below).

| **CONJUNCTIVE ADVERBS** |
|---|
| also, anyhow, as a result, besides, consequently, for example, furthermore, hence, henceforth, however, indeed, in fact, in addition, likewise, meanwhile, moreover, namely, nevertheless, notwithstanding, otherwise, so, still, then, therefore, thus |

☞**EXAMPLES:**

1. This is a difficult subject; **however**, you should be able to understand it if you study hard.

2. Mr. Brownley is a good teacher; **in fact**, he is the best teacher I have ever had.

3. I did my homework for two hours; **then** I went to bed.

4. They broke the rules; **consequently**, they must take the punishment.

5. The book has been damaged; **still** it is usable.

*6. I was, **nevertheless**, not in favor of the idea.

7. It may rain when you are at camp; **therefore**, you should take a raincoat with you.

8. His car was stolen; **as a result**, he could not get to work today.

*9. I plan, **moreover**, to attend a Christian college.

10. She clips and uses coupons; **thus** she saves several dollars on her grocery bills.

---

**Note:**  * In these examples the *conjunctive adverbs* are used parenthetically as sentence *interrupters.*

---

## VERBALS

One very important and widely used type of double-duty words is a group called **verbals**. Verbals are *verb forms that are used as other parts of speech.* English has three types of verbals: **participles** (present and past), **gerunds**, and **infinitives**. (You may recall that present and past participles are the second and fourth principal parts of verbs.) Study the following chart so that you will be able to recognize the different kinds of verbals used in sentences.

| VERBAL | WHAT IS IT? | EXAMPLES |
|--------|-------------|----------|
| **Present Participle** | A verb form used as an **adjective**. It always ends in *-ing*. | The auto racers got a *running* start. |
| **Past Participle** | A verb form used as an **adjective**. | Johnny hated *boiled* cabbage. |
| **Gerund** | A verb form used as a **noun**. It most often ends in *-ing*. | *Running* is good exercise. |
| **Infinitive** | A verb form that usually begins with "to" and is used as an **adjective, adverb,** or **noun**. | *To give* is *to receive*. (noun) The best time *to study* is when your mind is alert. (adjective) She came *to see* you. (adverb) |

## ■ *Verbal Modifiers:*

Because all verbals are *verb forms,* they can be modified by *adverbs.* Because gerunds and infinitives can be used as *nouns,* they also may be modified by *adjectives.*

## ■ *Verbal Spellings:*

Note on the chart that present participles and gerunds always end with *-ing*. Many past participles end with *-ed* or *-d*, but many others have their own unique spellings. Infinitives usually are preceded by the introductory word *to*, but there are exceptions.

✎ **EXERCISE A** Put an **X** in the box next to the answer that best identifies the word in **dark print** in each of the following sentences.

1.  All trucks weighing more than 5 tons must use the **truck** route.

    ☒ noun used as adjective        ☐ conjunctive adverb        ☐ adjective used as noun

2.  These books are **yours**.

    ☐ indefinite pronoun        ☐ pronoun used as adjective        ☐ demonstrative adjective

3.  **These** books are yours.

    ☐ demonstrative pronoun        ☐ demonstrative adjective        ☐ demonstrative adverb

4.  Mom said she would **iron** my wrinkled trousers.

    ☐ noun        ☐ verb        ☐ adjective

5.  The high wall around the estate had an **iron** gate.

    ☐ noun        ☐ verb        ☐ adjective

6.  The gate was made of **iron**.

    ☐ noun        ☐ verb        ☐ adjective

7.  **Certainly!** I would be happy to help you.

    ☐ adverb        ☐ adjective        ☐ interjection

8.  I would **certainly** be happy to help you.

    ☐ adverb        ☐ adjective        ☐ interjection

9.  I would certainly be happy **to help** you.

    ☐ infinitive        ☐ prepositional phrase        ☐ gerund

10. A **galloping** horse is a thing of beauty and gracefulness.

    ☐ present participle        ☐ past participle        ☐ gerund

11. The horse was **galloping** across the meadow.

    ☐ present participle used as a predicate adjective modifying "horse"

    ☐ present participle used in a verb phrase

    ☐ gerund used as predicate nominative renaming "horse"

12. **Galloping** at full speed is my favorite way to ride a horse.

☐ gerund            ☐ present participle          ☐ main verb

13. Goliath carried a huge **spear** as he came out to taunt the Israelites.

☐ verb              ☐ noun                        ☐ adjective

14. You can **spear** a fish if you have great patience and quick reflexes.

☐ verb              ☐ noun                        ☐ adjective

15. I tried **to spear** the last pickle at the bottom of the jar.

☐ verb              ☐ infinitive                  ☐ prepositional phrase

16. **Behold!** The king is coming, riding on a white horse.

☐ interjection      ☐ verbal                      ☐ verb

17. The mountain vista was a delight **to behold**.

☐ verbal            ☐ verb                        ☐ interjection

18. When we reach heaven, we shall **behold** God's glory.

☐ verb              ☐ verbal                      ☐ interjection

19. **Our** house is just around the corner.

☐ pronoun used as adverb    ☐ pronoun used as adjective    ☐ conjunctive adverb

20. The pie is baked; **however**, it is slightly burned.

☐ predicate adjective       ☐ conjunctive adverb           ☐ subordinating conjunction

21. The pie is **baked**; however, it is slightly burned.

☐ past participle           ☐ present participle           ☐ gerund

22. **Indeed**, that is a fine painting!

☐ interjection              ☐ subject                      ☐ conjunctive adverb

23. I cannot **picture** you wearing that dress.

☐ noun              ☐ adjective                   ☐ verb

24. She hung the **picture** on the west wall.

☐ noun              ☐ adjective                   ☐ verb

25. Early Egyptians and Indians communicated with **picture** writing.

    ☐ noun used as adjective          ☐ verb                    ☐ object of a preposition

26. **Fishing** is my father's favorite pastime.

    ☐ verb                    ☐ verbal: present participle      ☐ verbal: gerund

27. My mother was **fishing** for a complement.

    ☐ verb                    ☐ verbal: present participle      ☐ verbal: gerund

28. If you are over age 16, you will need a **fishing** license.

    ☐ verb                    ☐ verbal: present participle      ☐ verbal: gerund

29. She works for the **telephone** company.

    ☐ noun used as an object of a preposition
    ☐ noun used as an adjective
    ☐ infinitive without the introductory word "to"

30. Be sure **to telephone** us when you arrive.

    ☐ object of a preposition        ☐ infinitive              ☐ sentence's main verb

# LESSON 4: UNIT REVIEW

✎ **EXERCISE** Fill in the blanks below:

1.  All English words belong to one of _____ parts of speech.

2.  A(n) _____ is a word that names a person, place, thing, quality, or idea.

3.  A(n) _____ is a word that is used in place of a noun.

4.  A(n) _____ is a word that expresses action or state of being or that helps verbs complete
    their meanings.

5.  A(n) _____ is a word that modifies a noun or pronoun.

6.  A(n) _____ is a word that modifies a verb, adjective, or adverb.

7.  A(n) _____ is a word that shows the relationship of its object to others words in a sentence.

8.  A(n) _____ is a word that connects words, phrases, or clauses.

9.   A(n) _____ is an exclamatory word that has little or no grammatical connection to the rest of a sentence.

10.  The two main kinds of conjunctions are _____ and _____ conjunctions.

11.  A _____ _____ is an adverb usually used to connect independent clauses.

12.  The two kinds of nouns are _____ and _____ nouns.

13.  Proper nouns must begin with a _____ letter.

14.  When an interjection is punctuated by an exclamation mark or question, the next word should begin with a _____ letter.

15.  Possessive pronouns have the character of _____ because they modify nouns or pronouns.

16.  The eight types of pronouns are: _____, _____, _____, _____, _____, _____, _____, _____.

17.  _____ usually answer such questions as *how?, how much?, to what extent?, how often?, when?, where?* or *in which way?* about the words they modify.

18.  _____ answer the questions *what kind?, which one?, how many?,* or *how much?* about the nouns or pronouns they modify.

# Unit 2
# Using Phrases

---

> **A PHRASE is a group of related words that does not contain both a subject and a predicate.**

---

## LESSON 5: PHRASES CLASSIFIED ACCORDING TO USE

Phrases may be used anywhere in a sentence—in the beginning, at the end, or in the middle—to add information and interest to the main idea. A **phrase** functions as a single part of speech—usually fulfilling the functions of a *noun, verb, adjective,* or *adverb.* (Less common are groups of words functioning as *prepositions, conjunctions,* or *interjections.*) In this unit you will become familiar with the different types of phrases and how they are used in sentences. Study the chart below to understand how phrases can be used as various parts of speech within sentences.

| USE | EXPLANATION | EXAMPLES |
|---|---|---|
| **as a** <br><br> **NOUN** | A phrase may be used as a single noun is used—as a subject, object, predicate nominative, or appositive. | ***Boys and girls*** have separate gym classes at our school. *(subject)* <br><br> We enjoy ***playing football***. (direct object) |
| **as a** <br><br> **VERB** | A verb phrase consists of a main verb plus any helping verbs and modifiers. | I ***have been sleeping poorly lately***. <br><br> The engine ***is now running smoothly***. |
| **as an** <br><br> **ADJECTIVE** | A phrase may be used to modify a noun or pronoun in the same way that a single adjective would. | The people ***in the rear*** could not see well. *(modifies "people")* <br><br> ***A cold and violent*** storm was forecast for the area. *(modifies "storm")* <br><br> Now is a good time ***to pray for guidance***. (modifies "time") |

| USE | EXPLANATION | EXAMPLES |
|---|---|---|
| **as an** <br> **ADVERB** | A phrase may be used to modify a verb, adjective, or adverb in the same way that a single adverb would. | They were swimming *in the creek*. (modifies "were swimming") <br><br> We are hoping *to meet you soon*. (modifies "are hoping") <br><br> The racers ran swiftly *toward the finish line*. (modifies "ran") |
| **as a** <br> **PREPOSITION** | A group of words may serve as a single preposition. Such groups are usually called *compound prepositions*. | He was promoted *by reason of* his skills. <br><br> *Contrary to* rumors, I have not been sick. <br><br> I am writing *pertaining to* your inquiry. |
| **as a** <br> **CONJUNCTION** | A group of words may serve as a conjunction. This usually involves *subordinating conjunctions*, *conjunctive adverbs,* or *correlative conjunctions*. | I came *as soon as* you called. <br><br> *As a result*, you should begin to feel better. <br><br> We will, *in fact*, be there within the hour. |
| **as an** <br> **INTERJECTION** | An interjection may consist of a group of words. | For crying out loud! <br><br> Bah! Humbug! |

✎ **EXERCISE** In the blanks, write **noun, verb, adjective,** or **adverb** to identify which part of speech the phrases in **dark print** are. If the phrase is a noun phrase, write **S, O,** or **PN** above it to indicate whether it is used as a *Subject, Object, or Predicate Nominative.* If the phrase is an adjective or adverb phrase, underline the word or words it modifies.

_____*adjective*_____ 1. The <u>man</u> **from the cable-TV company** is coming to install the necessary wires.

_____ 2. All Scripture **is given** by inspiration of God.

_____ 3. All Scripture is profitable **for correction and instruction**.

_____ 4. **Eating the right food** will improve your health.

_____ 5. His parents were proud of **his many accomplishments**.

_____     6.  We **have been wondering** when you would be finished.

_____     7.  **The telephone directory** is in the drawer under the telephone.

_____     8.  The teacher assigned **the boys and girls** four chapters to read.

_____     9.  The receiver fumbled the ball **on the 10-yard line**.

_____    10.  It was **a warm, sunny day**.

_____    11.  The car **will cost** too much money.

_____    12.  I would be happy **to help you tomorrow**.

_____    13.  A noun is one of the parts **of speech**.

_____    14.  A verb is also one **of the parts** of speech.

_____    15.  A preposition usually comes **before its object**.

_____    16.  **Conjunctions and interjections** are parts of speech.

_____    17.  The boy **eating the apple** is my brother.

_____    18.  **My history textbook** has 340 pages.

_____    19.  **To become a professional baseball player** was his goal.

_____    20.  Her goal was **to become a playwright**.

_____    21.  We sold our old car **within one week**.

# LESSON 6: PHRASES CLASSIFIED ACCORDING TO FORM

Phrases may also be classified according to their *form,* or how they are constructed. They are named according to the initial or most important word in the phrase. Study the chart below to understand how the six most common kinds of phrases are constructed and how they are used in sentences:

| FORM | CONSTRUCTION | USE(S) | EXAMPLES |
|---|---|---|---|
| **PREPOSITIONAL** | Consists of a preposition followed by its object and any modifiers | Used as adjective, adverb, or noun | The church *around the corner* is a Baptist church. *(adjective)* <br><br> Dust collected *under the bed*. *(adverb)* <br><br> *On your feet* is the proper place for your shoes. *(noun)* |
| **PARTICIPIAL** | Begins with a present or past participle and includes any objects and modifiers | Used only as an adjective | *Having finished my soup*, I began the next course of the meal. *(modifies "I")* <br><br> The man *assembling the bicycle* is Tim's Dad. *(modifies "man")* |
| **GERUNDIAL** | Begins with a gerund* and includes any objects and modifiers <br><br> *Verb form ending in -ing | Used only as a noun | *Playing the drums* was his ambition. *(subject)* <br><br> You will not get your way by *throwing a temper tantrum*. *(object of a preposition)* |
| **PREPOSITIONAL GERUNDIAL** | A phrase introduced by a preposition which is followed by a gerund and other related words | Used as prepositional phrases are used—adjective, adverb, or noun | *After running the course*, the racers rested on the sidelines. *(adjective, modifies "racers")* <br><br> They rescued the drowning man *by throwing a life preserver to him*. *(adverb, modifies "rescued")* |
| **INFINITIVE** | Features an infinitive* and any objects and related words <br><br> *verb form beginning with to | Used as adjective, adverb, or noun | *To serve the Lord* is my chief desire. *(noun)* <br><br> The number *to call in case of emergency* is 9-1-1. *(adjective)* <br><br> She studied hard *to pass the test*. *(adverb)* |
| **ABSOLUTE** | A unique type of phrase consisting usually of a noun followed by and modified by a participle or participial phrase. | Modifies no particular word in the sentence of which it is a part, but it has a close thought relationship to the sentence or part of it | *The sun having set*, we walked back to our cabin. <br><br> Jody went to bed, *her homework being finished*. <br><br> *The last touches completed*, the artist stood back to examine the painting. |

✎ **EXERCISE A** In the blanks, write **prepositional, participial, gerundial, PG** (prepositional-gerundial), **infinitive,** or **absolute** to identify the **FORM** of the phrases in **dark print.**

_prepositional_    1. **Throughout the night**, the raindrops splashed against the window pane.

_____    2. **To win people's respect**, you must treat them with respect.

_____    3. The men **loading the relief supplies** were volunteers.

_____    4. I have learned the joy **of giving to others**.

_____    5. He turned on the radio **to hear the latest news**.

_____    6. **According to the report**, the storm did little damage.

_____    7. **The nominations being closed**, the members proceeded to vote.

_____    8. Mom hid our gifts **in her closet**.

_____    9. **After graduating**, he plans to attend a Christian high school.

_____   10. **To get a job** without experience is sometimes difficult.

_____   11. The old man, **muttering gruffly under his breath**, seemed upset about something.

_____   12. The meeting was adjourned, **no one else wishing to speak**.

✎ **EXERCISE B** Identify the **USE** in the sentence of the phrases in **dark print**. Write **S** (subject), **DO** (direct object), **IO** (indirect object), **OP** (object of a preposition), **PN** (predicate nominative), **PA** (predicate adjective), **Adj.** (other adjective), or **Adv.** (adverb).

_S_    1. **Winning or losing** is less important than how you play the game.

____    2. The woman **speaking with my mother** is Mrs. Donnan.

____    3. He disliked **studying after 10 p.m.**

____    4. She gave **playing intramural volleyball** her best effort.

____    5. His purpose was **to alert us** to the danger.

____    6. Nick drank water frequently **to avoid dehydration**.

_____ 7. Continue **in the things** which you have learned... *(2 Timothy 3:14).*

_____ 8. He went to the employment office to inquire about **getting a summer job.**

_____ 9. He went **to the employment office** to inquire about getting a summer job.

_____ 10. He went to the employment office **to get a summer job.**

_____ 11. **For best results**, hold the can upright when spraying.

# LESSON 7: RESTRICTIVE AND NON-RESTRICTIVE PHRASES

Adjective and adverb phrases can be called **restrictive** or **non-restrictive** depending on how they are used in a sentence. The phrase is restrictive if it is essential to completing the desired meaning of the sentence. It is called non-restrictive, however, if it is not essential to the meaning but merely adds more information.

| ESSENTIAL = RESTRICTIVE |
|---|
| NON-ESSENTIAL = NON-RESTRICTIVE |

## *PUNCTUATING RESTRICTIVE AND NON-RESTRICTIVE PHRASES:*

| Rule 2.1 | Non-restrictive phrases must be enclosed or set off with commas. Do not use commas to enclose restrictive phrases. |
|---|---|

☞**EXAMPLES:**

RESTRICTIVE—don't use commas:

The flight *from Chicago* will be delayed for twenty minutes.

The man *holding that briefcase* is a spy.

The package *arriving by special delivery tomorrow* will contain your urgent order.

(The highlighted phrases above are essential to understanding the sentence's meaning because they identify *which* flight, *which* man, and *which* package.)

NON-RESTRICTIVE—use commas:

The clerk, *looking quite puzzled,* asked me to repeat what I had said.

The Japanese bombed Pearl Harbor, *ending U.S. hopes to avoid war.*

*To afford a college education,* you should begin saving at an early age.

(The highlighted phrases above are not essential, but only give additional information.)

## ■ *Hints:*

When an adjective phrase *precedes* its modifier (sentence 3 immediately above), it is usually *non-restrictive.* When it *follows immediately after* its modifier (sentence 1), it can be either *restrictive or non-restrictive.* When it follows a *few words after* its modifier (sentence 2), it is usually *non-restrictive.*

Sometimes the *context* is the best clue as to whether a phrase is restrictive or non-restrictive. If the sentence makes complete sense without the phrase, the phrase usually is non-restrictive. If the essential meaning is lost without the phrase, the phrase is probably restrictive. Here are some examples:

☞**RESTRICTIVE**

The cowboys *with white hats on their heads* are usually the "good guys."

The President Roosevelt *holding office during World War II* was Franklin, not Teddy.

☞**NON-RESTRICTIVE**

The cowboys, *with white hats on their heads*, mingled with the rodeo fans.

President Roosevelt, *holding office during World War II*, joined Winston Churchill in representing the West at the Yalta Conference.

---

✎ **EXERCISE** Write **N** or **R** in the blanks to indicate whether the phrase in **dark print** is Non-restrictive or Restrictive. **Punctuate** the phrases as needed.

_N_     1. The White House, **located at 1700 Pennsylvania Avenue**, is the President's home.

_____     2. The white house **at 358 Maple Street** belongs to the Henry family.

_____     3. **Having reached age five** Ginny was eager to start kindergarten.

_____     4. **After receiving your gift** I feel indebted to you.

_____     5. Children **with infectious diseases** should stay home from school.

_____     6. **Viewed from a distance** the mountain resembles a sleeping giant.

_____     7. We closed our cottage **by the lake** for the winter.

_____     8. **Traveling by train** is not as popular now as it was in the 19th century.

_____     9. **At the top of each page** write your name and the name of the subject.

_____   10. The boys **eating the watermelon so vigorously** hope to win the contest.

_____   11. The boys **vigorously eating the watermelon with hopes of victory** finished instead only with tummy aches.

_____   12. **In catching twenty-one fish** Terry exceeded the legal limit by one.

_____   13. The lion attacked the gazelle **with a vengeance**.

_____   14. **Huffing and puffing with all his might** the wolf tried in vain to blow down the brick house.

_____   15. That person **in the mirror** is you.

# LESSON 8: SENTENCE FRAGMENTS

Read the definition of a *phrase* at the beginning of this unit. You will notice that a phrase is a group of words that does NOT contain both a subject and a predicate. This means that a phrase is NOT a sentence.

> **A SENTENCE is a group of words that expresses a complete thought.**

To express a complete thought, a sentence must have **both** of two parts—a *subject* and a *predicate*. The *subject* is a noun, pronoun, or noun-like group of words about which the sentence is making a statement. A *predicate*, which must contain a verb, is the statement the sentence is making about the subject.

A phrase can have a noun, pronoun, or noun-like expression which could serve as a subject. Or it can have a verb. However, because it does not have both a subject and a predicate, *a phrase cannot stand alone* as a sentence. *A phrase must be clearly connected to other words in the sentence*.

> **A SENTENCE FRAGMENT is a phrase or dependent clause that does not express completeness of meaning. It usually may not be written to stand alone as a sentence.**

In the following examples, the words in **dark print** are sentence fragments that cannot normally stand alone as a sentence. See how they should be combined with other words to form a complete thought in a sentence.

> *Always looking for a laugh.* Charlie was known as the class clown.
>
> Always looking for a laugh, Charlie was known as the class clown.

> The Founding Fathers signed the Declaration of Independence. *A remarkable document for its time.*
>
> The Founding Fathers signed the Declaration of Independence, a remarkable document for its time.

> I studied hard. *For my upcoming science test.*
>
> I studied hard for my upcoming science test.

## EXCEPTIONS

There are several grammatical situations in which it is acceptable to use a sentence fragment. In such cases, even if the expression does not contain both a subject and a predicate, a fairly complete idea is either expressed or implied. These special cases should be used sparingly and usually are employed by writers for special effects. The exceptions are as follows:

## ■ *Interjections*

Interjections can stand alone as complete "sentences," beginning with a capital letter and ending with punctuation.

Indeed! Oh, oh! Alas! Hush! Phooey! Sure!

## ■ *Greetings*

Good morning. Hello. Good-bye. Good afternoon. Greetings. Hi. Good night.

## ■ *Expressive or exclamatory statements*

What a day! Never again! Over my dead body!

## ■ *Transitional statements*

One further point. To summarize. Next item. Another point to ponder.

## ■ *Elliptical sentences*

Elliptical sentences have certain essential grammatical parts missing, but their meaning is complete as understood in context. They are frequently used in dialogue.

"Get a new car?"
"Yeah."
"Good price?"
"Not bad. Should be able to handle it."
"Like it so far?"
"Sure do."
"Pretty nice!"
"Thanks."

## ■ *Notes*

Sentence fragments are frequently employed in informal situations such as in catalogues or book notes, for the sake of brevity or saving space.

*Andrew Murray,* **The State of the Church,** *A challenging treatise on revitalizing the church for its ministry of intercession and completing the Great Commission. Speaks just as vividly to today's church and its spiritual needs as when first published around the turn of the century. Truly a great classic.*

(Adapted from Christian Literature Crusade catalogue, 1995-96)

---

✎ **EXERCISE A** Some of the following groups of words contain two complete sentences. Some contain at least one sentence fragment. Write **S** in the blank if the item has two complete sentences. Write **F** if the item contains any sentence fragments.

_____F_____  1.  I was ready to go out the door. When suddenly the phone rang.

_____  2.  I would rather not serve on the committee. Unless you can't find anyone else.

_____  3.  I like her. Even though she doesn't like me.

_____  4.  This song is one of my favorites. It reminds me of the week we spent at the beach.

_____  5.  If you look out the window, you will see it is raining. "Cats and dogs."

_____ 6. I attend Jordan Junior High School. The same school my parents attended.

_____ 7. The Spanish Armada had 130 ships. It was a large fleet for a 16th-century nation.

_____ 8. Around the garden, she planted marigolds. Which are useful for keeping bugs away.

_____ 9. The giant sequoias of California. Some are as much as 2,000 years old.

_____ 10. Thy Word is a lamp unto my feet. A light unto my pathway.

## CORRECTING FRAGMENTS

Sentence fragments can be corrected in one of the following ways:

- ■ **Attach fragments together and revise as necessary to make a complete sentence.**

- ■ **Attach a fragment to an otherwise complete sentence, if the result makes sense.**

- ■ **Revise each fragment so that it has its own subject and predicate.**

✎ **EXERCISE B** Correct all of the items in Exercise A that you marked with an **F**. Use one of the correction methods listed above.

1. _____*I was ready to go out the door when suddenly the phone rang.*_____

2. _____

_____

3. _____

_____

4. _____

_____

5. _____

_____

6. _____

_____

7. _____

_____

8. _____

_____

# LESSON 9: UNIT REVIEW

✎ **EXERCISE** Fill in the blanks below:

1.  A phrase is used as a single _____ ____ _____—usually fulfilling the functions of a

    _____, _____, _____, or _____.

2.  The six most common classifications of phrases according to *form* are these:

    _____   _____   _____


    _____   _____   _____

3.  What is a prepositional-gerundial phrase?

    _____

    _____

4.  What is an absolute phrase?

    _____

    _____

5.  Write a sentence containing an infinitive phrase used as a noun.

    _____

    _____

6.  Write a sentence containing a participial phrase.

    _____

    _____

7.  Why can a phrase NOT stand alone as a sentence?

    _____

    _____

8.  What is a non-restrictive phrase? What is a restrictive phrase?

    _____

    _____

    _____

9.  Which type of phrase should be enclosed or set off with commas?

    _____ restrictive      _____ non-restrictive      _____ both      _____ neither

# Unit 3
# Using Clauses

> **A CLAUSE is a group of words containing both a subject and a predicate and forming a part of a sentence.**

When a group of related words contains a subject and a predicate, it needs to be distinguished from the sentence as a whole. These are called clauses. Clauses come in two varieties: *independent* clauses and *dependent* clauses. Independent clauses may be called principal or main clauses, while dependent clauses may be called subordinate clauses.

## LESSON 10: INDEPENDENT CLAUSES

> **An INDEPENDENT CLAUSE expresses a complete thought and could stand alone if the rest of the sentence containing it were eliminated.**

Every complete sentence must have at least one independent clause. Sentences with one independent clause are called *simple sentences*. Sentences with two or more independent clauses are called *compound sentences*.

The following examples are sentences with independent clauses. The subject of each clause is underlined. The verb is double-underlined.

### ■ Simple Sentences (One Independent Clause)

The sun is shining.

The man from the insurance company is here to see you.

Nobody in his right mind would try to cross that raging stream without a life preserver.

### ■ Compound Sentences (Two Or More Independent Clauses)

The sun is shining and the wind is calm.

The man from the insurance company is here to see you, and he wants to explain his company's policies.

Nobody in his right mind would try to cross that stream unaided, but ropes and other safety gear should be used.

As the last example above shows, independent clauses may have more than one subject. A sentence or independent clause with one subject has a *simple subject*. A simple subject consists of one noun, pronoun, or noun-like expression about which the sentence makes a statement. A *complete subject* is the simple subject plus all of its modifying words and phrases. An independent clause with two or more subjects has a *compound subject*.

All sentences and clauses may also have *simple* and *compound predicates*. A *simple predicate* is the verb or verb phrase that makes a statement about the subject. A *complete predicate* is the simple predicate plus all of its objects and modifying words and phrases.

The following chart contains several simple sentences with the complete subjects and complete predicates separated. Even though some have compound subjects or compound predicates, they still contain only *one* independent clause. The simple or compound subject and predicate in each sentence are in **dark print**.

| SIMPLE SENTENCES (1 independent clause) ||
|---|---|
| **COMPLETE SUBJECT** | **COMPLETE PREDICATE** |
| The **sun** | **is shining** brightly. |
| My science **teacher** | always **explains** things thoroughly. |
| **Dogs** and **cats** | **are** the most common house pets. |
| My TV-loving **uncle** | always **eats** popcorn and **drinks** sodas during football games. |

The next chart contains several compound sentences with their independent clauses separated and the complete subjects and complete predicates also separated. The simple or compound subjects and predicates are in **dark print**.

| COMPOUND SENTENCES (2 or more independent clauses) |||||
|---|---|---|---|---|
| INDEPENDENT CLAUSE || CONNECTOR | INDEPENDENT CLAUSE ||
| **COMPLETE SUBJECT** | **COMPLETE PREDICATE** | | **COMPLETE SUBJECT** | **COMPLETE PREDICATE** |
| The bright, noonday **sun** | **is shining** right now, | and | the **sky** overhead | **is** a deep blue. |
| My science **teacher** | **explains** things well, | but | my math **teacher** | always **confuses** me. |
| The **price** and **size** | **are** acceptable; | however, | **we** | **cannot buy** the car right now. |
| This old **car** | neither **looks** good nor **runs** well | ; | my **brother** and I | **do** not **want** to keep it. |

## CONNECTORS AND PUNCTUATION

Independent clauses in compound sentences may be connected by *coordinating conjunctions* (simple or correlative conjunctions or conjunctive adverbs) or by a *semicolon*.

| Rule 3.1 | If a simple conjunction is used, it is preceded by a comma unless the independent clauses are very short and closely related in thought. (At times, a semicolon may be used instead of a comma; see page 186, Rule 9.54.) |
|---|---|

☞**EXAMPLE:**

We reached the fairground early in the day, **and** our father arrived in the afternoon.

| Rule 3.2 | If a conjunctive adverb with more than one syllable is used, it is preceded by a semicolon and followed by a comma. If a conjunctive adverb with one syllable is used, it is preceded by a semicolon and followed by no punctuation. |
|---|---|

☞**EXAMPLE:**

This is a difficult recipe; **however**, you should be able to make it.

I did my homework for two hours; **then** I went to bed.

✎ **EXERCISE A** Some of the groups of words in the following exercise express a complete thought and therefore could be a simple sentence or an independent clause in a compound sentence. Put a check mark ( ✓ ) in the blank before such statements. Write a *capital letter* at the beginning and a period at the end. Some of the groups of words are not complete thoughts. Put an ( ✗ ) in the blank before these incomplete statements.

___✓___ 1. <sup>T</sup>the tree in front of our school is an oak.

_____ 2. to become a great baseball player

_____ 3. with a smiling face, she accepted the award

_____ 4. the music of mozart

_____ 5. the engine was running

_____ 6. the dog with the black spots on his back

_____ 7. the baseball season is almost over

_____ 8. he plans to save the money earned last summer

_____ 9. this lesson is about independent clauses

_____ 10. a very good friend of mine

_____ 11. the power to give life or take it away

_____ 12. that lamp needs a new light bulb

✎ **EXERCISE B** Write five *compound sentences*, punctuating them correctly. Underline each independent clause. Circle the connecting word or punctuation mark. Try to include some compound subjects and/or predicates.

**EXAMPLE:**

Jan is an excellent singer, (and) she will perform at tonight's concert.

1. _____

    _____

2. _____

    _____

3. _____

    _____

4. _____

    _____

5. _____

    _____

# LESSON 11: DEPENDENT CLAUSES

> **A DEPENDENT CLAUSE contains a subject and verb but does not express a complete thought and cannot stand alone as a sentence.**

The second kind of clause is the *dependent clause*, also known as the *subordinate clause*. While dependent clauses do contain both a subject and a predicate, they do not express a complete and independent thought, usually because of their introductory words. The introductory words of dependent clauses "link" them to words in the independent clause. The thoughts that dependent clauses do express seem to "depend" on additional information which is not contained within the clause itself. The meaning of information in subordinate clauses is *dependent* upon information in an independent clause in the same sentence. This shows us that dependent clauses must always be part of a sentence which also contains at least one independent clause. Otherwise, they are just sentence fragments that cannot stand alone.

Sentences which contain a dependent clause are called *complex sentences*. A complex sentence consists of at least one independent clause and one or more dependent clauses. Different kinds of complex sentences are shown below. The words in regular type represent independent clauses. The words in **dark print** are dependent clauses.

☞ **EXAMPLES OF COMPLEX SENTENCES**

*While walking through the park this morning*, I met an old friend.

She is the kind of person *who is always willing to help others.*

My grandfather told me *that he would be happy to take me fishing.*

*Although I had not heard that song before*, it immediately became one of my favorites.

Dependent clauses may also **interrupt** independent clauses in a complex sentence. The chart below shows some examples.

| INDEPENDENT | DEPENDENT | INDEPENDENT (continued) |
|---|---|---|
| My teacher, | *who is always fair,* | gave me a reasonable score. |
| The barber | *who cuts my hair* | is an immigrant from Poland. |
| The television set | *which he bought* | has remote controls and stereo sound. |

## RESTRICTIVE AND NON-RESTRICTIVE CLAUSES

Like phrases, clauses can be *restrictive* and *non-restrictive*. **Restrictive clauses** are those which are *essential* to the meaning of the sentence. They are NOT set off with commas. **Non-restrictive clauses** are those which are *not essential* to the meaning of the sentence. Non-restrictive clauses ARE set off with commas. In the examples above, the first sentence contains a non-restrictive clause. The second and third contain restrictive clauses and therefore no commas are needed.

---

✎ **EXERCISE** Underline the dependent clauses in the following sentences. Punctuate the clause with a comma(s) if the clause is non-restrictive.

1. Your comment, <u>that you do not like math,</u> disappointed your teacher.

2. I will make a payment when I receive the order.

3. You seem to be less shy than I am.

4. The crops that the farmers planted last spring need moisture.

5. Able-bodied people who refuse to work should not be given free handouts.

6. My grandmother who was quite an accomplished pianist in her youth still enjoys music.

7. Jeff is the person whom I nominated for class president.

8.  Her latest album which was recorded last month is available on both compact disc and cassette.

9.  The textbook that we use in history class is written from a Christian perspective.

10. The time that you spent with our family was most enjoyable.

11. Our team which won all but one of its games will advance to the playoffs.

12. She is the kind of person whom you can always trust.

13. This sofa is more comfortable than that one.

14. My little brother seems to have adopted that stray dog which appeared at our house last week.

15. The dog which did not have a collar or identification tags appears to be a border collie.

16. Unless I am mistaken that girl is new to our school.

17. I will come as soon as I can get ready.

18. As long as you are going into the kitchen would you get me something to drink?

19. Take as much as you like, but eat all that you take.

20. Since you left I have been lonely.

21. The first person who finishes his slice of pie will be the winner.

# LESSON 12: ADJECTIVE CLAUSES

The next three lessons will explain the three types of dependent clauses: *adjective, adverb,* and **noun**. They are called this because they are used in sentences in the same way that individual adjectives, adverbs, and nouns are used.

In this lesson, we will consider adjective clauses.

> An **ADJECTIVE CLAUSE** is a dependent clause used as an adjective to modify a noun or pronoun.

## *RELATIVES*

**Adjective clauses** always begin with words known as *relatives*, which are either expressed or understood. A relative is a word that "relates" the adjective clause to the word or words it modifies. The following words are relatives:

☞**Relative pronouns:**

who, whom, which, that, whichever, whoever, whomever, whatever

whichsoever, whosoever, whomsoever, whatsoever

---

**Note:** *Whichsoever, whosoever, whomsoever,* and *whatsoever* are rarely used in modern English.

---

☞**Relative adjective:**

whose ("which" is occasionally also a relative adjective.)

☞**Relative adverbs:**

when, where

Relatives have no gender or number, that is, the same forms are used to modify masculine, feminine, or neuter nouns and pronouns, as well as both singular and plural nouns and pronouns. However, the antecedent of a relative pronoun does affect the choice of pronoun in other ways:

| Rule 3.3 | *who, whom, whoever,* and *whomever* refer only to people. |
|---|---|
| Rule 3.4 | *whose* and *that* may refer to people, places, things, or animals. |
| Rule 3.5 | *which* and *whichever* refer only to places, things, or animals, but not people. |

# ■ *Characteristics of Relatives*

Adjective clauses have one characteristic: the *whole clause* modifies a noun or pronoun. However, you should note and learn these characteristics of relatives:

■ **Relatives serve a grammatical function within the adjective clause itself** *(subject, object, adjective, adverb, etc.).*

■ **Relatives join the adjective clause which they introduce to an independent clause.**

■ **Relative pronouns refer to an antecedent in the independent clause.**

☞**EXAMPLES:** (The italicized words show the adjective clause.)

Jesus, **Who** *was born as a human baby,* is the Son of God.

**Note:** *Who* is the **subject of its clause** and refers to its antecedent in the independent clause, **Jesus;** the whole adjective clause modifies **Jesus,** the subject of the independent clause.

A person *to whom much is given* has special responsibilities to others.

**Note:** *Whom* is the **object of a preposition** within the adjective clause; it refers to its antecedent in the independent clause, **person;** and the whole adjective clause modifies the subject of the independent clause, **person.**

Yours is the best apple pie *that I have ever eaten.*

**Note:** *That* is the **direct object** of "have eaten" within the adjective clause; it refers to its antecedent, **pie,** in the independent clause; and the whole adjective clause modifies **pie,** the predicate nominative of the independent clause.

A Marxist is a person *whose philosophy is derived from the teachings of Karl Marx.*

**Note:** Within the adjective clause, *whose* is an **adjective** modifying "philosophy"; it refers to its antecedent, **person,** in the independent clause; and the whole adjective clause modifies **person,** the predicate nominative of the independent clause.

After dinner is the traditional time *when our family has prayer and Bible-reading.*

**Note:** Within the adjective clause, *when* is an **adverb** modifying the verb of the clause, "has"; it is a relative because it introduces the adjective clause and "relates" the clause to the word it modifies in the independent clause, **time.**

## ■ *Implied Relatives*

In some clauses, the relative introducing an adjective clause is ***implied or understood,*** rather than expressed.

☞**EXAMPLES:**

The wrench *I needed was missing.* = The wrench *[that] I needed was missing.*

He is the kind of person *you can trust.* = He is the kind of person *[whom] you can trust.*

# ■ *Who vs. Whom, etc.*

| **Rule 3.6** | Use *who* or *whoever* when the relative pronoun is the subject of the adjective clause. |
|---|---|

☞**EXAMPLE:**

Mike is the one ***who*** *deserves the award.*

| **Rule 3.7** | Use *whom* or *whomever* when the relative pronoun is an object in the adjective clause. |
|---|---|

☞**EXAMPLE:**

Am I the person *to **whom** you are speaking?*

| **Rule 3.8** | Use *whose* when the relative pronoun shows possession. |
|---|---|

☞**EXAMPLE:**

My sister, ***whose*** *hair is red,* does not have a temper.

| **Rule 3.9** | *That* and *which* may be used when the relative is either a subject or an object in the adjective clause. |
|---|---|

☞**EXAMPLES:**

This is an idea ***that*** *interests me. **(subject)***

This is an idea ***that*** *you will love. **(direct object)***

We saw the house ***which*** *your parents want to buy. **(direct object)***

We saw the house ***which*** *is for sale. **(subject)***

We saw the house *about **which** you spoke. **(object of a preposition)***

---

**Note:** Remember ***which*** and ***that*** may be used interchangeably, except ***which*** may not be used to refer to people.

---

## PLACEMENT OF ADJECTIVE CLAUSES

| Rule 3.10 | Adjective clauses usually should be placed immediately after the word they modify. |
|---|---|

Putting an adjective clause anywhere else results in what grammarians call a *misplaced modifier*. Misplaced modifiers create confusion—and, sometimes, silly results.

☞**MISPLACED AND SILLY:**

Mom fixed some food for the **team** *which smelled delicious*.

☞**CORRECTLY PLACED:**

Mom fixed for the team some **food** *which smelled delicious*.

☞**MISPLACED AND CONFUSING:**

Dad bought a **car** from a **junkyard** *which had been damaged*.

☞**CORRECTLY PLACED AND CLEAR:**

Dad bought from a junkyard a **car** *which had been damaged*.

✎ **EXERCISE A** Underline the adjective clauses in the following sentences. Circle the word or words they modify.

1.  Ernest Hemingway was a (novelist) whose life ended with suicide.

2.  The Pilgrims, who had been persecuted in England, went to Holland and then America.

3.  I know a quiet place where the wind seldom blows.

4.  An adjective clause is one which modifies a noun or pronoun.

5.  A facsimile ("fax") machine is a device which can transmit images over telephone lines.

6.  George Washington, whom we remember as the "Father of our Country," was a man of prayer.

7.  The person who receives the greatest number of votes will be declared the winner.

8.  He is a man whose name is unfamiliar to me.

9.  Aunt Carol, from whom I received my name, was my favorite relative.

10. Where is a man who will stand up for righteousness these days?

✎ **EXERCISE B** Underline the correct choice of relative in each of the following sentences. In the blank, tell how the relative is used within its clause (as a subject, direct object, object of a preposition, adjective, or adverb).

1.  My parents are the people to (who, <u>whom</u>) I am mostly indebted. *object of a preposition*

2.  John Foxe was a 16th-century English clergyman (who, whom) wrote the *Book of Martyrs*. _____

3.  O.J. Simpson, (who, whom) was once a football star and sportscaster, was tried in 1995 for the murder of his wife and another man. _____

4.  There is the clerk (who, whom) you must pay. _____

5.  The lamp (who, which) he broke was an antique. _____

6.  Your good name—(which, whom) name you must guard with great care—is one of your most precious assets. _____

7.  John Wesley, (who, whom) was one of the founders of Methodism, was a great evangelist. _____

8.  The next person (whose, who's) name I call will be the winner. _____

9.  The hour (when, which) I awoke was before daylight. _____

10. I would like to present Mrs. Clarkson, (who, whom) we honor tonight, as our special guest. _____

✎ **EXERCISE C** Rewrite the following sentences, correcting the misplacement of the adjective clauses.

1.   I petted the dog of my cousin that has fleas.

_____*I petted my cousin's dog, that has fleas.*_____

2.   My parents will be given a party whose anniversary is next week.

_____

_____

3.   Our teacher read a poem to our class that was written by Robert Burns.

_____

_____

4.   The boy put his bicycle into the garage that lives next door.

_____

_____

5.   The man was taken to a hospital that was in an accident.

_____

_____

# LESSON 13: ADVERB CLAUSES

Like phrases, dependent clauses may be used as adverbs. The second type of dependent clause we will consider, therefore, is the *adverb clause*. You will recall that adverbs answer such questions as *how?, when?, where?, why?, how much?, how long?, under what condition?, in what way?,* or *to what extent?* about the words they modify. Adverb clauses can answer those same kinds of questions.

> An **ADVERB CLAUSE** is a dependent clause which is used as an adverb to modify a verb, verb phrase, verbal, adjective, or adverb.

# *SUBORDINATING CONJUNCTIONS*

Adverb clauses are introduced by **subordinating conjunctions**. A subordinating conjunction relates the clause to the word it modifies. Following is a list of subordinating conjunctions that may come at the beginning of adverb clauses:

| SUBORDINATING CONJUNCTIONS | | | | |
|---|---|---|---|---|
| after | as long as | in order that | that | whenever |
| although | as soon as | lest | though | where |
| as | because | since | unless | wherever |
| as if | before | so that | until | whether |
| as much as | if | than | when | while |

## ■ *Conjunction, Preposition, Or Relative?*

You may notice that some of these words, such as *after, before, since,* and *until,* can also be used as prepositions. Similarly, the word *that* may be used as a relative pronoun. These words are subordinating conjunctions when they signal the beginning of an adverb clause which is "subordinate" to or "dependent" upon an independent clause and which modifies a verb, adjective, or adverb in the independent clause. Do not confuse prepositional phrases or adjective clauses for adverb clauses just because they may begin with one of these double-duty words. Check carefully how the group of words they introduce is *used* when determining what kind of phrase or clause the group of words is.

### ☞EXAMPLES OF ADVERB CLAUSES:

The subordinating conjunction is in bold italics.

> ***As long as*** *you persist in your stubbornness,* you will be denied your privileges.

The adverb clause modifies the verb in the main clause, "will be denied," and answers the question "how long?" or "to what extent?" about that verb.

> We must honor those who died in our country's wars, ***lest*** *we forget their sacrifice.*

The adverb clause modifies the verb in the main clause, "must honor," and answers the question "why?" about that verb.

> I will go ***where*** *You want me to go, dear Lord.*

The adverb clause modifies the verb in the main clause, "will go," and answers the question "where?" about that verb.

> We were certain ***that*** *you would not be able to come.*

The adverb clause modifies the predicate adjective of the main clause, "certain," and answers the question "in what way?" about that adjective.

> Your juice-maker seems to work better ***than*** *ours does.*

The adverb clause modifies the adverb "better" in the main clause and answers the question "to what extent?" about that adverb.

## PLACEMENT OF ADVERB CLAUSES

Unlike adjective clauses, which usually must be placed immediately after the word they modify, adverb clauses may be placed in *various locations* to add clarity, emphasis, or variety to the sentence. Quite often they are placed at the beginning of a sentence.

| Rule 3.11 | When adverb clauses introduce a sentence, they are followed by a comma. |
|---|---|

An adverb clause at the end of a sentence does not need a comma unless it is a non-restrictive clause, as in the case of the sentence you are now reading.

☞**EXAMPLES:**

*If you love me*, keep my commandments. (**introductory, with comma**)

Do not let the day end *while you are still angry*. (**end of sentence, restrictive, no comma**)

You do not have to wash the car now, *though I will not object if you do*. (**non-restrictive**)

---

**Note:** The adverb clause in the third sentence above under EXAMPLES has another adverb clause within it. Can you identify both?

---

## ELLIPTICAL CLAUSES

In some cases, part of an adverb clause may be omitted when the omitted part is clearly understood from the context of the sentence, especially from words in the main clause. Such clauses are called *elliptical clauses*.

☞**EXAMPLES:**

She can run faster *than I*.    =    She can run faster *than I* [*can run*].

*While praying*, he received a vision.    =    *While* [*he was*] *praying*, he received a vision.

*Although generally healthy*, I feel ill today.    =    *Although* [*I am*] *generally healthy*, I feel ill today.

Problems arise when the words omitted (but understood) in the adverb clause have no counterpart, reference, or basis in the independent clause. Such clauses are called *dangling elliptical clauses*. Here are two ways to correct dangling elliptical clauses:

■ **Insert into a dangling elliptical clause the subject and/or verb needed to make the sentence clear.**

■ **Change the subject and/or verb in the independent clause so they would be clear and logical if they were also expressed in the elliptical clause.**

☞**EXAMPLES:**

| | |
|---|---|
| DANGLING: | *When driving,* **traffic conditions** should be watched carefully.* |
| CORRECTED: | *When driving,* **you** should watch traffic conditions carefully. |
| DANGLING: | *Unless watered,* **gardeners** will not grow good vegetables.** |
| CORRECTED: | *Unless watered,* good **vegetables** will not grow. |

**Note: Optional Explanations for Advanced Students and Instructors**

* In this example, the clause **When driving** is an elliptical clause because the implied words "you are" have been omitted *(When [you are] driving …)*. However, in the incorrect version given first, there is no counterpart or reference to the implied word "you" in the main clause. This makes the elliptical clause "dangle," and the sentence appears to be saying that traffic conditions are doing the driving. The problem is corrected in the next sentence by the addition of the words "you should" *(When [you are] driving,* **you** *should …)*.

** In the dangling version, one cannot tell what the omitted (implied) words "they are" *(Unless [they are] watered …)* refer to in the main clause—gardeners or vegetables. The clause is made to seem like a nonsense adjective clause modifying "gardeners." In the corrected version, the sentence arrangement makes it clear that the antecedent to the implied "they" in the adverb clause is "vegetables" in the main clause, and the whole dependent clause is more clearly seen to be an adverb clause modifying "will grow."

✎ **EXERCISE A** Underline the adverb clauses in the following sentences. Circle the word or words they modify.

1. You should always remember to wash your hands <u>before you eat</u>.

**Note:** In this example, the underlined adverb clause modifies a verbal, an infinitive introducing an infinitive phrase used as a noun [direct object of the verb "should remember"]. Since verbals are verb forms, they may be modified by adverbs, including adverb clauses, even when used as nouns. Notice that the adverb clause is part of the whole infinitive phrase, "to wash your hands before you eat."

2. Although I slept until 9:30 this morning, I still feel tired.

3. The authorities will issue an "all clear" bulletin when the tornado has passed.

4. I have never been happier than I am now.

5. Jesus shed His blood in order that I might be saved from the penalty for my sin.

6. Please wait until I am finished.

7. Wherever you go, I will be thinking of you.

8.   I could not tell whether she understood me or not.

9.   She does not remember where she put her ring.

10.  Hannah called Jeannie after they had seen each other at church.

---

✎ **EXERCISE B** Underline the adverb clauses in the following sentences. Double-underline the subordinating conjunctions which introduce the clauses. (Some sentences may have more than one adverb clause.)

1.   I will let you know <u>if I can come</u>.

2.   Katie can sing better than I can.

3.   She acted as if she did not know me.

4.   As long as you are going to the store, would you mind picking up some snacks?

5.   They did it because they love you.

6.   Since you are smarter than I am, perhaps you can help me with this problem.

7.   I am certain that you did not write me a letter after I wrote my last one to you.

8.   "Take heed lest any man deceive you" (Mark 13:5).

9.   "Even a child is known by his doings, whether his work be pure, and whether it be right" (Proverbs 20:11).

10.  "...Who satisfieth thy mouth with good things; so that thy youth is renewed like the eagle's" (Psalm 103:5).

11.  Feel free to sit wherever you like.

12.  They hired their neighbor's boy to water the lawn while they were on vacation.

13.  As you may know, our guest speaker has authored several books.

14.  Adverb clauses at the end of a sentence do not require commas unless they are non-restrictive.

15.  Parts of an adverb clause may be omitted if no misunderstanding will occur.

✎ **EXERCISE C** Rewrite the following sentences, correcting errors in the use of the elliptical clauses.

1.  Though a good athlete, the coach did not put Tim on the team.

    _____ *Though a good athlete, Tim did not make the team.* _____

2.  While studying our homework, the lights went out.

    _____

    _____

3.  Before broken in, you can get blisters from new shoes.

    _____

    _____

4.  When still a toddler, my grandfather gave me a football.

    _____

    _____

5.  Though passing the course, his teacher says he needs extra study to fully grasp the subject.

    _____

    _____

6.  While in the Los Angeles area, Disneyland should be visited.

    _____

    _____

7.  Unless boiled for several minutes, you should not drink water directly from a stream.

    _____

    _____

# LESSON 14: NOUN CLAUSES

> **A NOUN CLAUSE is a dependent clause that serves the function of a noun within a sentence.**

The third type of dependent clause is the **noun clause**. This clause may be used in the same way as a noun is—as a subject, a direct object, an indirect object, a predicate nominative, an object of a preposition, or an appositive.

| USE OF CLAUSE | EXAMPLES |
|---|---|
| Subject | *What he said* was very confusing. |
| Direct Object | She promised *that she would work for me on Saturday*. |
| Indirect Object | We will send *whoever wants one* a free copy of our magazine. |
| Object of a Preposition | I would like to ask about *what you had in mind*. |
| Predicate Nominative | His comment was *that everyone is entitled to his own opinion*. |
| Appositive | Her remark, *that all men are brutes*, was ill-tempered and unfounded. |

## SIGNAL WORDS

Noun clauses are introduced by **signal words**. Following is a list of signal words that may come at the beginning of noun clauses:

| SIGNAL WORDS | | | | | |
|---|---|---|---|---|---|
| how | whatever | which | whom | what | whoever |
| if | when | whichever | whomever | whether | why |
| that | where | who | whose | | |

The signal words **that, whether,** and **if** are merely introductory words which serve no other grammatical function within the clause. The other signal words, however, in addition to introducing the noun clause, serve a particular grammatical function *within* the clause.

When a noun clause is a direct object, the signal word **that** is sometimes omitted (see last example below). Study the chart below to understand how noun clauses function within sentences and how the signal words are used within the clauses.

| SENTENCES WITH NOUN CLAUSES | USE OF CLAUSE WITHIN SENTENCE | USE OF SIGNAL WORD WITHIN THE NOUN CLAUSE |
|---|---|---|
| You should do *whatever* seems right. | direct object | *whatever* = subject of clause |
| Making friends is *what* I do best. | predicate nominative | *what* = direct object of "do" |
| She has a suggestion about *where* we should go for dinner. | object of a preposition | *where* = adverb modifying "should go" |
| Tell me *whether* you like my cookies. | direct object | *whether* = introductory word only |
| Our teacher said *[that]* we had done good work. | direct object | *[that]* = implied introductory word only |

✎ **EXERCISE A** Underline the noun clauses in the following sentences. In the blank, tell how the *clause* is used in the sentence. Refer to the preceding chart.

1.  <u>That he lied</u> is a certainty. <u>*subject*</u>

2.  The police asked what the witnesses had seen. _____

3.  When you come is not important. _____

4.  The map described where the treasure was buried. _____

5.  The circus announcer said who would perform the next act. _____

6.  The gun was found near to where the crime was committed. _____

7.  Whom you elect will make a difference in your policies. _____

8.  Which god you serve has eternal consequences. _____

9.  Your score will depend on how well you do on the final test. _____

10. Jefferson's idea, that all men are created equal, is expressed in the Declaration of Independence.

    _____

11. Whatever you do you should do with all your might. _____

12. You should do whatever you do with excellence. _____

✎ **EXERCISE B** In the blanks below, tell how the *signal word* is used *within each of the clauses* you underlined in Exercise A. Refer to the previous chart.

1.  _introductory word only_          7.  _____

2.  _____              8.  _____

3.  _____              9.  _____

4.  _____             10.  _____

5.  _____             11.  _____

6.  _____             12.  _____

# LESSON 15: UNIT REVIEW

✎ **EXERCISE A** Fill in the blanks below:

1.  A clause is a group of words containing both a _____ and a _____ and forming

    _____.

2.  There are two main classifications of clauses. These two are _____ and

    _____.

3.  A compound sentence consists of two or more _____ clauses.

4.  A complex sentence consists of at least one _____ clause and one or more

    _____ clauses.

5.  A(n) _____ clause modifies a noun or pronoun.

6.  A(n) _____ clause modifies a verb, verbal, adjective, or adverb.

7.  A(n) _____ clause may be used as a subject, object, predicate nominative, or appositive.

8.  Adjective clauses are introduced by words called _____.

9.  Adverb clauses are introduced by words called _____.

10. Noun clauses are introduced by words called _____ words.

11. Except for the words _____, _____, and _____, the words that introduce noun clauses serve a grammatical function within the clause.

12. Independent clauses in compound sentences may be connected by a _____ conjunction or by a _____.

✎ **EXERCISE B** Identify the clause in **dark print** as an *adjective clause, adverb clause,* or *noun clause*:

_____ 1.   This is an idea **that makes no sense.**

_____ 2.   **What you said about me** is very flattering.

_____ 3.   Do not leave the room **until you are finished.**

_____ 4.   That is the book about **which I was speaking.**

_____ 5.   Words **that express action** are called verbs.

_____ 6.   He is a man **whose words can be trusted.**

# Unit 4 Diagramming

Many students of grammar dislike diagramming sentences. They say that diagramming seems like a useless exercise because, in life, we do not speak or write in diagrams. It is true, or course, that our speech and writing is not in diagram form; but diagramming is very useful for learning how we really do communicate in real life. We use sentences, and, as we have seen, sentences are constructed in many different ways and have many different component parts. Here are some of the reasons for learning to diagram:

- **Diagramming helps you to see the *relationship* of sentence parts to one another.**

- **Diagramming sentences sharpens your analytical skills.**

- **By visualizing the structure of your sentences, you can more effectively write and speak them so that others will accurately understand what you say or write.**

- **Diagramming will highlight any difficulties you may have about the points of grammar discussed so far and alert you to areas you should review.**

In this unit, you will have opportunities to diagram the grammatical elements you have studied so far in this workbook.

## LESSON 16: DIAGRAMMING KEY WORDS

The *baseline* of any sentence diagram is a horizontal line. A vertical line crossing the baseline divides the subject from the predicate. In the examples below you will see how to add other lines to the baseline. When diagramming, retain all capital letters but delete punctuation marks.

---

### 1—2. Subject / verb:

Birds fly.                                              Listen.

| Birds | fly |

| X | Listen |

In sentence 2, the subject (*You*) is understood. Use an **X** to represent any word that is implied or understood.

### 3. Subject / action verb / direct object:

Boys like baseball.

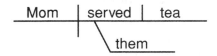

The direct object *baseball* is placed on the baseline after the verb and separated from it by a vertical line that does not extend below the baseline.

### 4. Subject / action verb / indirect object / direct object:

Mom served them tea.

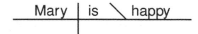

The indirect object *them* is placed below the verb and parallel to it. Draw a slanted line to connect it.

### 5. Subject / linking verb / predicate nominative:

I am he.

Both predicate nominatives and predicate adjectives are placed after the *verb* and separated by a line slanting to the left.

### 6. Subject / linking verb / predicate adjective:

Mary is happy.

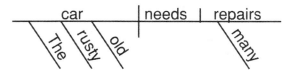

### 7. Adjectives:

The rusty old car needs many repairs.

Adjectives are placed on slanted lines under the word they modify. Remember that *a, an,* and *the* are adjectives too.

## 8. Adverbs modifying verbs:

They lived happily ever after.

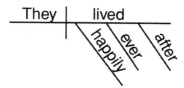

When adverbs modify verbs, place them on slanted lines under the *verb*.

## 9. Adverbs modifying adjectives:

Paula is a consistently cheerful woman.

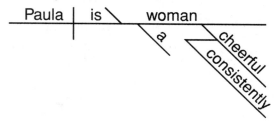

When an adverb modifies an adjective or another adverb, place it on a line connected to the modified word, as shown.

## 10. Adverbs modifying adverbs:

He writes fairly well.

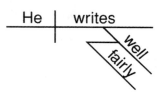

✎ **EXERCISE** Diagram the following sentences according to the examples given in this lesson.

1.   Many young girls prefer long hair.

2.   Tell me a funny story.

3.   My sickly grandmother hardly ever complains.

4.   The Bible is the most important book.

5.   The young racers ran quite swiftly.

6.   A sentence diagram is a useful grammatical tool.

7.   Ken gave the scouts some helpful hints.

# LESSON 17: DIAGRAMMING SENTENCES WITH PHRASES

Phrases are diagrammed as follows, according to their uses in a sentence. To review these phrase forms refer back to the chart in Lesson 6.

## 1. Prepositional phrase used as an adjective:

The girl in the blue sweat shirt is our camp counselor.

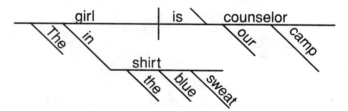

Draw a slanted line below the *noun* that the prepositional phrase modifies. Then draw a line parallel to the baseline. Place the preposition on the slanted line and the object of the preposition on the parallel line. Any words that modify the object of the preposition are placed on slanted lines below it.

## 2. Prepositional phrase used as an adverb:

You must love the Lord with a whole heart.

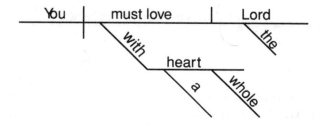

Locate the prepositional phrase underneath the *verb* it modifies and diagram in the same way as the preceding example.

## 3. Prepositional phrases used as nouns (subject and predicate adjective):

On Tuesday will be fine.                                This computer is out of date.

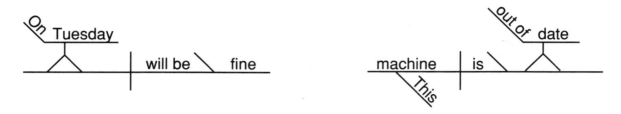

Draw a forked line on the *subject or predicate area* of the baseline. Place the prepositional phrase on the forked line.

## 4. Participial phrase:

The man opening the door for the lady is a gentleman.

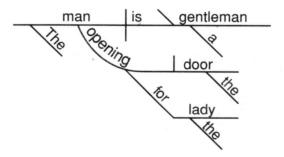

Place the participle *opening* on a curved line below the word it modifies—*man*. Diagram the rest of the participial phrase as you would for a direct object. The prepositional phrase modifies *opening*.

## 5. Gerundial phrase used as subject:

Learning grammar will improve your communications.

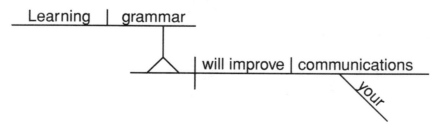

Recall that gerunds are verb forms used as **nouns**. The gerund phrase includes within it a direct object and possible modifiers. Diagram the gerund *learning* and its direct object *grammar* as shown, putting the whole noun phrase on a forked line as the **subject**. In examples 6 and 7, it is placed according to how it is used in the sentence—as a direct object or predicate nominative.

## 6. Gerundial phrase used as direct object:

He loves eating apple pie.

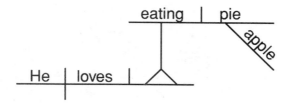

## 7. Gerundial phrase used as predicate nominative:

Commitment is giving your all for a cause.

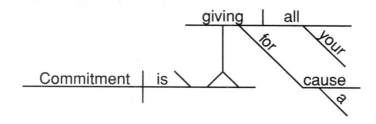

## 8. Infinitive phrases used as nouns:

**Used as subject**: To help others gives one a good feeling.

**Used as direct object**: Good grammar will help to improve your communication ability.

**As subject:**                          **As direct object:**

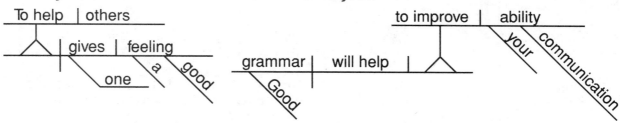

When infinitive phrases are used as nouns, they are diagrammed the same way as gerundial phrases.

## 9. Infinitive phrase used as adjective:

Obedience is the way to please God.

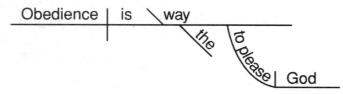

Place the infinitive on a curved line, showing its direct object, and attach the line to the *noun* it modifies.

## 10. Infinitive phrase used as adverb:

A true hero is a person worthy to be admired.

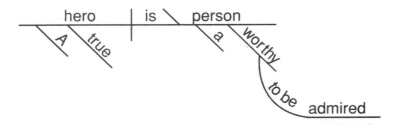

Attach the infinitive phrase (it has no direct object in this sentence) to the adjective it modifies—*worthy*.

## 11. Infinitive phrase ("clause") with its own subject:

Mom asked me to help her with the housecleaning.

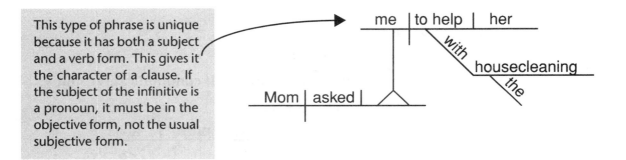

This type of phrase is unique because it has both a subject and a verb form. This gives it the character of a clause. If the subject of the infinitive is a pronoun, it must be in the objective form, not the usual subjective form.

This unique type of infinitive phrase is diagrammed as a subject–verb–direct object clause would be, and then placed on a forked line to function as the *direct object* of the sentence.

## 12. Prepositional-gerundial phrase (used as adverb):

The racers rested after running the course.

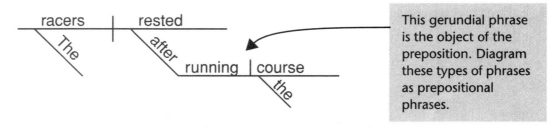

This gerundial phrase is the object of the preposition. Diagram these types of phrases as prepositional phrases.

## 13. Gerundial phrase used as an appositive:

The new policy, putting students on the honor roll, applies only to those with grades above B+.

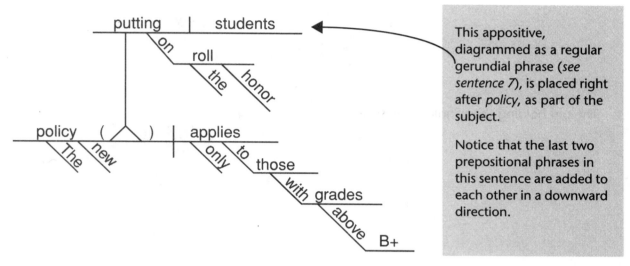

This appositive, diagrammed as a regular gerundial phrase (*see sentence 7*), is placed right after *policy*, as part of the subject.

Notice that the last two prepositional phrases in this sentence are added to each other in a downward direction.

## 14. Absolute phrase:

All things considered, the program was a success.

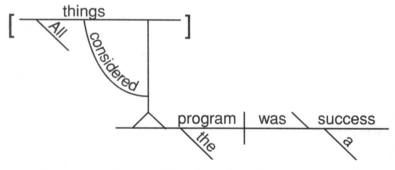

As in sentence 4, the participle *considered* is placed on a curved line below the **noun** it modifies—*things*. Put brackets around the entire absolute phrase (because it modifies no particular word) and place it on a forked line before the sentence subject.

✎ **EXERCISE** Diagram the following sentences containing various types of phrases. Draw your diagrams according to the appropriate examples given in this lesson.

1.   The lamp on the table is an antique.

2.    She covered the broccoli with melted cheese.

3.    The girl holding the candle is my sister.

4.    Putting your best foot forward is always a good policy.

5.    He always tries to give his all.

6.    To do his best for God was his goal in life.

7.   The woman playing the piano has great talent.

8.   Our work finished, we spent an hour playing basketball.

9.   Harry asked me to hand him the wrench.

10.  We heard a lecture about managing our money.

# LESSON 18: DIAGRAMMING SENTENCES WITH CLAUSES

## *COMPOUND SENTENCES*

Compound sentences (those with two or more independent clauses) are diagrammed like two simple sentences. The first independent clause is placed above the second, and the two clauses are connected by a dotted line. The connecting word is written along the dotted connecting line from verb to verb. If the clauses are joined by a semicolon, leave the connecting line blank.

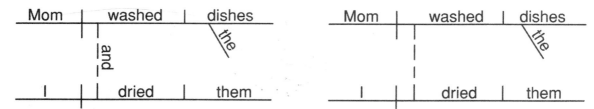

Mom washed the dishes and I dried them.          Mom washed the dishes; I dried them.

## COMPLEX SENTENCES

Complex sentences have at least one independent clause plus one or more dependent clauses.

### ■ Adjective and adverb clauses:

First diagram the independent clause. Then diagram the dependent clause *below* it. For adjective clauses, draw a dotted line from the **introductory word** of the dependent clause to the word the clause modifies. If necessary, review Lessons 12 and 13 on these types of clauses.

### 1. Adjective clause:

The law which was enacted by Congress was signed by the President.

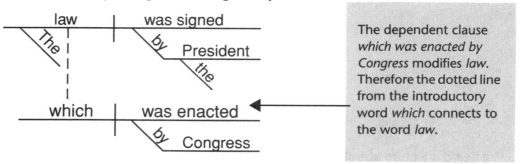

The dependent clause *which was enacted by Congress* modifies *law*. Therefore the dotted line from the introductory word *which* connects to the word *law*.

### 2. Adjective clause introduced by the implied relative pronoun "that":

The book I chose for my book report was not available.

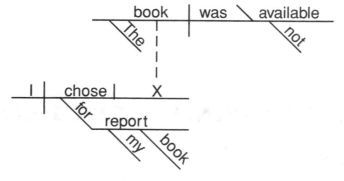

The **introductory word** (*that*) is implied in the dependent adjective clause *I chose for my book report*; this clause is positioned *below* and to the left of the independent clause. The implied relative pronoun "that" is shown as an **X**, and is connected with a dotted line to the word that it modifies (*book*) in the independent clause.

### 3. Adjective clause introduced by a relative pronoun used an object of a preposition:

He is the man about whom I was speaking.

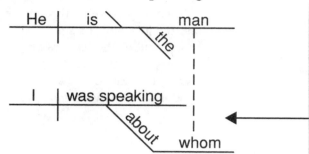

The introductory word *whom* is a relative pronoun used as an object of the preposition *about* in the dependent clause. This clause is placed *below* the independent clause, and the relative pronoun is connected with a dotted line to the noun *man* which it modifies.

### 4. Adjective clause introduced by a relative adjective:

An alto is a singer whose voice is low.

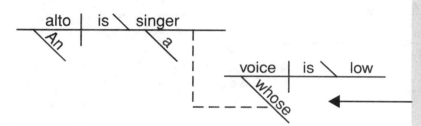

In order to connect the introductory word (*whose*) of the dependent clause to the noun *singer*, the dependent clause must be placed *below* and to the right of the independent clause.

### 5. Adjective clause introduced by a relative adverb:

We live in a town where everyone is friendly.

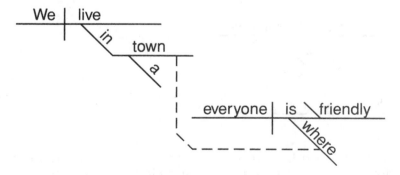

Likewise, in order to connect the **introductory word** (*where*) of the dependent clause to the word which it modifies (*town*), the dependent clause must be placed *below* and to the right of this noun in the independent clause. The relative adverb *where* is then connected with a dotted line to the object of the preposition—*town*.

---

**Note:** The prepositional phrase *in a town* is an adverbial phrase that modifies the verb *live* in the main clause.

---

## 6. Adverb clause modifying a verb:

We came when you called.

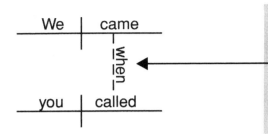

When diagramming this adverb clause, the dotted line with the subordinating conjunction *when* is drawn from the verb in the dependent clause (*you called*) to the word which it modifies in the independent clause; in this case, the verb *came*.

## 7. Adverb clause modifying an adjective:

I am happy that you came.

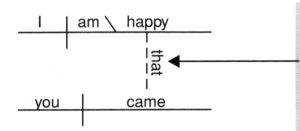

When diagramming this adverb clause, the dotted line with the subordinating conjunction *that* is drawn from the verb in the dependent clause (*you came*) to the word which it modifies in the independent clause; in this case, the predicate adjective *happy*.

## 8. Adverb clause (elliptical) modifying an adverb:

Jim can hit a baseball better than I.

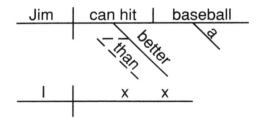

The omitted but implied words "can hit" in the elliptical clause are represented by X's. The subordinating conjunction *than* connects the dependent clause to the adverb *better*.

## ■ *Noun clauses*

The signal word of a noun clause is diagrammed according to its use within the clause. You will recall from Lesson 14 that the signal words ***that, whether***, and ***if*** have no grammatical function within their noun clauses. In diagramming a noun clause with one of these three signal words, place the signal word on a separate horizontal line *above* the noun clause. Connect the signal word to the *verb* of the noun clause with a dotted line. If the signal word is implied, rather than expressed, represent it with an **X**.

## 9. Noun clause used as a subject:

That he was an educated man was clear from his comments.

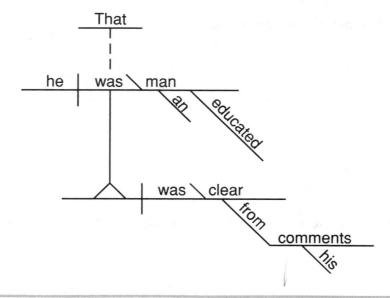

## 10. Noun clause used as a direct object (with implied signal word "that"):

The teacher said my answer was correct.

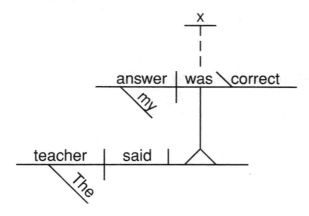

## 11. Noun clause used as an object of a preposition:

He reported about what he would do next.

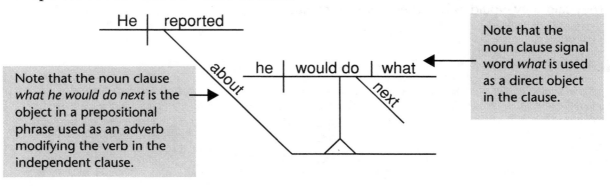

Note that the noun clause *what he would do next* is the object in a prepositional phrase used as an adverb modifying the verb in the independent clause.

Note that the noun clause signal word *what* is used as a direct object in the clause.

✎ **EXERCISE** Diagram the following compound or complex sentences according to the appropriate examples given in this lesson.

1.  We have been on vacation but we have returned.

2.  The immigrants came to America, and they contributed many things to our culture.

3.  Millard Fillmore is a president who is not well known in our day.

4.  They said they would arrive whenever they could.

5. The police reported nothing publicly about what they had discovered.

6. Whether we can leave depends upon the weather.

7. Catch me if you can. *(Write the implied subject "You" as an X in parentheses.)*

8. Give me all the money you have.

# LESSON 19: UNIT REVIEW

This unit has given you many examples of sentence diagrams. Study these examples again and use them to help you diagram the following sentences. This exercise will determine if you understand the proper word relationships given in the example diagrams, and how to apply this knowledge to diagramming various kinds of sentences. For each of the more difficult sentences, first decide which type of phrase or clause is used in the sentence, and then look for the appropriate example from Lessons 16-18.

✎ **EXERCISE A** Diagram the following sentences according to the examples given in Lesson 16.

1.   Faith is a gift of God.

2.   The Johnson's telephone was ringing constantly.

3.   Jay threw him the ball rather hard.

4.   Jessica memorized her verses quite rapidly.

5.   Pick up your clothes immediately.

✎ **EXERCISE B** Diagram the following sentences according to the examples given in Lesson 17.

1. Drinking water frequently removes impurities from your body.

2. On the night stand is her study Bible.

3. The student parking the car in the garage is a very good driver.

4. The sermon, "Giving All to Christ," convicted the congregation.

5.  After eating a wonderful meal, the family retired to the back porch.

6.  To start your own business takes a substantial amount of capital.

7.  Hard times forced the pastor to find a second job.

8.  Faith is believing God's promises.

✎ **EXERCISE C** Diagram the following compound or complex sentences according to the appropriate examples given in Lesson 18.

1. Nick worked in a company where the management fired all their consultants.

2. That is the proposal about which he was arguing.

3. Bill raked the leaves in the front yard while I mowed the grass behind the house.

4.  The sheep dogs worked the flock more than the shepherd.

5.  Philip claimed his brother broke the window.

6.  Renée told the class about what she did on vacation.

7.   Whether Sam was the choice for team captain was not revealed by the coach.

8.   A historian is an authority whose specialty is articulating the past.

✎ **EXERCISE D** Write a complex sentence of your own and diagram it below.

_____

_____

# Unit 5
# Writing Sentences

> A SENTENCE is a group of words consisting of a subject and predicate, expressing a complete thought, and capable of standing alone. A sentence begins with a capital letter and ends with a period, exclamation point, or question mark.

You have already learned a great deal about sentences during your study of the first four units of this book. The definition above is a common way of describing what a sentence is. We have already noted, however, that some expressions which do **not** meet all of the requirements of this definition are still able to express some fairly complete thoughts. For example, *independent clauses* express complete thoughts. They may stand alone as a sentence or be combined with other clauses to form a sentence. *Dependent clauses* express somewhat less complete thoughts because they depend on independent clauses for their fullest meaning. In addition, some expressions such as "Never!" or "Away with him!" or "Ticket, please" or "Anyone for tennis?" are quite understandable and sometimes stand alone as "sentences." However, for our study in this unit, we will use the word *sentence* in the strict grammatical sense indicated in the definition above.

## LESSON 20: SENTENCE CLASSIFICATION BY CLAUSE

There are a number of ways to classify sentences. In your study of clauses, you have already learned a great deal about the method discussed in this lesson: *classification according to the number and type of clauses,* in other words, having to do with their structure. You have learned about three types of sentences: *simple, compound,* and *complex.* There is a fourth type as well — the *compound-complex* sentence.

| CLASSIFI- CATION | NUMBER AND TYPE OF CLAUSES | EXAMPLES |
|---|---|---|
| Simple | **One independent clause** (*may have a compound subject and/or predicate*) | Bonnie and Alicia stayed overnight at Megan's house and had a good time together. |
| Compound | **Two or more independent clauses** (*each clause may have a compound subject and/or predicate*) | Megan stayed overnight at Bonnie's house, and they called Alicia on the telephone and laughed and talked for hours. |

| CLASSIFI-CATION | NUMBER AND TYPE OF CLAUSES | EXAMPLES |
|---|---|---|
| Complex | One independent clause<br><br>One or more dependent clauses<br><br>(each clause may have a compound subject and/or predicate) | Alicia, whose parents were out of town, stayed overnight at Bonnie's house, which is next door to Megan's house. |
| Compound-complex | Two or more independent clauses<br><br>One or more dependent clause<br><br>(each clause may have a compound subject and/or predicate) | Alicia, whose parents were out of town, stayed overnight at Bonnie's house, which is next door to Megan's house; and the three girls got together for a few hours. |

## WHEN TO USE EACH TYPE OF SENTENCE

| Rule 5.1 | A simple sentence is best used to express one or two simple ideas about one or more subjects. |
|---|---|

☞EXAMPLE:

Our street needs repair.

| Rule 5.2 | A compound sentence is best used to express two equally related parts of one main idea. |
|---|---|

☞EXAMPLE:

Our street needs repair, but the street department has no funds for the work.

| Rule 5.3 | A complex sentence is best used to express two ideas, one of which may not be as important as the other. |
|---|---|

☞EXAMPLE:

Our street, which is called Logan Street, is badly in need of repairs.

| Rule 5.4 | A compound-complex sentence is best used to express two equally related parts of one major idea and one or more ideas not as important as either of the two larger ideas. |
|---|---|

☞**EXAMPLE:**

Our street, which is called Logan Street, needs repair; but the street department, one of several financially strapped city agencies, has no funds for the work.

## ■ *Which Type Of Sentence Is The Following?*

(*The answer to this question is found after* LESSON 24: UNIT REVIEW.)

To be at home in all lands and ages; to count nature a familiar acquaintance, and art a familiar friend; to gain a standard for the appreciation of other men's work and the criticism of one's own; to carry the keys to the world's library in one's pocket and feel its resources behind one in whatever task he undertakes; to make hosts of friends among men of one's own age, who are the leaders in all walks of life; to lose one's self in generous enthusiasms, and to cooperate with others for common ends; to learn manners from students who are gentlemen, and to form character under professors who are Christian— these are the returns of a college for the best four years of one's life.

—William De Witt Hyde

✎ **EXERCISE A** In the blanks, write **S, CD, CX,** or **CC** to indicate whether the sentence is *simple, compound, complex,* or *compound-complex*. Underline all subjects in all clauses. Double-underline all predicate verbs (action or linking) in all clauses.

__S__    1. Oaks and maples line both sides of our street.

_____    2. Spoken words are sounds or combinations of sounds which represent ideas.

_____    3. In English, words fall into eight categories known as the parts of speech.

_____    4. Victor Telephone is a small company that serves two communities in a rural area.

_____    5. Fill out the enclosed application, and return it immediately if you wish to apply for the job.

_____    6. When it rains, I enjoy listening to the sound of raindrops; but I do not enjoy being out in the wet weather.

_____    7. On our class trip, we visited the state Capitol; and we met our senator and representative.

_____    8. People sometimes save money on their taxes by hiring a tax expert during preparation of their tax returns.

_____    9. People sometimes save money on their taxes when they hire a tax expert to prepare their tax returns.

_____    10. People sometimes save money on their taxes when they hire a tax expert to prepare their tax returns; however, other people prefer to complete their tax returns themselves.

✎ **EXERCISE B** The following sentences are all compound, complex, or compound-complex sentences. In the blanks below each sentence write each separate independent clause and each dependent clause, if any. If there are no dependent clauses, write *None* in the appropriate blanks.

1.  We may not always win, but we should try to do our best.

**Independent:**     *1. We may not always win*

                            *2. but we should try to do our best*

**Dependent:**     *None*

2.  People who love the Lord will desire to worship Him in the company of His people.

**Independent:** _____

_____

**Dependent:** _____

_____

3.  For our vacation this year, we again rented a cabin at the lake where we have gone for the past ten years.

**Independent:** _____

_____

**Dependent:** _____

_____

4.  Since the weather was good, we went for a hike; but we returned with blisters that hurt for several days thereafter.

**Independent:** _____

_____

**Dependent:** _____

_____

5.  Molly is a girl who always puts her homework ahead of extracurricular activities.

**Independent:** _____

_____

**Dependent:** _____

_____

6.   In my Bible, the words of Christ are printed in red; but my pastor reminded me that the entire Bible is the Word of God.

**Independent:** _____

_____

**Dependent:** _____

_____

7.   My tape player is a good one, but the headphones are broken.

**Independent:** _____

_____

**Dependent:** _____

_____

8.   The "Information Age" is filled with wonders, and the student who fails to learn computer skills may be left behind when he becomes an adult.

**Independent:** _____

_____

**Dependent:** _____

_____

9.   The filing cabinet which stands in my dad's office is made of steel, but it may not be entirely fireproof.

**Independent:** _____

_____

**Dependent:** _____

_____

10. October, which always has thirty-one days, has five Sundays this year; but three years ago it had only four.

Independent: _____

_____

Dependent: _____

_____

# LESSON 21: SENTENCE CLASSIFICATION BY PURPOSE

Sentences may also be classified according to the kind of statement they make, that is, according to their *meaning* or *purpose*. In this classification method, there are four types of sentences — **declarative**, **imperative**, **interrogative**, and **exclamatory**.

| CLASSIFICATION | PURPOSE | EXAMPLES |
|---|---|---|
| **Declarative** | **Makes a claim or a statement of fact, possibility, or condition.**<br><br>May be used for all kinds of narration, description, argument, or explanation. | The book I am reading has seventeen chapters.<br><br>It may be too late to come.<br><br>The sun's reflection shimmered across the rippling waves.<br><br>Narcotics are dangerous substances. |
| **Interrogative** | **Asks a question.**<br><br>May be used for direct inquiries or "rhetorical" questions (those for which the answer is obvious or already known) | How did you find me?<br><br>What is the name of that book you are reading?<br><br>Do you think you are smarter than I am? |
| **Exclamatory** | **Expresses strong feeling.**<br><br>May be used for special interest or effectiveness of expression. | Oh, if only I had studied for that test!<br><br>What a funny story that was! |
| **Imperative** | **Makes a request or states a command.**<br><br>May be used for giving orders, directions, or advice. | Please take a seat at this time.<br><br>Stop what you are doing! |

# DECLARATIVE SENTENCES

*Declarative sentences* simply make a *statement*, and end with a **period**. (*See examples above.*)

# INTERROGATIVE SENTENCES

*Interrogative sentences*, which ask questions, can be written in at least *four different ways*:

## 1. Place the subject after a helping verb.

☞**EXAMPLES:**

Do you care? Are you sleeping? Will you read me a story?

## 2. Begin with an interrogative pronoun or adverb.

☞**EXAMPLES:**

What am I doing? Where are my glasses? Who said that? Why speak now?

## 3. Add an interrogative statement to the end of a declarative or imperative statement.

☞**EXAMPLES:**

You are my friend, aren't you? Have a cookie, won't you?

## 4. Place a question mark at the end of a declarative statement.

☞**EXAMPLES:**

You're finished already? He's not going to church? She's ill? You're serious?

# EXCLAMATORY SENTENCES

*Exclamatory sentences* may also be written in different ways:

## 1. Use the following word order: exclamatory word + complement (predicate nominative or adjective, direct object, etc.) + subject + predicate.

☞**EXAMPLES:**

How beautiful you look tonight!

What a rough time we had!

What a tall boy you are!

Such bad weather this is!

2.  Exclamatory "sentences" are the only "sentences" that may consist of merely a word, a phrase, or a dependent clause.

☞**EXAMPLES:**

Danger! Your attention, please!   Many thanks!    Good grief!

Ouch! A thousand times, no!    Out with you!

## IMPERATIVE SENTENCES

In *imperative sentences*, the subject is usually the pronoun *"You,"* either singular or plural, although it is usually merely understood, NOT EXPRESSED. In most cases, a helping verb with an imperative idea, such as *must, should, ought (to),* or *need (to),* is also implied.

☞**EXAMPLES:**

(**You must**) Stop what you are doing! (**You need to**) Take a bath.

(**You should**) Read this article. (**You ought to**) Do your homework.

Usually, in imperative sentences, the implied subject "You" suggests that the sentence is being directly addressed to the person to whom one is speaking or writing. In some imperative sentences using the words *let* or *may*, however, the "You" is more vague or not implied at all; and the sentence is not really addressed directly to a reader or listener. Instead, the sentence makes a more general request or exhortation, but is still considered imperative.

☞**EXAMPLES:**

Let us pray.

"Whosoever will come after me, let him deny himself..." (Mark 8:34).

May we always be true to our beliefs.

## ENDING PUNCTUATION

Use the appropriate kind of ending punctuation for each type of sentence.

| Rule 5.5 | Declarative sentences always end with a period. |
|----------|--------------------------------------------------|
| Rule 5.6 | Imperative sentences may end with either a period (for mild requests) or an exclamation point (for strong commands). |
| Rule 5.7 | Interrogative sentences always end with a question mark. |
| Rule 5.8 | Exclamatory sentences always end with an exclamation point. |

# SENTENCE COMBINATIONS:

Some sentences appear to be combinations of two or more classifications, each clause having a different character. In such cases, the sentence is classified according to its most prominent or significant feature.

☞**IMPERATIVE:**

Act now, or you will lose your opportunity.

**Note:** The overall thrust of the sentence is a command, even though the second clause has a declarative character.

☞**INTERROGATORY:**

You are still my friend, aren't you?

**Note:** The main purpose of the sentence is to make an inquiry, even though the first clause has a declarative character.

✎ **EXERCISE** In the blanks, write **Decl., Imp., Int.,** or **Excl.** to indicate whether the sentence is *declarative, imperative, interrogative,* or *exclamatory*. Place the correct punctuation mark at the end of the sentence. (If the sentence is imperative, use your best judgment in deciding whether a period or exclamation point is appropriate.)

*Imp.*    1.  Please accept my apology.

_____    2.  What a busy little fellow you have been

_____    3.  Can you recite John 3:16 from memory

_____    4.  Finish your homework, or you will not be allowed to watch television tonight

_____    5.  The price of that item is $14.95

_____    6.  What do you think you are doing

_____    7.  What time is it

_____    8.  Put your trust in God

_____    9.  Never, ever speak to me in that way again

_____  10.  Have you finished reading chapter four

_____  11.  We must learn from our mistakes

_____  12.  When you come to the end of your life, what will you have to show for your efforts

_____  13.  Answer the telephone; it's ringing

_____  14.  Whoever would enjoy long life, let him be sure he honors his parents

_____  15.  May I take your coat

_____  16.  A hearty welcome to you

_____  17.  In the first chapter of the Gospel of John, who is called "The Word"

_____  18.  At what time does the varsity game begin

_____  19.  Never spit into the wind

_____  20.  May his every wish come true

# LESSON 22: SENTENCE CLASSIFICATION BY EMPHASIS

Sentences may also be classified according to *how their content is arranged*. Different arrangements cause different points of *emphasis*. The three most common classifications are **loose,** **periodic,** and **balanced**. Most of the sentences we speak or write are loose, but periodic and balanced sentences can be used to provide variety and interest to our communications.

| CLASSIFICATION | DESCRIPTION | EXAMPLES |
|---|---|---|
| **Loose** (normal emphasis) | The sentence is arranged in such as way that the primary idea or meaning is known before the end of the sentence. | She enjoyed knitting, a skill she learned from her mother.<br><br>Autumn is the time to plant tulip and daffodil bulbs.<br><br>Your mother is calling. |
| **Periodic** (creates suspense) | The sentence is arranged in such a way that the main idea or meaning becomes clear only toward the *end* of the sentence. | If you love Me, keep My commandments *(John 14:15).*<br><br>Hungry, tired, and sore from their long ordeal, the lost hikers were flown out of the wilderness by the rescue helicopter. |
| **Balanced** (variation of loose or periodic) | The sentence is written in such a way that similar or opposing ideas have *parallel grammatical phrasing.* | When pride comes, then comes shame *(Proverbs 11:2a).*<br><br>On Monday I have gym; on Tuesday I have choir.<br><br>The wise forgive, fools never. |

In a **loose** sentence, the main idea is typically *followed by* details, modifiers, and dependent clauses. Usually, in **periodic** sentences, a dependent clause comes *before* the main clause *(see example 1 of the periodic sentences in the chart above)*. However, this is not always the case *(see example 2 above)*. In a **periodic** sentence the reader has to wait for the main idea until he has comprehended the details upon which the main idea is based.

## TWO CLASSIC (and very long) SENTENCES

| PERIODIC | BALANCED |
|---|---|
| If you can keep your head when all about you | To everything there is a season, |
| Are losing theirs and blaming it on you; | A time for every purpose under heaven: |
| If you can trust yourself when all men doubt you, | A time to be born, |
|  But make allowance for their doubting too; | And a time to die; |
| If you can wait and not be tired by waiting, | A time to plant, |
| Or, being lied about, don't deal in lies, | And a time to pluck what is planted; |
| Or, being hated, don't give way to hating, | A time to kill, |
| And yet don't look too good, nor talk too wise; | And a time to heal; |
| If you can dream—and not make dreams your master; | A time to break down, |
| If you can think—and not make thoughts your aim; | And a time to build up; |
| If you can meet with triumph and disaster | A time to weep, |
| And treat those two impostors just the same; | And a time to laugh; |
| If you can bear to hear the truth you've spoken | A time to mourn, |
| Twisted by knaves to make a trap for fools, | And a time to dance; |
| Or watch the things you gave your life to broken, | A time to cast away stones, |
| And stoop and build 'em up with worn-out tools; | And a time to gather stones; |
| If you can make one heap of all your winnings | A time to embrace, |
| And risk it on one turn of pitch-and-toss, | And a time to refrain from embracing; |
| And lose, and start again at your beginnings | A time to gain, |
| And never breathe a word about your loss; | And a time to lose; |
| If you can force your heart and nerve and sinew | A time to keep, |
| To serve your turn long after they are gone, | And a time to throw away; |
| And so hold on when there is nothing in you | A time to tear, |
| Except the Will which says to them: "Hold on"; | And a time to sew; |
| If you can talk with crowds and keep your virtue, | A time to keep silence, |
| Or walk with kings—nor lose the common touch; | And a time to speak; |
| If neither foes nor loving friends can hurt you; | A time to love, |
| If all men count with you, but none too much; | And a time to hate; |
| If you can fill the unforgiving minute | A time of war, |
| With sixty seconds' worth of distance run— | And a time of peace. |
| Yours is the Earth and everything that's in it, | *— Ecclesiastes 3:1-8, NKJV* |
| And—which is more—you'll be a Man, my son! | |
| *— Rudyard Kipling* | |

✎ **EXERCISE** In the blanks, write **L**, **P**, or **B** to indicate whether the sentence is *loose, periodic* or *balanced.* Some discretion is involved; be prepared to defend your answer.

_L_    1.  Our conversations contain several different types of sentences.

____    2.  "You can take a man out of the country; you can't take the 'country' out of a man" *(Anonymous).*

____    3.  When you hear two knocks on the door, it will be me.

____    4.  "To believe in immortality is one thing, but it is first needful to believe in life" *(Robert Louis Stevenson).*

____    5.  If you do not like this kind of salad, please tell me so.

____    6.  The parking lot was resurfaced with a fresh layer of asphalt.

____    7.  "He who despises the word will be destroyed, but he who fears the commandment will be rewarded" *(Proverbs 13:13).*

____    8.  "Success is never final and failure never fatal" *(George F. Tilton).*

____    9.  "An atheist's most embarrassing moment is when he feels profoundly thankful for something and can't think of anybody to thank for it" *(Anonymous).*

____    10. "Without faith a man can do nothing; with it all things are possible" *(William Osler).*

____    11. The *Declaration of Independence*, which was written in 1776, contains a few memorable phrases and the statement of many grievances with which few people are familiar today.

____    12. "Faith is to believe what we do not see, and the reward of this faith is to see what we believe" *(St. Augustine).*

____    13. "Nothing can be done without hope" *(Helen Keller).*

____    14. The author of the book I am reading was born in Australia.

____    15. "Two people unselfish and considerate, tactful and warmhearted, and salted with humor, who are in love, have the most essential of all qualifications for a successful marriage—they have character" *(William Lyon Phelps).*

____    16. This chair needs a new coat of paint, but the old paint should be removed first.

____    17. "Music is well said to be the speech of angels" *(Thomas Carlyle).*

____    18. "One man with courage is a majority" *(Andrew Jackson).*

# LESSON 23: DIAGRAMMING COMPOUND-COMPLEX SENTENCES

Compound-complex sentences may seem difficult to diagram. The task is made easier when each independent clause and dependent clause is considered separately and diagrammed as a unit. The independent clauses are then connected with dotted lines from verb to verb.

Here is a sentence from the Bible which has four independent clauses and one dependent (adjective) clause. Two of the independent clauses have compound predicates. Recall that "not" is an adverb.

☞**EXAMPLE:**

They that wait upon the Lord shall renew their strength; they shall mount up with wings as eagles; they shall run, and not be weary; they shall walk, and not faint. (Isaiah 40:31)

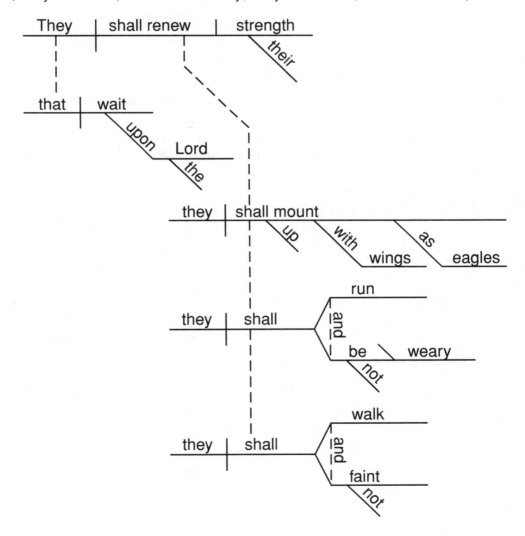

The next sentence contains two independent clauses and one dependent (adverb) clause. The second independent clause contains an infinitive phrase used as a direct object. Diagram the first independent clause (*we cannot win ...*) with its attached dependent clause. Underneath, diagram the second independent clause and attach the two clauses, verb to verb, with a dotted line and the conjunction.

☞**EXAMPLE:**

We cannot win unless we score more points, and we hope to score at least five more.

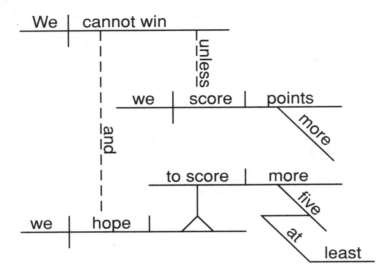

---

✎ **EXERCISE** Diagram the following compound-complex sentences, according to the examples given in this lesson and in Unit 4.

1.   Think before you speak, and you will avoid conflicts.

2. That our father is a righteous man has been a blessing to our family; moreover, he sets an excellent example for his children.

3. The article which appeared in our school paper carried my byline, but the reporting was a group effort.

4.  After we leave school, we will do our homework; and we will then meet you at the hamburger shop.

5.  Treating people who are disagreeable in a loving manner is a challenge, but it is something that we must do.

# LESSON 24: UNIT REVIEW

✎ **EXERCISE** Fill in the blanks below:

1.  What are the four classifications of sentences according to number and type of clauses?

    _____    _____

    _____    _____

2.  What are the four classifications of sentences according to purpose or meaning?

    _____    _____

    _____    _____

3.  What are the three classifications of sentences according to emphasis or arrangement of content?

    _____    _____

    _____

4.  A(n) _____ sentence asks a question or makes an inquiry.

5.  A(n) _____ sentence makes a command or request.

6.  A(n) _____ sentence expresses strong feeling.

7.  A(n) _____ sentence states a claim, fact, possibility, or condition.

8.  In a _____ sentence, the full meaning or idea is not entirely made clear until the end of the sentence.

9.  In a _____ sentence, the main idea is stated early and followed by details, modifiers, or dependent ideas.

10. In a _____ sentence, similar or opposing ideas have similar or parallel grammatical phrasing.

11. A _____ sentence has one independent clause.

12. A _____ sentence has two or more independent clauses.

13. A _____ sentence has one independent clause and one or more dependent clauses.

14. A _____ sentence has two or more independent clauses and one or more dependent clauses.

15. What punctuation mark(s) may end an imperative sentence? _____

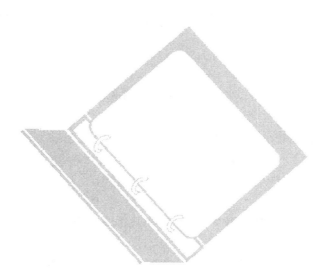

ANSWER TO THE QUESTION ON PAGE 79: Complex

# Unit 6 Building Vocabulary

To be more effective in your use of language—whether in speaking, listening, writing, or reading—you should continually try to increase and improve your vocabulary. To *increase* it means you should strive to add more and more words to your communications. Building a vocabulary takes a long time and can be accomplished by frequent use of the dictionary and other word books, as well as by expansive reading—taking note of new words as you read. To *improve* your vocabulary means to precisely and accurately select and use words to convey exact meanings. This too can be accomplished through use of a dictionary, thesaurus and other word books, and through reading.

> **VOCABULARY is the sum or stock of words used in a language by an individual or class of people, or in a field of knowledge.**

As you read, take note of how accomplished authors express exact meanings by the careful selection of just the right words. Read good literature, not necessarily the most popular or common fare. Other means of increasing and improving your vocabulary include the study of foreign languages (especially those which have contributed significantly to English), listening to good speakers (in person or via the mass media), avoiding excessive exposure to and imitation of poor speakers and writers (including those who constantly use faddish or ungrammatical language), and paying close attention to word components (such as prefixes, suffixes, and roots). This unit includes some lessons to help you increase or improve your vocabulary.

## LESSON 25: PREFIXES

> **A PREFIX is a syllable or syllables united with the beginning of a word or a word root to modify (change) its meaning.**

The English language has dozens of prefixes. By attaching these syllables to the beginnings of words or word roots, our stock of words can be greatly increased, thus adding to the available word choices we can make to express our thoughts more precisely. The word **prefix** itself is an example of a word with a prefix. The first three letters of this word (*pre-*) express the idea *"before."* This prefix helps us understand the meaning of the word *prefix*. We could say that the word means something that is "fixed" or "fastened" "before."

On the following pages is a chart listing some of the prefixes used in English words. Learn the meaning of the prefixes and study the example words.

| PREFIX | MEANING | EXAMPLES OF WORDS USING THE PREFIX |
|---|---|---|
| un- | "not" gives a negative meaning to the root word | unhappy, unwieldy, unguarded, unkept, unknown, unravel, unsteady, untimely, unwilling<br><br>"Un-" can be attached to almost any adjective |
| in-<br>il-<br>im-<br>ir- | "not" gives a negative meaning to the root word | incurable, inevitable, ineffective<br><br>illegal, illiterate, illegitimate<br><br>impatient, immortal, improbable<br><br>irresistible, irreligious, irrelevant, irreverent |
| dis- | "not" "the opposite of" "opposite to" | disorder, discredit, disregard, disinfect, disconnect, disfavor, disloyal, dishonor, disarray, disbelief, dissatisfied, disable |
| pre-<br>fore- | "before" "in front of" | predict, preview, preconceived<br><br>forecast, foretaste, foresight |
| ante-<br>pro- | "before" "in front of" | ante-bellum, antediluvian, antemeridian<br><br>proceed, prospect |
| a-<br>ab-<br>de- | "from," "apart" "down," "without" **de-** is used to intensify the meaning of the root. | avert, adrift, allay, afloat, apathy<br><br>abort, abate, abrupt, abduct, absent<br><br>deflect, deflate, dethrone |
| ad-<br>af-<br>al-<br>an-<br>ap-<br>as- | "to" | adjoin, adverb, adhere, adjust, adopt<br><br>affix, affirm, affair, afflict, affront<br><br>allure, allude, allege, alliterate, allow<br><br>annex, annotate, annihilate, announce, annul<br><br>appoint, appraise, appear, apparatus, apply<br><br>associate, ascend, assemble, aspire, assist |

| co- | "with" | cooperate, commingle, coordinate |
| col- | "together" | collapse, collect, collate, collide, collusion |
| con- | | confront, contract, congregation, consist |
| com- | | committee, combine, commerce, commit |
| cog- | | cognizant, cogent, cognate, cognition |
| cor- | | correspond, correct, correlative, corrupt |
| e- | "out of" | evade, evoke, elapse, egress, elect |
| ex- | "without" "away from" | export, expose, exempt, exact, examination |
| per- | "through" "throughout" "thoroughly" | pervade, perceive, permeate, percolate, percussion, perfect, perplex, perspective, perspire |
| trans- | "across" "beyond" | transport, transpire, translate, transform, transcend, transpose |
| inter- | "between" | interracial, intervene, intersperse, interpose, interlude, interfere |
| intra- | "within" | intrastate, intramural, intramuscular, intravenous |
| infra- | "below" | infrared, infrastructure, infralapsarian |
| super- | "above" "over" | supersede, supernatural, superior, supercharger, superfluous |
| supra- | | supratemporal, supralapsarian, supranasal |
| sub- | "under," "below" | subhuman, subside, subject, submerge, submarine |
| suc- | "almost" "somewhat" | succumb, succeed, succinct, succor |
| suf- | "slightly" "after," "less than" | suffocate, suffer, sufficient, suffix, suffocate |
| sup- | | suppress, supplicate, suppose, supplant, supply |
| sus- | | suspend, suspect, sustain, susceptible |
| circum- | "around" | circumference, circumnavigate, circumspect, circumvent |
| contra- | "against," "oppose" | contradict, contraindicate, contravene, contraband |
| counter- | "substitute," "contrast" | counterpart, counterpoint, countermand, counterfeit, counterbalance |

| PREFIX | MEANING | EXAMPLES OF WORDS USING THE PREFIX |
|--------|---------|-----------------------------------|
| uni- | "one" (united) | universe, unison, uniform |
| mono- | "one" (alone) | monotone, monologue, monopoly |
| bi- | "two" | biannual, biennial, bicycle, bisect, bicameral, bipartisan |
| tri- | "three" | trinity, tripod, triple, triplex, tripartite, trilogy |
| en-<br><br>em- | "to make," "put in"<br>"in," "within"<br>"into," "toward"<br>"through" | enable, engross, encamp, enthrone, endanger, entangle, entrust, enrapture, envelop, envelope<br>embolden, empower |
| in-<br><br>im-<br><br>il-<br><br>ir- | "to make"<br>"put in," "put on"<br>"in," "within"<br>"into," "onto"<br>"toward"<br>"through" | inflate, install, instill, infiltrate<br>impute, impel, impend, import<br>illustrate, illumine, illusion,<br>irrigate, irruption, irradiate |
| be- | "to make or fill," "on,"<br>"over," "against," "at"<br>"about" | begrudge, belittle, bespeckled, besmirch, beseech, beguile, bedeck, becalm |
| non- | "no," "not"<br>"reverse of"<br>"absence of" | nonresident, nonpayment, nonessential, nonrestrictive, nonfiction, nonsense, nonpartisan, nonexistent, nongovernmental |
| post- | "after"<br>"mail" | postdate, postpone, postmortem, postlude, postmark, postman |
| mis- | "ill," "wrong,"<br>"incorrect," "unlawful" | misfortune, miscount, mistake, misquote, misconceive, misdirect, misbehave, misstate, miscalculate, misunderstand, misguided |
| re-<br><br>retro- | "back," "again,"<br>"anew," "backward,"<br>"behind" | reclaim, repress, redeem, recommit, reconcile, reforest, redraw, restate, reform, reiterate<br>retrospect, retrogress, retroactive |
| anti- | "against"<br>"opposite" | antisocial, antiwar, anti-Semitic, antiaircraft, antigovernment |
| auto- | "self" | automatic, automobile, autograph, autobiography |

| hyper- | "beyond the ordinary" | hypersensitive, hyperactive, hypercritical, hyperbole, hypertension |
| hypo- | "under," "beneath," "less than ordinary" | hypodermic, hypoactive, hypocritical, hypotenuse, hypothesis, hypoacidic |
| peri- | "all," "around" | perimeter, periphery, period, periscope, periodontal |
| poly- | "many" | polygram, polysyllable, polygraph, polygamy, polygon |
| syn- | "with" | synthesis, synonym, synchronize, syncretism, syncopation |

✎ **EXERCISE A** In the center space, write a definition of your own for each word, based on the literal meaning of the prefix and root word or syllable(s). Then look the word up in a dictionary and write the dictionary's definition. Compare your definition with the meaning given in the dictionary.

**My Definition**                                  **Dictionary's Definition**

1. polyphonic    *having many sounds*                *having or consisting of*
                                                 *many sounds or voices*

2. antisocial

3. misfortune

4. autograph

5. irresistible

6. allure

7. antedate

8. impractical    _____        _____

                  _____        _____

9. transform      _____        _____

                  _____        _____

10. contradict    _____        _____

                  _____        _____

✎ **EXERCISE B** On the left, in *dark print*, are several root words. In parentheses is the literal meaning of a prefix which could be attached to the root word. Write a word which fits the combined meaning.

1.  **human** (greater than)_____ *superhuman* _____

2.  **racial** (between)_____

3.  **form** (with) _____

4.  **form** (again, over) _____

5.  **form** (across) _____

6.  **form** (one) _____

7.  **respond** (with, together) _____

8.  **portion** (to) _____

9.  **fixed** (to) _____

10. **thought** (before) _____

11. **press** (under) _____

12. **press** (back) _____

13. **press** (together) _____

14. **able** (to make) _____

15. **able** (not) _____

16. **pod** (three) _____

# LESSON 26: SUFFIXES

> **A SUFFIX is a syllable or syllables added to the end of a word or word root to modify the meaning of the word or root.**

Below are some of the most common suffixes in English words. Learn their meanings and study the examples.

| SUFFIX | MEANING | EXAMPLES OF WORDS WITH THE SUFFIX |
|---|---|---|
| -al | "pertaining to," "proceeding from" | parental, devotional, traditional |
| -ual | | spiritual, intellectual |
| -et | "little" | floweret, eaglet, violet, tablet |
| -ette | | statuette, kitchenette, gazette |
| -let | | ringlet, wavelet, piglet |
| -ling | | duckling, fledgling, darling, yearling |
| -ule | | globule, cellule |
| -able | "capable of being" | blamable, tolerable, vulnerable, movable, notable |
| -ible | | responsible, flexible, reversible, indivisible, corruptible |
| -ous | "full of," "having" | monotonous, populous, poisonous, disastrous |
| -ious | | furious, delicious, anxious, atrocious |
| -eous | | righteous, courteous |
| -ty | "being," "state of being" | divinity, liberty, morality, nobility, sanity, opportunity |
| -ety | | propriety, gaiety |
| -ity | | infirmity, adversity, equality |
| -ness | "state of being" | happiness, loneliness, wilderness, godliness |
| -age | | bondage, pilgrimage |

| SUFFIX | MEANING | EXAMPLES OF WORDS WITH THE SUFFIX |
|---|---|---|
| **-ancy** **-ency** | "state of being" | buoyancy, poignancy<br>frequency, potency |
| **-sion** **-tion** | "the act of," "state of being" | succession, extension, explosion<br>temptation, inspiration, contribution, consolation, obligation |
| **-ive** | "able to," "having power to," "serving to" | progressive, attentive, submissive, protective, negative, positive, executive, affirmative, declarative, instructive |
| **-ize** | "to make," "to place into," "to practice" | equalize, legalize, symbolize, civilize, humanize, realize, authorize, magnetize, fertilize, harmonize |
| **-fy** | "to make," "to make like," "to give the qualities of" | magnify, nullify, clarify, citify, sanctify, glorify, ratify, purify, liquefy, justify, beautify, diversify, disqualify |
| **-er** **-or** | "maker," "doer" | appointer, conferrer<br>nominator, mortgagor, guarantor |
| **-ee** | "receiver" | nominee, mortgagee, guarantee, appointee, conferee |
| **-ic** | "relating to," "characterized by," "belonging to," "connected with," "consisting of," "associated with" | domestic, dramatic, realistic, demonic |
| **-ary** **-ory** | "relating to," "characterized by," "belonging to," "connected with," "consisting of," "associated with" | contrary, arbitrary, military, stationary<br>transitory, compulsory |
| **-ish** | "like," "pertaining to," "in a small degree" | childish, reddish, dampish, feverish, Swedish, British |
| **-some** | "full of," "very" | lonesome, gladsome, wearisome, burdensome |
| **-dom** **-hood** **-ment** | "state or quality of being," "that which" | kingdom, martyrdom<br>childhood, motherhood<br>establishment |

| -ism | "state or quality of being," "that which" | heroism, capitalism |
| -mony | | matrimony |
| -tude | | aptitude |
| -ine | "of," "like," "pertaining to" | canine, bovine |
| -ile | | infantile, mercantile |
| -id | | squalid, fervid |
| -ist | "one who" | communist, linguist |
| -eer | | engineer |
| -ent | | resident |
| -ard | | drunkard |
| -y | "full of" | syrupy, runny |
| -ose | | verbose |
| -ful | | eventful, graceful |
| -ent | | confident |
| -logy | "study of" | geology, biology, psychology, sociology, methodology |
| -graph | "writing" | monograph, paragraph |
| -graphy | | geography, typography |

✎ **EXERCISE** Write a word with one of the **suffixes from the chart** that fits the description or definition given below. The answer may or may not be one of the words on the chart.

_____*Temptation*_____   1.   the act of being **tempted**

_____   2.   the state of being **perverted**

_____   3.   the state of being **connected**

_____   4.   having the quality of **eloquence**

_____   5.   having the quality of **luxury**

_____   6.   having the quality of **relevance**

_____   7.   able to **submit**

_____   8.   serving to **decide**

_____ 9.   having the power to **execute**

_____ 10.  to make **equal**

_____ 11.  to make **legal**

_____ 12.  to make **magnetic**

_____ 13.  to make **pure**

_____ 14.  to give the quality of **beauty**

_____ 15.  to make **liquid**

_____ 16.  one who receives an **appointment**

_____ 17.  one who **guarantees**

_____ 18.  relating to **drama**

_____ 19.  characterized by **realism**

_____ 20.  of or pertaining to a **revolution**

_____ 21.  characterized by **vision**

_____ 22.  having to do with **Britain**

# LESSON 27: TROUBLESOME CHOICES

There are several sets of words which are often the source of confusion, causing the writer or speaker to make a wrong vocabulary choice. The following list clarifies the meaning of some of these sets of troublesome words. Examples follow to show how each is properly used.

## SIT or SET?

**sit, sat, (have) sat** ⇒ to sit down, to be in a place, to occupy a seat

   No one wants to **sit** in the front row.

   That idea does not **sit** well with him.

**set, set, (have) set** ⇒ to place, to put something down, to decide, to determine

   She **set** the food on the table.

   They **set** a date for their wedding.

## LIE or LAY?

**lie, lay, (have) lain** ⇒ **to recline, to rest in a horizontal position**

My book is **lying** on the table.

I think I will **lie** down for a short rest.

**lay, laid, (have) laid** ⇒ **to place something down**

I will **lay** your book on the table.

The bag of trash was **laid** in the garage.

## BRING or TAKE?

**bring, brought, (have) brought** ⇒ **to show movement toward the speaker (think: _"come"_)**

Please **bring** me that magazine.

She **brought** me a list of contributors.

**take, took, (have) taken** ⇒ **to show movement away from the speaker (think: _"go"_)**

**Take** that smelly thing away from me!

Let's **take** this specimen to science class tomorrow.

## LEAVE or LET?

**leave, left, (have) left** ⇒ **to depart, to go away, to keep something where it is**

We plan to **leave** on the 2:15 flight.

Please **leave** that vicious dog alone.

**let, let, (have) let** ⇒ **to allow, to permit**

Do not **let** that happen again.

Mom and Dad **let** us attend the party last night.

## AFFECT or EFFECT?

**affect, affected, (have) affected** ⇒ **verb: to influence; participle: fake, contrived**

We hope our ideas will **affect** future decisions.

He has an **affected** manner of speech.

**effect, effected, (have) effected, effect** ⇒ **verb: to accomplish, bring about; noun: a result**

The social workers tried to **effect** change in conditions.

We see the **effect** of sin all around us.

## ADVERSE or AVERSE?

**adverse ⇒ unfavorable, harmful**

We frequently have **adverse** weather during winter.

**averse ⇒ opposed to, unwilling**

They were **averse** to testifying before the committee.

## ALLUDE or ELUDE?

**allude, alluded, (have) alluded ⇒ to refer to**

In his speech, he **alluded** to a poem of T.S. Eliot.

**elude, eluded, (have) eluded ⇒ to escape from, to avoid**

The bank robber **eluded** capture.

## ALLUSION or ILLUSION?

**allusion ⇒ an indirect reference**

The book was filled with **allusions** to the Bible.

**illusion ⇒ a false belief, idea, or vision**

She was under the **illusion** that he loved her.

## AMOUNT or NUMBER? MUCH or MANY?

**amount, much ⇒ used with quantities or substances that *cannot* be counted**

She put too **much** sugar in her coffee.

The desert has a small **amount** of water.

**number, many ⇒ used with quantities or items that *can* be counted**

They had **many** excuses for their behavior.

He had only a small **number** of customers.

## FEW or LITTLE? LESS or FEWER?

**little, less ⇒ used with quantities or substances that *cannot* be counted**

We have only a **little** milk left for breakfast.

The foreman wanted more results and **less** dawdling.

**few, fewer ⇒ used with quantities or items that *can* be counted**

She has **few** worries in life.

The trees had **fewer** apples on them after the storm.

## COMPRISE or COMPOSE?

comprise ⇒ to include or contain

The Senate **comprises** 100 members from 50 states.

compose ⇒ to make up, to form

The Senate is **composed** of 100 members.

## CONTINUAL or CONTINUOUS?

continual, continually ⇒ again and again at regular intervals

Shuttle buses run **continually** between the parking lot and the stadium.

continuous, continuously ⇒ constant, in an unbroken way

A **continuous** flow of water was released from the dam throughout the summer.

## DISINTERESTED or UNINTERESTED?

disinterested ⇒ impartial, neutral

We need a **disinterested** referee to settle this.

uninterested ⇒ not interested or concerned

I am **uninterested** in your proposal.

## CAN or MAY?

can ⇒ to be able, to have ability

**Can** you climb a tree?

may ⇒ to have permission

Mom, **may** I climb that tree?

## ANXIOUS or EAGER?

anxious ⇒ filled with worry, dread, concern

He is **anxious** about his history test tomorrow.

eager ⇒ looking forward with keen desire

He is **eager** to start the race.

## EMIGRATE or IMMIGRATE?

emigrate ⇒ to leave a native country

Many Jews **emigrated** from Russia in the 1980's.

immigrate ⇒ to enter a new country

The Chang family **immigrated** here to America.

## EMINENT or IMMANENT

**eminent** ⇒ famous, prominent

Albert Einstein was an **eminent** scientist.

**immanent** ⇒ inherent, indwelling

Pantheists believe God is **immanent** in everything.

## EMANANT or IMMINENT

**emanant** ⇒ issuing from or flowing forth

Water **emanant** from the earth is usually pure.

**imminent** ⇒ about to happen

Some people believe the Second Coming is **imminent**.

## ELICIT or ILLICIT?

**elicit** ⇒ verb: to draw out, to bring forth

The reporter tried to **elicit** a comment from him.

**illicit** ⇒ adjective: unlawful, illegal

Federal agents tried to halt the **illicit** drug traffic.

## AMONG or BETWEEN?

**among** ⇒ usually refers to more than two

The offering plate was passed **among** those attending.

**between** ⇒ usually refers to only two

The distance **between** here and there is short.

## ACCEPT or EXCEPT?

**accept** ⇒ verb: to receive, to agree to

We are happy to **accept** your invitation.

**except** ⇒ preposition: excluding; verb: to exempt, to exclude

No one **except** the doctor was allowed into the room.

No one may be **excepted** from the test.

## FLAUNT or FLOUT?

**flaunt** ⇒ **to show off proudly**

He likes to **flaunt** his great wealth.

**flout** ⇒ **to reject, to scorn**

You cannot **flout** the law without consequences.

## INFER or IMPLY?

**infer** ⇒ **to draw a conclusion from facts**

From the evidence, I can **infer** that you are guilty.

**imply** ⇒ **to suggest**

Are you **implying** that I took the cookies?

## BESIDE or BESIDES?

**beside** ⇒ **along side of**

Flowers were growing **beside** the walkway.

**besides** ⇒ **in addition to**

Didn't you bring any food **besides** these hot dogs?

✎ **EXERCISE** Underline the correct word in parentheses in each of the following sentences.

1. (Can, <u>May</u>) I have permission to visit the school nurse?

2. A judge must be (disinterested, uninterested) in the cases which are tried in his court.

3. The United States of America is (comprised, composed) of fifty sovereign states.

4. Lake Michigan (lies, lays) (among, between) Michigan and Wisconsin.

5. We may have no other god (beside, besides) Jehovah.

6. May I ask you to (bring, take) me a glass of water?

7. The message of redemption is a (continual, continuous) thread running throughout every part of Scripture.

8. A high fever can be one (effect, affect) of influenza.

9.  The criminal's boyish looks created the (allusion, illusion) of innocence.

10. She had an (adverse, averse) reaction to the medication.

11. In advising me, he (eluded, alluded) to his own father's wise counsel.

12. She was (anxious, eager) to eat her favorite foods again.

13. The (eminent, imminent, emanant) artist was too humble to (flaunt, flout) his talents.

14. (Less, Fewer) people attended the conference this year than last year.

15. She has been unable to (illicit, elicit) a reasonable response from her students.

16. Because of oppression, thousands have (emigrated, immigrated) from their native lands.

17. From my remarks, do not (imply, infer) that I do not trust you.

18. (Leave, Let) sleeping dogs (lie, lay).

19. I think I will just (sit, set) here and think for awhile.

20. We have a large (number, amount) of books stored in our warehouse.

21. The warring parties have (laid, lain) down their arms.

22. Our suggestions did not (sit, set) well with the committee.

# LESSON 28: TRICKY DICTION

> **DICTION is the choice of words for the expression of ideas.**

In addition to the troublesome sets of words you studied in the previous lesson, there are a number of other words and expressions which frequently give rise to faulty diction. In this lesson, we will examine some of these problem areas. Learning to avoid these diction pitfalls will improve your vocabulary and your ability to communicate with effectiveness and eloquence.

## ain't

This is a substandard contraction. Do not use it except to purposely represent substandard speech.

WRONG:     This **ain't** the right way to do things.

CORRECT:     This **isn't** the right way to do things.

OKAY:     "This hyar ol' tin lizzie **ain't** runnin' like she wuz."

## aren't I

This is an ungrammatical construction. It is improper to use "are" with the first person, singular pronoun "I."

WRONG:     I'm acting silly, **aren't I**?

CORRECT:     I'm acting silly, **am I not**?

## all right, alright

There is no such word as *alright*. The correct form is *all right*.

WRONG:     I hope everything is **alright**.

CORRECT:     I hope everything is **all right**.

## all the farther, all the faster

These and similar expressions are objectionable when they are used to mean *as far as, as fast as*, etc.

WRONG:     This is **all the farther** I can go today.

This is **all the faster** this old car can go.

CORRECT:     This is **as far as** I can go today.

This is **as fast as** this old car can go.

## a lot, alot, lots

"Alot" is not an acceptable word. "A lot" and "lots," used to mean *many* or *a great number or amount*, should be used only in *informal* settings.

WRONG:     He has **alot** of money.

INFORMAL:   He has **a lot** of money. He has **lots** of money.

FORMAL:     He has **a large amount** of money.

## all ready, already

*All ready* means "everyone or everything is ready." *Already* means "by this time," or "previously."

CORRECT:     We are **all ready** to leave on our hike.

They have **already** left on their hike.

## amount up to

Omit the preposition *up* in uses such as the following:

WRONG:        Our yard-sale receipts **amounted up to** $257.35.

CORRECT:     Our yard-sale receipts **amounted to** $257.35.

## anywhere, nowhere, somewhere

Do not add an "*s*" to the end of these words.

WRONG:        I can't find my shoes **anywheres**. They must be **somewheres**.

CORRECT:     I can't find my shoes **anywhere**. They must be **somewhere**.

## as, because, that, whether

Avoid the use of *as* as a substitute for *because, that,* or *whether*.

POOR:          My sneakers were stolen, **as** I left my locker open.

WRONG:        I cannot say **as** I know that song.

BETTER:       My sneakers were stolen **because** I left my locker open.

CORRECT:     I cannot say **that** I know that song.

                  I cannot say **whether** I know that song.

## bad, badly

Use *bad* only as an adjective (including as a predicate adjective). Use *badly* only as an adverb modifying a verb, adjective, or adverb.

WRONG:        I feel **badly** about your loss.

                  My watch is running **bad**.

CORRECT:     I feel **bad** about your loss. (predicate adjective following linking verb)

                  My watch is running **badly**. (adverb modifying an action verb)

## being as, being that

Do not use these expressions to mean *because* or *since*.

WRONG:        **Being that** your parents have more wisdom, you should listen to them.

CORRECT:     **Because** your parents have more wisdom, you should listen to them.

## better, had better

Do not use *better* in place of *had better*.

WRONG:        You **better** see a doctor.

CORRECT:     You **had better** see a doctor.

## center around

This expression is illogical. Things can be around a center, but a center cannot be around anything. Use *center on, center in,* or *center at.*

| | |
|---|---|
| WRONG: | His talk **centered around** the true meaning of Christmas. |
| CORRECT: | His talk **centered on** the true meaning of Christmas. |
| | The conference was **centered at** the company's headquarters. |
| | Our hope is **centered in** Christ's work of redemption. |

## complected

The correct form is *complexioned.*

| | |
|---|---|
| WRONG: | Most native Polynesians are **dark-complected** people. |
| CORRECT: | Most native Polynesians are **dark-complexioned** people. |

## different from, different than

Use *different from* before a simple noun or pronoun. It is increasingly acceptable to use *different than* before a clause, but it is better to reword the sentence to avoid this construction.

| | |
|---|---|
| WRONG: | Your book is **different than** mine. |
| CORRECT: | Your book is **different from** mine. |
| DOUBTFUL: | His story was **different than** we had first heard. |
| BETTER: | His story was **not the same one** we had first heard. |

## double subject

Do not use a double subject.

| | |
|---|---|
| WRONG: | My mom **she** can surely bake great pies. |
| CORRECT: | My mom can surely bake great pies. |

## enthused

This is an incorrect word. Do not use this counterfeit participle when you mean the adjective *enthusiastic.*

| | |
|---|---|
| WRONG: | We are not very **enthused** about your proposal. |
| CORRECT: | We are not very **enthusiastic** about your proposal. |

## equally as

Drop the *as.*

| | |
|---|---|
| WRONG: | Her essay was good, but his was **equally as** well written. |
| CORRECT: | Her essay was good, but his was **equally** well written. |

## expect

Do not use as a substitute for *suppose* or *suspect*.

    WRONG:      I **expect** you will want a shower after your workout.

    CORRECT:    I **suppose** you will want a shower after your workout.

## had of, had ought, could of, would of, should of, etc.

Do not use *of* after *had*. Do not use *had* with *ought*.
Do not use *of* as a substitute for the helping verb *have*.

    WRONG:      If only I **had of** known about your need, I **could of** helped.

                You **had ought** to get that broken pipe repaired.

    CORRECT:    If only I **had** known about your need, I **could have** helped.

                You **ought** to get the broken pipe repaired.

## heighth

*Depth* and *width* are words, but *heighth* is not. The correct form is *height*.

    WRONG:      The **heighth** of the community Christmas tree was sixty feet.

    CORRECT:    The **height** of the community Christmas tree was sixty feet.

## hopefully

*Hopefully* is an adverb meaning "in a hopeful manner." It is widely misused to mean *"I hope."*
Avoid this usage if you want to be grammatically precise.

    WRONG:      **Hopefully** we will have enough money for this project.

                *(Literal Meaning: We will have in a hopeful manner enough money ...)*

    CORRECT:    We **hope** we will have enough money for this project.

## irregardless

This is an incorrect form of *regardless* (*without regard*). The prefix *ir-* and the suffix *-less* both
have negative meanings, making *irregardless* an unacceptable double negative.

    WRONG:      The meeting will be held **irregardless** of how many people attend.

    CORRECT:    The meeting will be held **regardless** of how many people attend.

## irritate, aggravate

These two words are often used interchangeably, but they should not be so used because they have different meanings. *Irritate* means "to make angry." *Aggravate*, which means "to make worse," is often used to mean "to make angry." It should be used with the latter meaning only in informal speech.

INFORMAL:    Your constant twitching is really **aggravating** me.

STANDARD:    Your constant twitching is really **irritating** me.

CORRECT:    The cold weather is **aggravating** her arthritis pains.

## kind of, sort of; kind of a, sort of a

*Kind of* and *sort of* are acceptable only in informal speech when meaning *somewhat*. Adding the word *a* to these expressions is redundant and should be avoided even in informal speech.

INFORMAL:    This box is **kind of** heavy.

FORMAL:    This box is **somewhat (or quite)** heavy.

WRONG:    What **kind of a** person are you, anyway?

CORRECT:    What **kind of** person are you, anyway?

## liable, apt, likely

These words are not always interchangeable, as some think. *Liable* means "exposed to something adverse." *Apt* suggests "appropriateness" or "fitness." *Likely* suggests "probability." *Likely* and *apt* can sometimes be interchanged (as when the meaning is "prone") but not to mean "probable."

WRONG:    It is **apt** to snow tomorrow.

It is **liable** to snow tomorrow.

CORRECT:    It is **likely** to snow tomorrow.

He proved himself **apt** in logical thinking.

They were held **liable** for the damages.

## like, as, as if

Do not use the preposition *like* as a substitute for the subordinating conjunctions *as* and *as if* to introduce an adverb clause. (*Like* and *as* are sometimes interchangeable as *prepositions*, but not as subordinating conjunctions.)

WRONG:    It looks **like** it is going to rain.

Do this exactly **like** you were told to do it.

CORRECT:    It looks **as if** it is going to rain.

Do this exactly **as** you were told to do it.

An alligator looks somewhat **like** a crocodile. *(like = preposition)*

A screwdriver should not be used **as** a paint-can opener. *(as = preposition)*

## mad

This word should be used to mean "angry" only in informal usages. Its formal meaning is "insane."

INFORMAL:    Don't be **mad** at me for losing your necklace.

FORMAL:      Her guilt was driving her **mad**.

## media, phenomena

These are the *plural* forms of *medium* and *phenomenon*.

WRONG:       The news **media is** too liberal.

CORRECT:     The news **media are** too liberal.

## outside of, inside of

Omit the preposition *of*.

WRONG:       The residents stood in horror **outside of** their burning building.

CORRECT:     The residents stood in horror **outside** their burning building.

## real, really

Do not use the adjective *real* in place of the adverb *really*.

WRONG:       This is **real** good coffee.

CORRECT:     This is **really** good coffee.

## reason...is because

This expression contains a redundancy. Use *reason is that* or *because*.

WRONG:       The **reason** we cannot come **is because** we will be out of town.

CORRECT:     The **reason** we cannot come **is that** we will be out of town.

             We cannot come **because** we will be out of town.

## try and, sure and

Do not use *and* with *try* or *sure*. Use *to* after these words.

WRONG:       I must **try and** get some sleep.

             Be **sure and** send me a postcard when you get there.

CORRECT:     I must *try to* get some sleep.

             Be **sure to** send me a postcard when you get there.

## type

This word is a noun. Do not use it as an adjective.

WRONG:     What **type** books do you enjoy reading?

CORRECT:     What **type of** books do you enjoy reading?

## used to could

Do not use this expression when you mean *used to be able*.

WRONG:     My uncle **used to could** yodel.

CORRECT:     My uncle **used to be able to** yodel.

## wait on, wait for

Do not use *wait on* to mean *wait for*. "Wait on" means "to serve or attend to."

WRONG:     We've been **waiting on** you for an hour.

CORRECT:     We've been **waiting for** you for an hour.

The sales clerk **waited on** her customers with courtesy and skill.

## want in, want on, want out, want through

Do not use these expressions. Insert an appropriate verb form.

WRONG:     The dog **wants in**.

Another passenger **wants on** the bus.

Excuse me, I **want through**.

Does anybody **want out**?

CORRECT:     The dog **wants to come in**.

Another passenger **wants to get on** the bus.

Excuse me, I **want to get through**.

Does anybody **want to go out**?

## way, ways

Do not add an *"s"* to "way" when referring to distance.

WRONG:     We still have a long **ways** to go.

CORRECT:     We still have a long **way** to go.

## why...for, what...for

Do not use *why...for.* It is redundant.

WRONG:      **Why** did he do that **for?**

CORRECT:    **Why** did he do that?

            **What** did he do that **for?**

## where vs. that; where...at, where...to; where, when

Do not use *where* to mean *that.*
*At* and *to* are unnecessary after *where.*
Do not use *where* or *when* in stating a definition.

WRONG:      I heard **where** eating certain kinds of cholesterol is beneficial.

            **Where** are my shoes **at?** He doesn't seem to know **where** he's going **to.**

            A ventriloquist is **where** someone can "throw his voice."

            An intercom is **when** you have a device for wireless voice transmission.

CORRECT:    I heard **that** eating certain kinds of cholesterol is beneficial.

            **Where** are my shoes? He doesn't seem to know **where** he's going.

            A ventriloquist is someone **who** can "throw his voice."

            An intercom is a device for wireless voice transmission.

---

✎ **EXERCISE** Rewrite the following sentences correcting any examples of faulty diction.

1.  You look pale. Are you feeling alright? You ain't sick are you?

    _____

    _____

2.  I am invited, aren't I? If not, I'll be real aggravated.

    _____

    _____

3.  I think this is all the farther we should go into this cave.

    _____

    _____

4. You seem to be under the allusion that Joyce Kilmer, author of "Trees," is a woman.

   _____

   _____

5. We took alot of side roads in order to allude our pursuers.

   _____

   _____

6. Between them all, the twelve girls consumed a large amount of doughnuts.

   _____

   _____

7. We were anxious to sail anywheres a fair breeze might blow us.

   _____

   _____

8. As we like all type pizzas, we ordered four different kinds to be delivered.

   _____

   _____

9. I don't know as eating that many pizzas is a good idea. It might make your stomach feel badly.

   _____

   _____

10. Being as you have been ill, you better not exercise too heavily today.

   _____

   _____

11. The testimony centered around a light-complected woman seen leaving the crime scene.

   _____

   _____

12. My sister she is different than I am. She's always so enthused about everything.

_____

_____

13. I expect I am equally as qualified as you are, even though I have had less experiences.

_____

_____

14. If you had of notified me, I would of attended the meeting.

_____

_____

15. To light a match inside of a hay barn is the heighth of folly. Hopefully, you will never do that.

_____

_____

16. Irregardless of his lowly background, he was kind of a snob. He acted like he owned the place.

_____

_____

17. The reason my father is mad is because he thinks the news media distorts the truth.

_____

_____

18. We are apt to lose the game unless our star player begins to improve. He used to could score twenty points per game. He should try and reach that goal again.

_____

_____

19. For a half hour, we waited on the store to open; now we want in.

_____

_____

20. We heard on television where a bear market is looming. A bear market is when stock prices decline for a long period.

_____

_____

# LESSON 29: EXPAND YOUR VOCABULARY

✎ **EXERCISE** Improve your vocabulary by learning the meaning of these words:

(Use a dictionary, if necessary, and write a definition in the blanks.)

1.  altruistic_____

    _____

2.  antithesis_____

    _____

3.  arbitrary_____

    _____

4.  autocratic _____

    _____

5.  capricious _____

    _____

6.  cynical _____

    _____

7.  dogmatic_____

    _____

8.  eccentric _____

    _____

9.  enigmatic _____

_____

10. eulogy _____

_____

11. extraneous_____

_____

12. garrulous _____

_____

13. gregarious _____

_____

14. impeccable _____

_____

15. innocuous _____

_____

16. insatiable _____

_____

17. insidious_____

_____

18. loquacious_____

_____

19. lucrative _____

_____

20. malevolent _____

_____

21. meticulous _____

_____

22. mitigation _____

_____

23. mollify _____

_____

24. omniscient _____

_____

25. perfunctory _____

_____

26. precocious _____

_____

27. propitiate _____

_____

28. reticent _____

_____

29. sinister _____

_____

30. vacillation _____

_____

# Unit 7
# Agreement in Sentences

As you may have noticed in your study of grammar so far, grammatical elements often have a number of different forms. Selecting the correct form for various grammatical situations is important for clear and effective communication. You have also learned that thought expressions are made complete by combining words with different functions into a harmonious whole called a sentence. Harmony is best achieved in a sentence when the various words and other grammatical elements agree with one another in form. Making the proper match is called **agreement**. Agreement in form is necessary in two main areas—subjects and verbs must agree in several different respects, and pronouns must agree with their antecedents. Usually, matching of forms comes quite automatically. But there are a few obstacles to agreement over which many people stumble. We will explore the matter of grammatical matchmaking in this unit.

## LESSON 30: SINGULAR AND PLURAL (NUMBER)

One of the ways sentence elements must agree is in **number**.

> **NUMBER is the form taken by nouns, pronouns, and verbs showing whether one or more than one is indicated.**

Number in grammar is designated as either *singular* or *plural*. When a word refers to *one* person, place, thing, quality, or idea, it is **singular**. When a word refers to *more than one*, it is **plural** in number.

| Rule 7.1 | Most nouns change from singular to plural by adding -s or -es. |
|---|---|
| Rule 7.2 | If a word ends in -y preceded by a consonant, change the "y" to "i" before adding *-es*. |
| Rule 7.3 | If a word ends in -sh, -ch, -x, -z, or -s, the plural ending is usually *-es*. |

| Rule 7.4 | The plural of letters, numbers, signs, and words—used as particular terms in a sentence—is formed by adding 's. |
|---|---|
| Rule 7.5 | Personal pronouns and some nouns change from singular to plural by changing their spelling, taking altered forms, or remaining unchanged, or by the use of different words. |
| Rule 7.6 | Most action verbs and some linking verbs end in -s or -es in their present singular form and change to plural by dropping the -s or -es. |
| Rule 7.7 | Linking verbs which are a form of "to be" take distinctive forms for singular and plural. |

The following chart shows some examples of changes in form according to number.

| NOUNS | | | |
|---|---|---|---|
| **SINGULAR** | **PLURAL** | **RULE** | **CHANGES IN FORM** |
| boy | boys | 1 | ADDS -S |
| horse | horses | 1 | ADDS -S |
| box | boxes | 3 | ADDS -ES |
| mouse | mice | 5 | DIFFERENT WORD |
| deer | deer | 5 | NO CHANGE |
| candy | candies | 2 | ALTERED BEFORE -ES |
| man | men | 5 | SPELLING CHANGE |
| woman | women | 5 | SPELLING CHANGE |
| democracy | democracies | 2 | ALTERED BEFORE -ES |
| essay | essays | 1 | ADDS -S |
| sheep | sheep | 5 | NO CHANGE |
| people | peoples | 1 | ADDS -S |
| **PERSONAL PRONOUNS** <br> Note that only *you* stays the same in both singular and plural. | | | |
| I | we | 5 | DIFFERENT WORD |
| me | us | 5 | DIFFERENT WORD |
| you | you | 5 | NO CHANGE |
| he | they | 5 | DIFFERENT WORD |

| PERSONAL PRONOUNS (cont.) | | | |
|---|---|---|---|
| SINGULAR | PLURAL | RULE | CHANGES IN FORM |
| she | they | 5 | DIFFERENT WORD |
| it | they | 5 | DIFFERENT WORD |
| him | them | 5 | DIFFERENT WORD |
| her | them | 5 | DIFFERENT WORD |
| **ACTION VERBS (PRESENT TENSE)** | | | |
| runs | run | 6 | ADDS OR DROPS -S |
| muddies | muddy | 2 | ALTERED BEFORE -ES |
| talks | talk | 6 | ADDS OR DROPS -S |
| has | have | | SPELLING CHANGE |
| catches | catch | 6 | ADDS OR DROPS -ES |
| rushes | rush | 6 | ADDS OR DROPS -ES |
| fixes | fix | 6 | ADDS OR DROPS -ES |
| buzzes | buzz | 6 | ADDS OR DROPS -ES |
| **ACTION VERBS (PAST TENSE)** | | | |
| ran | ran | | NO CHANGE |
| muddied | muddied | | NO CHANGE |
| talked | talked | | NO CHANGE |
| had | had | | NO CHANGE |
| caught | caught | | NO CHANGE |
| rushed | rushed | | NO CHANGE |
| fixed | fixed | | NO CHANGE |
| buzzed | buzzed | | NO CHANGE |
| **LINKING VERBS** The first five sets of singular and plural verbs are forms of the verb "to be." | | | |
| am | are | 7 | DIFFERENT WORD |
| are | are | | NO CHANGE (using the pronoun *you*) |
| is | are | 7 | DIFFERENT WORD |
| was | were | 7 | DIFFERENT WORD |
| were | were | | NO CHANGE (using the pronoun *you*) |
| seems | seem | 6 | ADDS OR DROPS -S |
| becomes | become | 6 | ADDS OR DROPS -S |
| appears | appear | 6 | ADDS OR DROPS -S |

✎ **EXERCISE A** Write **S** or **P** in the blanks to indicate whether the nouns or pronouns below are Singular or Plural. Write **B** if the word is the same in both singular and plural.

| | | | | | |
|---|---|---|---|---|---|
| _S_ | 1. culture | _____ | 10. pictures | _____ | 19. congregation |
| _____ | 2. picnics | _____ | 11. oxen | _____ | 20. moose |
| _____ | 3. cure | _____ | 12. people | _____ | 21. doubts |
| _____ | 4. you | _____ | 13. crowd | _____ | 22. love |
| _____ | 5. opponents | _____ | 14. mistakes | _____ | 23. we |
| _____ | 6. blast | _____ | 15. boxes | _____ | 24. beauty |
| _____ | 7. brushes | _____ | 16. dice | _____ | 25. children |
| _____ | 8. magazines | _____ | 17. chairmen | _____ | 26. nation |
| _____ | 9. key | _____ | 18. they | _____ | 27. press |

✎ **EXERCISE B** Change the following nouns or pronouns from singular to plural or from plural to singular. Check a dictionary if you are in doubt.

| | | | | | |
|---|---|---|---|---|---|
| 1. gallery | _galleries_ | 12. sisters | _____ | 23. us | _____ |
| 2. gentlemen | _____ | 13. carrier | _____ | 24. discs | _____ |
| 3. galaxy | _____ | 14. female | _____ | 25. painting | _____ |
| 4. ax | _____ | 15. nights | _____ | 26. breeze | _____ |
| 5. hike | _____ | 16. brace | _____ | 27. glass | _____ |
| 6. he | _____ | 17. elite | _____ | 28. well | _____ |
| 7. trout | _____ | 18. delicacy | _____ | 29. church | _____ |
| 8. grain | _____ | 19. we | _____ | 30. units | _____ |
| 9. trawler | _____ | 20. lesson | _____ | 31. party | _____ |
| 10. four | _____ | 21. clock | _____ | 32. bunny | _____ |
| 11. notebook | _____ | 22. worms | _____ | 33. club | _____ |

# LESSON 31: AGREEMENT IN NUMBER

## *SUBJECTS AND VERBS*

> **Rule 7.8**    Subjects and verbs must agree in number. Singular subjects must have singular verbs. Plural subjects must have plural verbs.

☞ **SINGULAR SUBJECT, SINGULAR VERB:**

The *cow* **is** a Holstein.

An honest *man* **sleeps** well.

A purple *iris* **was growing** in her flower bed.

☞ **PLURAL SUBJECT, PLURAL VERB:**

The *cows* **are** all Holsteins.

Honest *men* **sleep** well.

Purple *irises* **were growing** in her flower bed.

As we noted in the introduction to this unit, most literate people, or those for whom English is their first language, usually do not have trouble getting their subjects and verbs to agree in number. There are a few situations, however, which cause problems for many people. Some of them are discussed below.

## *INTERVENING PHRASES AND CLAUSES*

Sometimes a phrase or clause comes between the subject and the verb. Even if another noun in that intervening phrase is closer to the verb than the subject is, the verb must still agree in number with the subject.

☞ **EXAMPLES:**

The *cows* in the meadow **are** all Holsteins. (*Cows*, not *meadow*, is the subject.)

The *boy* who sits behind me in history and English classes **is** very intelligent. (*Boy*, not *classes*, is the subject.)

Our *teacher*, together with other teachers from our school, **is attending** a conference this week. (*Is attending* agrees with the singular subject *teacher*.)

The old *car*, along with several hard-to-find spare parts, **was sold** for $500. (*Was sold* agrees with the singular subject *car*.)

This year's *crop* of oranges *is being threatened* by an early frost. (*Crop*, not *oranges*, is the subject.)

The *pitter-patter* of a thousand raindrops **was sounding** upon the tin roof. (*Pitter-patter* is the subject, not *raindrops*.)

## PREDICATE NOMINATIVES

In the case of predicate nominatives following subjects, a verb must agree in number with its *subject*, NOT with the predicate nominative which may follow it—even if that predicate nominative (in **bold**, below) is different in number from the subject and verb (in ***bold italics***).

☞**EXAMPLES**

*One* of my favorite fruits *is* **bananas**. (*One*, not *bananas*, is the subject.)

*Diseases are* often a **result** of unsanitary conditions.

The collected *works* of Shakespeare *make* a fine **gift** for any lover of literature.

## "DELAYED-SUBJECT" OR "TURNAROUND" SENTENCES

Questions and sentences beginning with "Here" and "There" usually have subjects that come *after* their verbs. This often poses a problem for subject-verb agreement. You must "look ahead" or "think ahead" to determine which word is the subject before choosing the verb. If you are still confused, mentally change the word order so that the subject comes before the verb.

☞**EXAMPLES:**

| | | |
|---|---|---|
| *Is Tom building* his own house? | = | *Tom is building* his own house. |
| *Do blondes* really *have* more fun? | = | *Blondes* really *do have* more fun. |
| *Aren't they* taller than the others? | = | *They are* (not) taller than the others. |
| Here *are* the *plans* we have drawn. | = | The *plans* we have drawn *are* here. |
| Here *is* the *book* you loaned to me. | = | The *book* you loaned me *is* here. |
| There *are* many exciting *tales* to be told. | = | Many exciting *tales are* to be told. |
| There *is* a *man* at the door to see you. | = | A *man is* at the door to see you. |

The contractions ***Here's***, ***There's***, and ***Where's*** should only be used with *singular* subjects because these contractions are formed with the singular verb *is*.

☞**WRONG:**

*Where's* my shoes?

*Here's* the CD's you ordered.

*There's* his books.

☞**CORRECT:**

*Where are* my shoes? /or: *Where's* my shoe?

*Here are* the CD's you ordered. /or: *Here's* the CD you ordered.

*There are* his books. /or: *There's* his book.

## COMPOUND SUBJECTS

Learn the following rules to ensure subject-verb agreement when the subject is compound.

| | |
|---|---|
| Rule 7.9 | **Subjects joined by *and* take a plural verb (unless the two subjects refer to a single person or entity).** |
| Rule 7.10 | **Singular subjects joined by *or, nor, either...or,* or *neither...nor* take a singular verb.** |
| Rule 7.11 | **Plural subjects joined by *or, nor, either...or* or *neither...nor* take a plural verb.** |
| Rule 7.12 | **When a singular subject is joined to a plural subject by *or, nor, either...or,* or *neither...nor,* the verb must agree with the subject nearer the verb in the sentence.** |

☞**EXAMPLES:**

*Harry and* the other *men* **are attending** a men's retreat sponsored by their church.

---

**Note:** Example of single-entity exception: Our *Lord and Savior is* Jesus Christ.

---

A *sweater or* a light *jacket* **is** appropriate to wear for the outdoor concert.

*Neither movies nor* television *programs* adequately **depict** most classic books' full content.

*Either* a ten-dollar *bill or* two five-dollar *bills* **are** acceptable.

## SINGULAR IN MEANING, PLURAL IN FORM

❑ **Certain words are singular in meaning but plural in form.**

Such words take singular verbs. Some of them are said to be plural in form because they end with -*s*. Others use a plural ending taken from an ancient root language, such as Latin.

☞**EXAMPLES:**       **USED WITH SINGULAR VERBS**

mumps           *Mumps* **is** a painful childhood disease.

measles         *Measles* **is** a disease that is now controlled by vaccinations.

molasses        *Molasses* **gives** cookies a special taste.

news            No *news* **is** good news.

stamina         His *stamina* **seems** to have no bounds.

whereabouts     The *whereabouts* of the lost dog **was** not **known**.

❏ **Certain academic terms are singular in meaning but plural in form.**

Words ending with *-ics* are often singular in meaning when they refer to a *science* or *course of study*. Such words take singular verbs.

☞**EXAMPLES:**         **USED WITH SINGULAR VERBS**

economics       Free-market *economics* **was advocated** by Ludwig von Mises.

physics          *Physics* **was** the realm of Albert Einstein.

dramatics       *Dramatics* **is** a course which would-be actors often take.

mathematics    *Mathematics* **is** an ancient science.

ethics            *Ethics* **is** a science of behavior according to a moral code.

❏ **Some of these terms may be plural in meaning and take a plural verb.**

At other times, words ending with *-ics* refer to a quality, physical activity, or behavior, in which case they take plural verbs.

☞**EXAMPLES:**         **USED WITH PLURAL VERBS**

gymnastics      The quarterback's limber *gymnastics* always **help** him elude tacklers.

ethics            His business *ethics* **are** questionable.

economics       The *economics* of a multinational corporation **are** complex.

## COLLECTIVE NOUNS

❏ **Collective nouns are those which name a group but are singular in form.**

These nouns may take either a singular verb or a plural verb. They are *singular* when the group is considered as a *single unit*. They are *plural* when the group is considered according to the *individual members* of the group.

☞**EXAMPLES:**         **CONSIDERED AS A UNIT (USED WITH SINGULAR VERBS)**

crowd            The *crowd* **was** larger than police had anticipated.

jury             The *jury* **has returned** to its deliberations.

class            The *class* **has decided** on its motto.

☞**EXAMPLES:**         **CONSIDERED AS INDIVIDUALS (USED WITH PLURAL VERBS)**

crowd            The *crowd* attending the baseball game **were given** souvenir hats.

jury             The *jury* **are discussing** their individual opinions before voting.

class            The *class* **are suggesting** various ideas for a fund-raiser.

❏ **Collective nouns may also be plural in form and take a plural verb.**

Of course, collective nouns may also have *plural forms* which indicate more than one group of the same kind. In these cases, they always take *plural verbs*.

☞**EXAMPLES:**            **PLURAL IN FORM WITH PLURAL VERBS**

crowds          Disorderly *crowds* **are** a police department's nightmare.

families        Several Christian *families* **are forming** a private school.

teams           *Teams* from several districts **are playing** in the tournament.

groups          Twenty pro-life *groups* annually **sponsor** a rally at the State Capitol.

## TITLES AND NAMES

❑ **Titles and names are singular in meaning but are often plural in form.**

Titles of books, publications, works of art, etc. and names of cities, organizations, countries, etc. are usually considered singular even if they contain plural words.

☞**EXAMPLES:**            **USED WITH SINGULAR VERBS**

Cedar Rapids            *Cedar Rapids* **is** a city in Iowa.

General Motors          *General Motors* **has** opened a new plant in Mexico.

The New York Times      *The New York Times* **is** one of America's few national newspapers.

"Trees"                 *"Trees"* **is** a poem by Joyce Kilmer.

Boy Scouts of America   The *Boy Scouts of America* **holds** annual Jamborees.

United Nations          The *United Nations* **was** formed in 1945.

United States           The *United States*** **provides** billions of dollars in foreign aid.

---

**Note:** In the early days of America, the Founders of the country usually referred to their new nation in a plural sense —*The United States of America are…*—indicating their understanding that each state is individually sovereign and the nation is a federated union of these states. Some advocates of states' rights still prefer today to use the name "United States" in this plural sense.

---

## INDEFINITE PRONOUNS

Matching indefinite pronouns to the correct form of verbs is a problem for many people. That is because some indefinite pronouns are singular, some are plural, and some can be either singular or plural, depending upon the *number* of the noun to which they refer.

❑ **Certain indefinite pronouns require singular verbs.**

☞**EXAMPLES:**            **PRONOUNS USED WITH SINGULAR VERBS**

anybody         *Anybody* **is** welcome to participate.

anyone          *Anyone* **is** eligible for the contest.

each            *Each* **has** had a share of the candy.

either          *Either* **is** correct.

neither         *Neither* **is** correct.

everybody       *Everybody* **wants** one of these.

| | |
|---|---|
| everyone | *Everyone* **wonders** what will happen next. |
| many a one | *Many a one* **has** longed for the olden days. |
| nobody | *Nobody* **likes** a quitter. |
| no one | *No one* **sings** better than she. |
| one | *One* of us **has** to be wrong. |
| somebody | *Somebody* **is** at the door. |
| someone | *Someone* **was** sitting in my chair. |
| another | *Another* **has** taken your place. |

## ❑ Some indefinite pronouns are plural in form and take plural verbs.

☞**EXAMPLES:**          **PRONOUNS USED WITH PLURAL VERBS**

| | |
|---|---|
| both | *Both* **are** acceptable answers. |
| few | *Few* **have had** such an exciting experience. |
| many | *Many* **were** not pleased with the idea. |
| several | *Several* **have expressed** their opposition. |

## ❑ Other indefinite pronouns may be either singular or plural.

These pronouns may take either a singular or plural verb, *depending upon the number of the key word in a modifying phrase* or the *intended meaning* of the pronoun (see the examples marked with * below).

☞**EXAMPLES:**          **PRONOUNS USED WITH SINGULAR VERBS**

| | |
|---|---|
| some | *Some* of the *bread* **has become** moldy. |
| all | *All* of the *money* **has been spent.** |
| half | *Half* of the *roadway* **is covered** with water. |
| none* | *None* of the *milk* **has been poured.** |
| | *None* (not one)* of the *students* **wishes** to go. |

☞**EXAMPLES:**          **PRONOUNS USED WITH PLURAL VERBS**

| | |
|---|---|
| some | *Some* of *us* **are going** to the mountains tomorrow. |
| all | *All* of the *children* **are** ready for bed. |
| half | *Half* of the *men* **were** Asians. |
| none* | *None* of the *berries* **have been picked.** |
| | *None* (not any)* of the *students* **wish** to participate. |

---

**Note:** *According to certain studies, accomplished writers use plural verbs about as frequently as singular verbs with the pronoun *none*.

---

## RELATIVE PRONOUNS

You will recall that relative pronouns are the words that introduce adjective clauses. They often serve as the subjects of the clauses. One cannot tell from these pronouns themselves whether they are singular or plural. We must look to the nouns to which they refer to tell what their number is. The following rule applies:

| | |
|---|---|
| Rule 7.13 | **Relative pronouns referring to singular nouns require singular verbs; relative pronouns referring to plural nouns require plural verbs.** |

☞**EXAMPLES:**

SINGULAR: My uncle restored an antique *car* **which was built** in 1923.

PLURAL: The club elected its new *officers*, **who serve** a term of two years.

✎ **EXERCISE A** Underline the correct verb in parentheses in each of the following sentences.

1. There (<u>isn't</u>, aren't) enough room in this box for all of those books.

2. Several of my classmates (is, are) members of the school band.

3. Neither of the two students (was, were) able to spell the word.

4. Every one of the girls (wants, want) join the chorus.

5. Each of these items (cost, costs) six dollars.

6. Not one of the answers (was, were) correct.

7. Civics (was, were) my father's favorite subject when he was in school.

8. Neither the teacher nor the students (agree, agrees) with the book's analysis.

9. The row of chairs (was, were) out of alignment.

10. The computer, along with associated peripherals, (were, was) the latest model.

11. Where (were, was) they found?

12. Anyone who (has, have) two or more cars (receive, receives) a multi-vehicle discount on his insurance.

13. (There's, There are) 1,000 pieces to this jigsaw puzzle.

14. *The Federalist Papers* (is, are) one of the most neglected collections of American historical documents.

15. Her hysterics (do, does) not impress anyone.

16. Why (don't, doesn't) he want to be on the team?

17. One of the jars (is, are) empty.

18. Here (come, comes) the parade.

19. Here (come, comes) the floats and marching bands.

20. Either Sherlock Holmes or Miss Marple (is, are) my favorite detective character.

21. There (isn't, aren't) any peanut butter in this jar.

22. (Is, Are) manned or unmanned space flights more beneficial?

23. Good relations with other countries (are, is) the prime objective of our foreign policy.

24. I am one of those people who (need, needs) a full night's sleep.

25. Our gym teacher and coach (are, is) Mr. Roberts.

26. The team (has, have) elected its new captain.

## PRONOUNS AND ANTECEDENTS

> **An ANTECEDENT is a noun or noun-like word or expression to which a pronoun refers.**

Not only must pronoun subjects agree with their *verbs* in number, but all pronouns must also agree with their *antecedents* in number. Singular pronouns have singular antecedents. Plural pronouns have plural antecedents.

| SINGULAR PRONOUNS AND ANTECEDENTS | PLURAL PRONOUNS AND ANTECEDENTS |
|---|---|
| Every *student* has *his* own locker. | All *students* have *their* own lockers. |
| *No one* was prepared for *his* test. | *Many* were unprepared for *their* tests. |
| The *bride* had *her* hair styled just before the wedding. | The *bridesmaids* had *their* hair styled just before the wedding. |

If a pronoun has two antecedents, it must agree in number with the nearer of them.

☞ **EXAMPLES:**

> The **bride** and **bridesmaids** had **their** hair styled just before the wedding.
> (*Their* must agree with *bridesmaids*, which is nearer.)

> Either the team **members** or the **coach** will have **his** picture in the school paper.

## ■ *Collective Nouns*

If a collective noun is an antecedent of a pronoun, the pronoun will be either singular or plural, depending on whether the collective noun is considered as a unit or as individual members separately.

☞ **EXAMPLES:**

> The **class** raised **their** hands. (The class acted as individuals.)

> The **class** elected **its** new president. (The class acted as a whole.)

## ■ *Indefinite Pronouns*

Pronouns that have singular indefinite pronouns as antecedents are singular. Pronouns with plural indefinite pronouns as antecedents are plural. (See the examples starting on page 133 to see which indefinite pronouns are singular and which are plural.)

☞ **EXAMPLES:**

> Is **anyone** finished with **his** meal?

> **Few** have written **their** names on the roster.

When the sense of a singular indefinite pronoun such as *everyone, everybody, anyone,* etc. is *many* or *all,* a personal pronoun referring to it may be plural (even when the indefinite pronoun takes a singular verb), as in the sentence *"Everybody is doing **their** part."* Such usage helps to avoid somewhat awkward approaches as *"Everybody is doing **his or her** part."* Of course, it would also be acceptable to use the singular generic masculine *(his)* pronoun in the preceding example sentence, since this pronoun form, also known as the *common gender* form, may be used in such situations to refer to both males and females (see the next lesson).

✎ **EXERCISE B** Underline the correct pronoun and/or verb in parentheses in each of the following sentences.

1. Most of the schools in our town (has, <u>have</u>) (<u>their</u>, its) own football team.

2. Most of the car (has, have) lost (its, their) paint.

3. Each of the soldiers hiked with (his, their) full eighty-pound pack on (his, their) back.

4. All of the witnesses came forward with (his or her, their) own pet peeves.

5. Every woman expressed (their, her) individual preference.

6. Volunteer firemen (is, are) people who (is, are) willing to give freely of (their, his) time for the safety of the community.

7. A volunteer fireman (is, are) someone who (is, are) willing to give freely of (their, his) time for the safety of the community.

8. (Has, Have) anyone made up (his, their) mind yet?

9. Every boy wishing to attend the training program must decide whether (they, he) (is, are) willing to raise (his, their) support money.

10. Neither Mr. Frederick nor any of his coworkers (has, have) received (his, their) bonus checks yet.

11. Every animal in the herd seemed to have a mind of (their, its) own.

# LESSON 32: PERSON AND GENDER

Sentence elements must also agree in *person*, when applicable, and in *gender*.

> **PERSON is any one of three relations in discourse:**
> **the one speaking (first person),**
> **the one spoken to (second person), or**
> **the one spoken about (third person).**
>
> **GENDER is the form taken by nouns and pronouns indicating whether they are male, female, common, or neuter.**

## *SUBJECT-VERB AGREEMENT*

### ■ *Person*

**Person** is not an issue in *subject-verb* agreement when a subject is a **noun**. All nouns may be thought of as being in the *third person*. Verbs used with nouns must therefore also be in their *third-person form*.

The main problem in getting subjects and verbs to agree in **person** comes when the subject is a **personal pronoun**. The form of *present-tense verbs* changes, depending upon the person of the pronoun. Here are some examples:

| PERSONAL PRONOUNS | SINGULAR | PLURAL |
|---|---|---|
| **FIRST PERSON** | I **am** | we **are** |
| | I **have** | we **have** |
| | I **run** | we **run** |
| | I **sleep** | we **sleep** |
| | I **fidget** | we **fidget** |
| **SECOND PERSON** | you **are** | you **are** |
| | you **have** | you **have** |
| | you **run** | you **run** |
| | you **sleep** | you **sleep** |
| | you **fidget** | you **fidget** |
| **THIRD PERSON** | he, she, it **is** | they **are** |
| | he, she, it **has** | they **have** |
| | he, she, it **runs** | they **run** |
| | he, she, it **sleeps** | they **sleep** |
| | he, she, it **fidgets** | they **fidget** |

You can see from the above chart that, except for the linking verb *to be* (and its various forms—*am, is, are, was, were*), the only change in verb form is with personal pronouns in the ***third person, singular***. This is true for most action verbs and for linking verbs other than *to be*.

## ■ *Gender*

In English, *gender* is not an issue in *subject-verb* agreement; that is, the gender of the subject does not affect the form of the verb. Verbs do not have gender.

## *PRONOUN-ANTECEDENT AGREEMENT*

Pronouns must agree with their antecedents not only in *number* but also in ***person*** and ***gender***.

## ■ *Person*

### ☞ FIRST PERSON:

I am aware of **my** shortcomings.

Please give **me my** book.

**We** finished **our** picnic in the rain.

He gave **us** only what was **ours**.

☞**SECOND PERSON:**

**You** look very much like **your** uncle.

I will tell **you** what **your** score is.

**You** may all now take **your** seats.

☞**THIRD PERSON:**

The **dog** chased **its** tale.

**She** lost **her** way.

**He** is **his** own worst critic.

**They** sold **their** house.

# ■ *Gender*

| Rule 7.14 | Antecedents of MASCULINE gender are referred to by *he, him,* or *his.* |
|---|---|

☞**EXAMPLE:**

The *man* lost **his** job because *he* was irresponsible in meeting **his** duties.

| Rule 7.15 | Antecedents of FEMININE gender are referred to by *she, her,* or *hers.* |
|---|---|

☞**EXAMPLE:**

*Karen* cleaned **her** room even though **her** mother had not asked **her** to do it.

| Rule 7.16 | Antecedents of NEUTER gender are referred to by *it* or *its.* |
|---|---|

☞**EXAMPLE:**

The *flower* lost *its* petals.

| Rule 7.17 | Antecedents of COMMON GENDER are referred to by *he, him,* or *his.* |
|---|---|

When an antecedent includes both males and females, use the masculine pronouns.

☞**EXAMPLE:**

Each *contestant* must fill out **his** own application. (Awkward: his or her own...)

| Rule 7.18 | Antecedents that name animals are usually referred to by the NEUTER pronouns (*it* or *its*). |
|---|---|

The *common-gender* pronouns may be used, however, to create more personal interest in the animal. The *masculine* and *feminine* pronouns may be used when the sex of the animals is significant.

☞**EXAMPLES:**

The *horse* ate *its* hay.

The injured cowboy's beloved *horse* found *his* way back home.

The black *stallion* tossed *his* head in defiance.

The *mare* helped *her* colt to *its* feet.

✎ **EXERCISE** Underline the correct pronoun in parentheses. Circle the antecedent.

1.  Has (anyone) forgotten (<u>his</u>, their) notebook?

2.  All in favor of the motion please raise (his or her, their, his) right hands.

3.  Each girl will have (her, his, their) own private lesson.

4.  The tigress led (its, her) cubs into the thicket.

5.  Several of the soldiers found (his, their) way behind the lines.

6.  Most of the house has lost (its, their) roofing as a result of the storm.

7.  Most of the houses have lost (its, their) roofs as a result of the storm.

8.  The sunshine on the lake's ripples gives (it, them) a glittering look.

## LESSON 33: MORE PRONOUNS AND ANTECEDENTS

### *RELATIVE PRONOUNS*

Relative pronouns must agree with their antecedents in kind. *Who* and *whom* usually refer only to *persons*. *Which* usually refers only to *things* or *animals*. *That* refers to *persons, animals, or things*.

| RELATIVE PRONOUN | REFERS TO THESE ANTECEDENTS | EXAMPLES |
|---|---|---|
| who whom whoever whomever | Persons | He is the man **who** bought our car. We are the people **whom** God has blessed. |
| which | Things or animals | The Titanic is a ship **which** sank in the North Atlantic. Our dog, **which** we call Morty, is a bulldog. |
| that | Persons, animals, or things | The family **that** prays together stays together. There is the dog **that** bit me. This is the game **that** counts most. |

| Rule 7.19 | When a relative pronoun has more than one antecedent, it agrees with the antecedent nearer to it. |
|---|---|

☞**EXAMPLES:**

*People* and *things which* are related to the theater interest Tom.

*Things* and *people who* are related to the theater interest Tom.

## COMPOUND PRONOUNS

Compound ("self") pronouns cannot stand alone without antecedents. Do not use them unless a reflexive or intensive idea is present in the sentence.

☞**WRONG:**

Dylan and *myself* will attend the conference.

This is a matter that should be kept between you and *myself*.

*Herself* will do the honors.

☞**CORRECT:**

Dylan and *I* will attend the conference.

This is a matter that should be kept between you and *me*.

*She* (or: *She herself*) will do the honors.

## USELESS REPETITION

Avoid placing a personal pronoun immediately after its antecedent. The highlighted pronouns in the following examples are repetitive and unnecessary.

☞**WRONG:**

My cousins *they* live in Cleveland.

Uncle Bob *he* is a good fisherman.

## IMPLIED REFERENCES

The relationship between a pronoun and its antecedent should be obvious. *Implied reference* occurs when the antecedent is not actually expressed but must be inferred from the context or from previous or subsequent statements. Many excellent writers use implied references effectively. If you use this device, you must be careful to avoid confusing the reader.

Pronouns such as *it, which, this,* and *that* and demonstrative adjectives such as *this, that,* and *such* are often used to refer to an entire preceding statement, rather than to some specific noun or pronoun antecedent. Be careful that the reference is clear and unmistakable.

If the pronoun *it* is used indefinitely or impersonally (as in *"it is possible that…" "it is unclear to me…"*) another *it* referring to a definite antecedent should not be used in the same sentence, in order to avoid confusion.

☞**DOUBTFUL:**

Whenever I think of what happened last night, I get *that* sinking feeling.

My friend believes in evolution. *That* is a theory which seems implausible to me.

I lost your telephone number, *which* is the reason I didn't return your call.

He was in *that* silly mood again.

In *this* book, *it* says the League of Nations was a good idea.

*This* guy says to me, "Can I give you a ride?"

My coat is missing, and *it* is possible that *it* was stolen.

☞**IMPROVED:**

Whenever I think of what happened last night, I get a sinking feeling. **OR**
Whenever I think of what happened last night, I get *that* sinking feeling which comes from shame.

My friend believes in evolution, a theory which seems implausible to me.

I lost your telephone number and therefore could not return your call.

He was in a silly mood. **OR**
He was in that silly mood which often comes over him.

A book that I am reading says that the League of Nations was a good idea.

A man whom I didn't know said to me, "Can I give you a ride?"

My coat is missing, and *it* may possibly have been stolen.

# DOUBLE REFERENCES

*Double reference* occurs when a single pronoun has two possible antecedents, leaving the reader or listener confused. Rework the sentence to make the pronoun-antecedent relationship clear. If a pronoun has two possible noun references and the antecedent is nevertheless clear from the context, the sentence is acceptable.

☞**DOUBTFUL:**

When a *pastor* counsels a *parishioner*, *he* should seek biblical answers. *(who is "he?")*

*John* told *Jim* that *he* works too hard. *(who is "he?")*

☞**IMPROVED:**

A pastor who counsels a parishioner should seek biblical answers for his counselee.

John told Jim, "You work too hard."

OR: John told Jim, "I work too hard."

OR: John told Jim that he (Jim) works too hard.

OR: John told Jim that he (John) works too hard.

OR: John advised Jim not to work so hard.

OR: John promised Jim not to work so hard.

☞**CLEAR:**

My *mother* told my *grandmother* that *she* would visit *her* at the nursing home.

✎ **EXERCISE** Rewrite the following sentences, correcting errors or points of confusion involving pronouns and antecedents.

1. In two weeks our class will have another field trip. They are always enjoyable.

   *In two weeks our class will have another field trip. Field trips are always enjoyable.*

2. Central High and Washington High renewed its basketball rivalry last night.

3. The media refuses to blame itself for the public's attitudes.

4.  The teacher which teaches English in our school he has a master's degree.

    _____

    _____

5.  When the phone rings, it might be for me.

    _____

6.  Our car is the one who has a flat tire.

    _____

    _____

7.  In this magazine, it says that the "simple-living" movement is not as simple as some advocates have said.

    _____

    _____

8.  My stapler it needs a refill of staples.

    _____

9.  Larry and myself are planning a camping trip.

    _____

10. The filly that won the Breeder's Cup race was photographed with his trainer.

    _____

    _____

11. Joel loaned Mark his bicycle for his paper route because his had a flat tire.

    _____

    _____

12. I just had this great idea.

   _____

13. My dad, which earned a doctorate in physics, now teaches the subject at the university. That is
   my goal also.

   _____

   _____

14. It's that time of the year again; let's get ready for Thanksgiving.

   _____

   _____

# LESSON 34: UNIT REVIEW

✎ **EXERCISE** Fill the blanks below:

1.  *Number* in grammar is designated as either _____ or _____.

2.  When a word refers to one person, place, thing, quality, or idea, it is _____ in num-
    ber.

3.  When a word refers to more than one, it is _____ in number.

4.  Singular subjects take verbs that are _____ in number. Plural subjects take verbs that
    are _____ in number.

5.  The number of a verb is not affected by any _____ or _____ which comes
    between the subject and the verb.

6.  Subjects joined by "and" take a _____ verb (unless the two subjects refer to
    _____).

7. Singular subjects joined by "or," "nor," "either...or," or "neither...nor" take a _____ verb. Plural subjects joined by these conjunctions take a _____ verb.

8. When a singular subject is joined to a plural subject by "or," "nor," "either...or," or "neither...nor," the verb must agree with _____.

9. Words ending with *-ics* are often singular in meaning when they refer to a _____ or _____. When such words refer to a quality, physical activity, or behavior, they usually take verbs that are _____ in number.

10. Collective nouns take a verb that is _____ in number when they refer to a group that is considered as a unit or whole. They take a verb that is _____ in number when the group to which they refer is considered according its individual members.

11. The pronoun "someone" is _____ in number.

12. The pronoun "both" is _____ in number.

13. Relative pronouns referring to singular subjects require verbs that are _____ in number. Relative pronouns referring to plural subjects require verbs that are _____ in number.

14. Pronouns must agree with their antecedents in _____, _____, and _____.

15. Verbs used with noun subjects must be in the _____-person form.

16. Present-tense action verbs and some linking verbs change their forms when written in which person and number? _____ person, _____ number

17. Antecedents of masculine gender are referred to by the pronouns ____, ____, or ____.

18. Antecedents of feminine gender are referred to by the pronouns ____, ____, or ____.

19. Antecedents of neuter gender are referred to by the pronouns ____ or ____.

20. Antecedents of common gender are referred to by the pronouns ____, ____, or ____.

21. The relative pronouns _____ and _____ usually refer only to persons. The relative pronoun _____ usually refers only to things or animals. The relative pronoun _____ refers to persons, animals, or things.

# Unit 8
# Conjugating Verbs

Many people think that their communications will be more interesting, meaningful, or powerful if they season their sentences with colorful adjectives and adverbs. Experienced writers know, however, that the expressions which really sparkle are those with concrete nouns and dramatic verbs. Since verbs are words that express action or state of being, they are the words that especially give movement and posture to your messages. Understanding verbs and knowing how to use them is, therefore, a vital component of your study of grammar. Before you begin this unit, review the basic facts you learned about verbs in Unit 1. In the present unit, you will learn more details about these basic facts.

## LESSON 35: THE PRINCIPAL PARTS OF VERBS

> **PRINCIPAL PARTS** are the most basic forms of verbs from which all other verb forms and uses are created.

In the next lesson (Lesson 36), we will study something called verb *tense*. Tense is a term that describes how different *times* are expressed in the action of a verb. Before we look at the details of tense, however, we should review the *four principal parts* of verbs. All of the different forms that verbs take to express tense employ one or another of these four principal parts. The following table shows the four principal parts of verbs:

| 1ST PRINCIPAL PART: Present (to...) | 2ND PRINCIPAL PART: Present Participle | 3RD PRINCIPAL PART: Past | 4TH PRINCIPAL PART: Past Participle (have, has, or had) + |
|---|---|---|---|
| love | loving | loved | loved |
| call | calling | called | called |
| look | looking | looked | looked |
| murder | murdering | murdered | murdered |
| flee | fleeing | fled | fled |
| eat* | eating* | ate* | eaten* |
| crunch | crunching | crunched | crunched |
| splatter | splattering | splattered | splattered |
| climb | climbing | climbed | climbed |
| choose* | choosing* | chose* | chosen* |

There are several things to note about the examples given in the table on the previous page.

## ■ *1st Principal Part*

First, look at the examples of the first principal part (*present* form). The simplest form of the verb is the first principal part. It is often referred to as the *infinitive* form because it is this form that is used to create an infinitive; that is, an infinitive is created by using the word "to" plus the first principal part (present form) of the verb.

## ■ *2nd Principal Part*

Next look at the column containing examples of the second principal part, the *present participle*. Notice that all of the examples end with *-ing*. This feature makes the second principal part easy to recognize. The present participle form is used in creating the idea of on-going action in verbs *(I am eating...)*. It is also used when a verb form *(verbal)* is needed to function as an adjective *(a dancing bear...)*. Review the material about verbals in Unit 1.

## ■ *3rd Principal Part*

You will notice from the examples of the third principal part (*past* form) that many of them end with *-ed*. Thousands of English verbs create their past form by adding *-ed* or, if the verb already ends with an "e," by adding only *-d*. A few verbs of this kind add the ending *-t*. These are all called **regular** verbs. You will also notice that some of the examples (marked with an \*) in this column do not end this way. These are called **irregular** verbs.

## ■ *4th Principal Part*

The *past participle* form (fourth principal part) of *regular* verbs is the same as the past form. For some *irregular* verbs, the fourth principal part is the same as the present and/or past form. For other *irregular* verbs, the fourth part is entirely different. Again, you must simply memorize these verbs. Notice, however, that there is something consistent about the past participles. When used as verbs in the predicate of a sentence, they are always preceded by some form of the helping verb *to have (have, has,* or *had)*, for example, as in *I have eaten....* The past participle may also be used as an adjective *(the chosen few...)*.

## *REGULAR AND IRREGULAR VERBS*

> **REGULAR VERBS are verbs that create their past forms by adding *-ed, -d,* or *-t*.**

The principal parts of most verbs are easy to learn because they follow a regular pattern. These verbs are therefore called regular verbs. Most English verbs create their past form by adding *-ed* or, if the verb already ends with an "e," by adding only *-d*. (A few regular verbs add the ending *-t*).

> **IRREGULAR VERBS do not follow any set pattern in forming their past or past-participle forms.**

Because irregular verbs have no regular pattern, you must simply memorize all of the various forms. The chart below contains examples of many irregular verbs. (***The second princi-***

*pal part is not shown because all present participles end in* -ing.)

| PRESENT | PAST | PAST PARTICIPLE | PRESENT | PAST | PAST PARTICIPLE |
|---|---|---|---|---|---|
| arise | arose | arisen | go | went | gone |
| bear | bore | borne, born | grow | grew | grown |
| beat | beat | beaten | hang (*object*) | hung | hung |
| become | became | become | hear | heard | heard |
| begin | began | begun | know | knew | known |
| bind | bound | bound | lay (*to place*) | laid | laid |
| bite | bit | bitten | lead | led | led |
| blow | blew | blown | lend | lent | lent |
| break | broke | broken | let | let | let |
| bring | brought | brought | lie (*to recline*) | lay | lain |
| burst | burst | burst | lose | lost | lost |
| buy | bought | bought | meet | met | met |
| cast | cast | cast | pay | paid | paid |
| catch | caught | caught | prove | proved | proven, proved |
| come | came | come | put | put | put |
| cut | cut | cut | rise | rose | risen |
| dig | dug | dug | ride | rode | ridden |
| dive | dove (*or* dived) | dived | ring | rang | rung |
| do | did | done | run | ran | run |
| draw | drew | drawn | say | said | said |
| drink | drank | drunk | see | saw | seen |
| drive | drove | driven | set | set | set |
| fall | fell | fallen | sit | sat | sat |
| feel | felt | felt | shine | shone | shone |
| find | found | found | show | showed | shown, showed |
| flee | fled | fled | shrink | shrank, shrunk | shrunk |
| fly | flew | flown | sing | sang | sung |
| forget | forgot | forgotten | sink | sank | sunk |
| freeze | froze | frozen | sleep | slept | slept |
| get | got | gotten | speak | spoke | spoken |
| give | gave | given | spend | spent | spent |

| PRESENT | PAST | PAST PARTICIPLE | PRESENT | PAST | PAST PARTICIPLE |
|---|---|---|---|---|---|
| spring | sprang | sprung | throw | threw | thrown |
| stand | stood | stood | wake | woke, waked | woken, waked |
| steal | stole | stolen | wear | wore | worn |
| swim | swam | swum | win | won | won |
| swing | swung | swung | wind | wound | wound |
| take | took | taken | work (to form) | wrought | wrought |
| tear | tore | torn | wring | wrung | wrung |
| think | thought | thought | write | wrote | written |

## PRINCIPAL PARTS OF LINKING AND HELPING VERBS

The linking verb *to be* is somewhat more complicated. Its four principal parts are usually given as *be (am, is, are)*, *being*, *was (were)*, *been*. The various forms which must be used depend upon the *person* of the subject with which this linking verb is used.

### ■ Linking Verb: "to be"

| PERSON | PRESENT | PRESENT PARTICIPLE | PAST | PAST PARTICIPLE |
|---|---|---|---|---|
| 1st Person | be, am, are | *(am, are, was, were)* **being** | was, were | *(have, had)* **been** |
| 2nd Person | are | *(are, were)* **being** | were | *(have, had)* **been** |
| 3rd Person | is, are | *(is, are, was, were)* **being** | was, were | *(has, have, had)* **been** |

Verbs such as *to be, to have,* and *to do* can be either **action verbs** or **helping verbs**. When they are action verbs, they have the usual four principal parts. When they are helping verbs, however, "have" and "do" do not have all of the four principal parts. Other helping verbs also have only a limited number of principal parts. Here are some examples of helping verbs:

### ■ Helping Verbs

| PRESENT | PRESENT PARTICIPLE | PAST | PAST PARTICIPLE |
|---|---|---|---|
| be, am, is, are | being | was, were | been |
| do | ------- | did | ------- |
| have | having | had | ------- |
| shall, should | ------- | ------- | ------- |
| will | ------- | would | ------- |

| PRESENT | PRESENT PARTICIPLE | PAST | PAST PARTICIPLE |
|---------|--------------------|------|-----------------|
| may | ------- | might | ------- |
| can | ------- | could | ------- |
| must, ought | ------- | ------- | ------- |
| dare | ------- | dared | ------- |

✎ **EXERCISE A** Above each of the verbs in **dark print**, write *1, 2, 3,* or *4* to indicate which principal part of the verb is being used (*1 = present*, *2 = present participle*, *3 = past*, *4 = past participle*). **Underline all helping verbs.** Note: some verbs are used in predicates; some are used as modifying participles (verbal adjectives); some are used in their infinitive form.

$\overset{2}{}$
1. We <u>have been</u> **working** hard on our research papers.

2. You should not be **running** on this wet floor.

3. She had **telephoned** to **say** she could not **come**.

4. Crystal and Diane have **gone** to church.

5. We had been **rollicking** in the park.

6. You should not be **prejudiced** against those who **disagree** with you.

7. The prisoners were **taken** to their cells.

8. Many Northerners have never **eaten** okra.

9. What can be **done** with these leftovers?

10. We will be **asking** for permission to **enter** the contest.

✎ **EXERCISE B** Write the three other principal parts of the following verbs. If you are not sure, check a dictionary or the lists in this lesson. NOTE: This exercise continues on the following page.

| | Present | Present Participle | Past | Past Participle |
|---|---------|--------------------|------|-----------------|
| 1. | give | _____ | _____ | _____ |
| 2. | hurt | _____ | _____ | _____ |
| 3. | suppose | _____ | _____ | _____ |
| 4. | water | _____ | _____ | _____ |
| 5. | put | _____ | _____ | _____ |

| 6. | sing | _____ | | |
|----|------|-----------|---|---|
| | **Present** | **Present Participle** | **Past** | **Past Participle** |
| 7. | lie (falsify) | _____ | _____ | _____ |
| 8. | lie (recline) | _____ | _____ | _____ |
| 9. | forecast | _____ | _____ | _____ |
| 10. | mean | _____ | _____ | _____ |
| 11. | drown | _____ | _____ | _____ |
| 12. | climb | _____ | _____ | _____ |
| 13. | bid (auction) | _____ | _____ | _____ |
| 14. | bid (command) | _____ | _____ | _____ |
| 15. | drag | _____ | _____ | _____ |
| 16. | drug | _____ | _____ | _____ |
| 17. | pass | _____ | _____ | _____ |
| 18. | whistle | _____ | _____ | _____ |
| 19. | attack | _____ | _____ | _____ |
| 20. | worship | _____ | _____ | _____ |
| 21. | freeze | _____ | _____ | _____ |
| 22. | burn | _____ | _____ | _____ |
| 23. | build | _____ | _____ | _____ |
| 24. | hang (person) | _____ | _____ | _____ |
| 25. | hang (object) | _____ | _____ | _____ |
| 26. | wound (injure) | _____ | _____ | _____ |
| 27. | wind | _____ | _____ | _____ |
| 28. | hear | _____ | _____ | _____ |
| 29. | lend | _____ | _____ | _____ |

# LESSON 36: TENSE AND VERB FORMS

> **TENSE is the time of action or state of being expressed in a verb.**

Verbs take different forms to indicate the *time* of the action or condition expressed by the verb. These various forms are known as *tenses*. Most action and linking verbs have six tenses—three *simple* tenses and three *perfect* (completed) *tenses*.

| TENSE | *EXPRESSES ACTION OR CONDITION...* | EXAMPLES |
|-------|-----------------------------------|----------|
| **Present** | ...in the present time (now). | I *see* the painting. |
| **Past** | ...in past time (before now). | I *saw* the painting yesterday. |

| Future | ...future time (after now). | I *shall see* the painting tomorrow. |
| **TENSE** | *EXPRESSES ACTION OR CONDITION...* | **EXAMPLES** |
| **Present perfect** | ...which began at some time in the past and is continuing now. | I *have seen* this painting. |
| **Past perfect** | ...which began at some time in the past and was completed at some later time in the past. | I *had seen* that painting before. |
| **Future perfect** | ...which begins in the present or future and will end at some time later in the future. | I *shall have seen* the painting for the third time. |

## CONJUGATION OF VERBS

To write verbs in all their forms indicating *tense, number, person, voice, tone,* and *mood* is to **conjugate** the verb. By way of illustration, **conjugation tables** for the verb **to see** are used on subsequent pages. Although we will study more about **voice** and **tone** later (see Lessons 37 and 39), learn the following definitions to help you understand these conjugation tables and to help you with the ending exercise:

**CONJUGATION is the various changes in the form and use of the verb to signify tense, voice, number, person, and mood.**

**ACTIVE VOICE is the form of the verb showing that the subject is the doer of the action of the verb.**

**PASSIVE VOICE is the form of the verb showing that the subject is the receiver of the action of the verb.**

**SIMPLE TONE is the ordinary form of the verb indicating simple time and emphasis.**

**PROGRESSIVE TONE is the form of the verb indicating that the action is on-going.**

**EMPHATIC TONE is the form of the verb indicating special emphasis.**

**MOOD is a characteristic of verbs, revealing how action or expression is thought of by the subject; indicative (fact), subjunctive (hypothetical), and imperative (command).**

# ■ *Conjugation of the verb "to see"* (<u>Active Voice</u>, *Indicative Mood*)

**Principal parts:** *see, seeing, saw, seen*

| Number: | Singular | | | Plural | | |
|---|---|---|---|---|---|---|
| Tone: | Simple | Progressive | Emphatic | Simple | Progressive | Emphatic |
| **Present Tense** | | | | | | |
| 1st per. | I see | I am seeing | I do see | we see | we are seeing | we do see |
| 2nd per. | you see | you are seeing | you do see | you see | you are seeing | you do see |
| 3rd per. | he, she, it sees | he, she, it is seeing | he, she, it does see | they see | they are seeing | they do see |
| **Past Tense** | | | | | | |
| 1st per. | I saw | I was seeing | I did see | we saw | we were seeing | we did see |
| 2nd per. | you saw | you were seeing | you did see | you saw | you were seeing | you did see |
| 3rd per. | he, she, it saw | he, she, it was seeing | he, she it, did see | they saw | they were seeing | they did see |
| **Future Tense** | | | | | | |
| 1st per. | I shall see | I shall be seeing | | we shall see | we shall be seeing | |
| 2nd per. | you will see | you will be seeing | | you will see | you will be seeing | |
| 3rd per. | he, she, it will see | he, she, it will be seeing | | they will see | they will be seeing | |
| **Present Perfect Tense** | | | | | | |
| 1st per. | I have seen | I have been seeing | | we have seen | we have been seeing | |
| 2nd per. | you have seen | you have been seeing | | you have seen | you have been seeing | |
| 3rd per. | he, she, it has seen | he, she, it has been seeing | | they have seen | they have been seeing | |
| **Past Perfect Tense** | | | | | | |
| 1st per. | I had seen | I had been seeing | | we had seen | we had been seeing | |
| 2nd per. | you had seen | you had been seeing | | you had seen | you had been seeing | |
| 3rd per. | he, she, it had seen | he, she, it had been seeing | | they had seen | they had been seeing | |
| **Future Perfect Tense** | | | | | | |
| 1st per. | I shall have seen | I shall have been seeing | | we shall have seen | we shall have been seeing | |
| 2nd per. | you will have seen | you will have been seeing | | you will have seen | you will have been seeing | |
| 3rd per. | he, she, it will have seen | he, she, it will have been seeing | | they will have seen | they will have been seeing | |

# ■ *Conjugation of the verb "to see" (**Passive Voice**, Indicative Mood)*

| Number: | Singular | | Plural | |
|---|---|---|---|---|
| Tone*: | Simple | Progressive | Simple | Progressive |
| **Present Tense** | | | | |
| 1st per. | I am seen | I am being seen | we are seen | we are being seen |
| 2nd per. | you are seen | you are being seen | you are seen | you are being seen |
| 3rd per. | he, she, it is seen | he, she, it is being seen | they are seen | they are being seen |
| **Past Tense** | | | | |
| 1st per. | I was seen | I was being seen | we were seen | we were being seen |
| 2nd per. | you were seen | you were being seen | you were seen | you were being seen |
| 3rd per. | he, she, it was seen | he, she, it was being seen | they were seen | they were being seen |
| **Future Tense** | | | | |
| 1st per. | I shall be seen | I shall be being seen | we shall be seen | we shall be being seen |
| 2nd per. | you will be seen | you will be being seen | you will be seen | you will be being seen |
| 3rd per. | he, she, it will be seen | he, she, it will be being seen | they will be seen | they will be being seen |
| **Present Perfect Tense** | | | | |
| 1st per. | I have been seen | | we have been seen | |
| 2nd per. | you have been seen | | you have been seen | |
| 3rd per. | he, she, it has been seen | | they have been seen | |
| **Past Perfect Tense** | | | | |
| 1st per. | I had been seen | | we had been seen | |
| 2nd per. | you had been seen | | you had been seen | |
| 3rd per. | he, she, it, had been seen | | they had been seen | |
| **Future Perfect Tense** | | | | |
| 1st per. | I shall have been seen | | we shall have been seen | |
| 2nd per. | you will have been seen | | you will have been seen | |
| 3rd per. | he, she, it will have been seen | | they will have been seen | |

**Note:** * There are no emphatic-tone forms for verbs in the passive voice. There are no progressive-tone forms for verbs in the perfect tenses, passive voice. Although, technically, progressive forms could be constructed for the perfect tenses, they would be awkward and are not generally used.

## ■ *The Verbal Form of "to see"*

### ❏ Verbals are verb forms used as another part of speech.

*Verbals* have only the following forms:

| Voice: | Active Voice | | Passive Voice |
|---|---|---|---|
| Tone: | Simple | Progressive | Simple |
| Present infinitive | to see | to be seeing | to be seen |
| Perfect infinitive | to have seen | to have been seeing | to have been seen |
| Present participle | seeing | ------- | being seen |
| Past participle | seen | ------- | ------- |
| Perfect participle | having seen | having been seeing | having been seen |
| Present gerund | seeing | ------- | being seen |
| Past gerund (see below) | seen | ------- | ------- |
| Perfect gerund | having seen | having been seeing | having been seen |

### ❏ Past gerunds refer to persons or things which have been acted upon.

Even though *past gerunds* are not common, they are used of persons or things which have been acted upon. The past gerund *seen* may be used as follows: They were numbered among the *seen*. By definition, these verbals are always used as nouns; therefore they can be used as *subjects*, *direct objects*, *objects of prepositions*, *predicate nominatives*, and *appositives*. Past gerunds normally end with the suffix *-ed*, unless they take an irregular ending.

☞**EXAMPLES:**

The *hospitalized* were released today. (past gerund—used as a *subject*)

They comforted the *wounded*. (past gerund—used as a *direct object*)

✎ **EXERCISE A** In the blanks, identify the **tense, voice,** and **tone** of the verbs in **dark print.** Compare the verbs with the preceding charts, if necessary.

1.  I **shall be attending** the concert tonight. *future, active, progressive*

2.  We **have been watching** the football game. _____

3.  He **was** last **seen** in Chicago. _____

4.  Frank **has been known** to be forgetful. _____

5.  We **are known** by our deeds. _____

6.  Men **shall be judged** for what they have done. _____

7.  I **did do** my homework. _____

8.  By 5:15 p.m., we **shall have been talking** for an hour. _____

9.  Who **murdered** Julius Caesar? _____

10. The woman **has been seeing** a psychiatrist. _____

11. They **will be finished** at 6 p.m. _____

12. They **will have been married** for fifty years. _____

13. Elijah **was taken** up to heaven in a fiery chariot. _____

14. I **was eating** when you called. _____

15. I was eating when you **called**. _____

16. When **do** you **arrive**? _____

17. We **shall decide** the winner tomorrow. _____

18. You **will have done** that for the last time. _____

---

✎ **EXERCISE B** Review the section about **verbals** in Lesson 3, and study the chart on verbal forms in this lesson and back in Lesson 3. Then identify the type and tense of the verbals in **dark print** in the sentences below.

1.  The firemen tried to help the **injured**. _____*past gerund*_____

2.  The **injured** victims were taken to a hospital. _____

3.  **Seeing** is believing. _____

4.  **To be** or not to be, that is the question. _____

5.  The **surging** waves crashed upon the shore. _____

6.  **Being saved** is the greatest experience in life. _____

7.  **Being saved** by the bell, the boxer returned to his corner. _____

8.  Jesus healed the **crippled** and the blind. _____

9.  **To have been talking** with you has been a pleasure. _____

10. The old cabin had no **running** water. _____

# LESSON 37: ACTIVE AND PASSIVE VOICE

> **VOICE is the form or use of a verb indicating whether its subject is the doer (active) or the receiver (passive) of the verb's action.**
>
> **ACTIVE VOICE is the form of the verb showing that the subject is the doer of the action of the verb.**
>
> **PASSIVE VOICE is the form of the verb showing that the subject is the receiver of the action of the verb.**

## ACTIVE VOICE

A verb form is in the active voice when the subject is the doer of the action and the direct object is the receiver of the action.

☞**EXAMPLES:**

*Johnny* **hit** the ball.

*Washington Irving* **wrote** the story of Rip Van Winkle.

The *orchestra* **gave** a great performance.

## PASSIVE VOICE

A verb form is in the passive voice when the subject is the receiver of the action and the object of the preposition "by" is the doer of the action. A verb in the **passive voice** consists of a form of the verb **be** *(am, is, are, was, were, be, being, been)* followed by the *past participle* of a main verb. One clue for identifying a passive-voice verb is that it is followed by a phrase, either expressed or implied, beginning with the preposition **by**, indicating the doer of the action.

☞**EXAMPLES:**

The *ball* **was hit** by Johnny.

The *story* of Rip Van Winkle **was written** by Washington Irving.

A great *performance* **was given** by the orchestra.

The *roll call* **was taken** (by -------). (Doer implied.)

---

✎ **EXERCISE** Write **A** or **P** in the blank to indicate whether the verb in **dark print** is Active or Passive. Before answering, ask yourself, "Who or what is the doer of the action? Is the subject of the verb the doer or receiver of the action?"

_A_  1. He **will compete** in the chess tournament tomorrow.

____  2. The assignment **must be completed** before Friday.

____  3. I **have been studying** my history lesson.

____  4. This sweater **has been damaged** by moths.

____  5. We **have been wondering** what you meant by that.

____  6. We have been wondering what you **meant** by that.

____  7. We **shall see** Jesus someday if we have been saved.

____  8. We shall see Jesus someday if we **have been saved**.

____  9. The document **has been typed**.

____  10. The secretary **is typing** the document.

____  11. We **are experiencing** technical difficulties; please stand by.

____  12. We are experiencing technical difficulties; please **stand** by.

____  13. The sun **has been shining** for three weeks straight.

____  14. Some light **has been shed** on the mystery by this latest discovery.

____  15. This new discovery **has shed** some light on the mystery.

____  16. The music to which I **am listening** is very peculiar.

____  17. When Christ returns, He **will be acknowledged** as Lord by all men.

____  18. When Christ returns, every knee **shall bow** before Him.

____  19. The telephone **is ringing**.

____  20. You **are being called** to active duty.

# LESSON 38: TRANSITIVE AND INTRANSITIVE VERBS

> **TRANSITIVE VERBS are characterized by or involve transfer or passing of action to a receiver of the action.**
>
> **INTRANSITIVE VERBS are not able to transfer action to a receiver.**

Verbs are classified as either *transitive* or *intransitive*. When we speak of verbs having a *receiver* of their action, we are speaking of transitive verbs. *Transitive verbs* are those which have their action passed from a *doer* to a *receiver*. Transitive verbs can be either *active* or *passive*, because their action can be "passed" either from their subject to their direct object *(active voice)*, or from the object of the preposition "by" to the subject *(passive voice)*.

*Intransitive verbs* have *only doers*; they have *no receivers or objects* of their action. Because of this, intransitive verbs cannot be written or spoken in passive voice. Their action is not "passed" to anyone or anything.

| EXAMPLES | |
|---|---|
| **TRANSITIVE**<br>(action transfers to a receiver) | You *may start* the *engine*. (active voice)<br>She *lit* the *candle*. (active voice)<br>The *cow was milked* by the farmer. (passive voice) |
| **INTRANSITIVE**<br>(no receiver of the verb's action) | The engine *is running*. (active voice)<br>The sun *rose* at 5:30 a.m. (active voice)<br>The dog *sat* in my lap. (active voice) |

Of course, since only transitive verbs can transfer action, only *action verbs* can be *transitive*. All *linking verbs* are considered *intransitive*. Some action verbs, however, may be transitive in one sentence but intransitive in another. In the example above, *The engine is running*, "is running" is considered intransitive because it has no object or receiver of its action. But in the sentence *The foreman is running the factory*, the verb is transitive because now it has a receiver of its action.

---

✎ **EXERCISE** In the blanks, write **T** or **I** to indicate whether the verbs in **dark print** are Transitive or Intransitive. Before answering, ask yourself, "Is there an expressed or implied receiver of the action?" If not, the verb is likely *intransitive*. If the verb is *transitive*, underline the receiver of its action.

_T_     1. The women **baked** <u>cookies</u> for the social.

____     2. The light **is shining** brightly.

____ 3. The river **has risen** by two feet during the last twelve hours.

____ 4. You **may come** out now.

____ 5. Please **put** the mail on my desk.

____ 6. The frog **was changed** into a handsome prince.

____ 7. They **should be** here any minute.

____ 8. The plane **arrived** late.

____ 9. "The Word **became** flesh."

____ 10. Gold **was discovered** at Sutter's Mill in the foothills of the Sierra Nevada.

____ 11. He **claimed** his right to speak before the assembly.

____ 12. Many types of birds **fly** south for the winter.

____ 13. Pilots **fly** airplanes.

____ 14. That pizza **smells** good.

____ 15. This **seems** to be the proper course of action to take.

____ 16. The motor **is operating** well.

____ 17. The motor **is operating** the machine.

____ 18. The audience **applauded** enthusiastically.

____ 19. The audience **applauded** the performance.

____ 20. The performers **were given** a standing ovation by the audience.

# LESSON 39: TONE OF VERBS

> **TONE is a characteristic of verb tenses precisely indicating simple time, emphasis, or progress.**

Another way to describe how verbs are used is to speak about their *tone.* In some tenses, verbs may have one of three tones. The three tones are illustrated in the following chart:

| TONE | EXPRESSES | EXAMPLES |
|---|---|---|
| Simple | ...ordinary tense or time | We always *pray* before meals. |
| Progressive | ...on-going action or state of being | We *are praying* for you. |
| Emphatic | ...special emphasis. (Also used in questions.) | *Do* you *pray* for us? Yes, we *do pray* for you often. |

## ■ *Simple Tone*

This describes ordinary tense or time, using the *present* and *past* forms of the verb.

## ■ *Progressive Tone*

As you can see from studying the following chart, to create the progressive form of an *active-voice* verb, use an appropriate tense of the helping verb *to be* plus the *present participle* (*-ing* form) of the main verb.

To create the progressive form of a *passive-voice* verb use a form of the helping verb *to be* plus the word *being* plus the *past participle* of the main verb.

| ACTIVE VOICE: | | |
|---|---|---|
| | Present progressive: | am (are, is) + seeing |
| | Past progressive: | was (were) + seeing |
| | Future progressive: | shall (will) be + seeing |
| | Present perfect progressive: | have (has) been + seeing |
| | Past perfect progressive: | had been + seeing |
| | Future perfect progressive: | shall (will) have been + seeing |
| PASSIVE VOICE: | Present progressive: | am (are, is) + being + seen |
| | Past progressive: | was (were) + being + seen |
| | Future progressive: | shall (will) be + being + seen |
| | Present perfect progressive: | (none) |
| | Past perfect progressive: | (none) |
| | Future perfect progressive: | (none) |

## ■ *Emphatic Tone*

The *emphatic tone* is used only in the present and past tenses, active voice. It is created by using the present or past form of the helping verb *to do* (*do, does,* or *did*) plus the present form of the main verb.

| ACTIVE VOICE: | | |
|---|---|---|
| | Present emphatic: | do see, does see |
| | Past emphatic: | did see |
| PASSIVE VOICE: | Present emphatic: | (none) |
| | Past emphatic: | (none) |

✎ **EXERCISE A** In the blanks, write the tense and tone of the verbs in **dark print**, using the terms from the middle column of the preceding two charts.

1.  We **have been fishing** all morning. _____*present perfect progressive*_____

2.  What **are** you **trying** to tell me? _____

3.  The boy **did tell** the truth. _____

4.  They **have been** our friends for years. _____

5.  He **is known** as a genius. _____

6.  The gauge **indicates** that the tank is empty. _____

7.  **Does**n't he ever **stop** his complaining? _____

8.  They **will have been traveling** for two weeks._____

9.  **Do** not **allow** yourselves to be tempted. _____

10. He **was being bitten** by mosquitoes._____

11. He **had been observed** fleeing from the scene._____

12. The program **is seen** daily on Channel 6. _____

13. I **have been wondering** where you were. _____

14. We **are having** a good time. _____

✎ **EXERCISE B** In the margin to the left of each of the sentences in Exercise A, write **A** or **P** to indicate whether the verb in **dark print** is in *Active* or *Passive voice.*

# LESSON 40: UNIT REVIEW

✎ **EXERCISE** Fill in the blanks below:

1.  The four principal parts of verbs are _____, _____, _____, and

    _____.

2.  The second principal part of verbs always ends with the suffix _____.

3.  The third principal part of *regular* verbs ends with the suffix _____, _____, or _____.

4.  The fourth principal part of verbs is preceded by the helping verb _____, _____, or _____.

5.  The six tenses are _____, _____, _____,

    _____, _____, and _____.

6.  To write verbs in all their forms indicating tense, number, person, voice, tone, and mood is to

    _____ the verb.

7.  The form or use of a verb indicating whether its subject is the doer or the receiver of the verb's

    action is called _____.

8.  When the subject is the doer of the verb's action, the verb is in _____ voice.

9.  When the subject is the receiver of the verb's action, the verb is in _____ voice.

10. Verbs that do not pass their action from a doer to a receiver are called _____.

11. Only _____ verbs can be transitive.

12. The characteristic of some verb tenses indicating progress, emphasis, or simple time is called

    _____.

# Unit 9
# Using Punctuation

Proper *punctuation* of sentences is a necessary tool for correct, clear, and effective writing because it helps to make the relationships of words and thoughts clear to the reader. The *marks of punctuation* reflect the pauses and voice changes in our spoken communications. These voice inflections are an essential part of our meaning. Punctuation accomplishes the same purposes in written expressions. Use of punctuation marks varies somewhat among individual writers, but some basic rules have arisen from common usages throughout the years. These basic rules help us all to understand one another, and any variations should be employed only when they help, rather than hinder, the communication of ideas.

> **PUNCTUATION is a method or system of written symbols designed to make communications clear.**

The most important marks of punctuation are: the period, the question mark, the exclamation point, the comma, the semicolon, the colon, the dash, the hyphen, the apostrophe, parentheses, brackets, quotation marks, and other special marks and foreign symbols. These will be discussed in the lessons of this unit.

## FOUR USES OF PUNCTUATION

The *four main uses* or purposes of punctuation are to end, introduce, separate or enclose parts of a sentence.

| Rule 9.1 | **Use punctuation to indicate the end of a statement. There are three ending marks for this purpose: the period, the question mark, and the exclamation point.** |
| --- | --- |

☞**EXAMPLES:**

The time to speak out has come**.**

Who is our next contestant**?**

What a funny story**!**

| Rule 9.2 | **Use punctuation to introduce material that follows. The three marks of introduction used for this purpose are the comma, the colon, and the dash.** |
| --- | --- |

☞**EXAMPLES:**

One person has been the foundation of our family, my father.

Take the following with you: a notebook, a pen or pencil, and an eraser.

The law of God is simple——to love God above all and to love your neighbor as yourself.

| Rule 9.3 | **Use punctuation to separate parts of a sentence or word. The five marks of separation are the comma, the semicolon, the dash, the hyphen, and the apostrophe.** |
|---|---|

☞**EXAMPLES:**

If you love Me, keep My commandments.

Some like it hot; some like it cold.

Love, joy, peace, patience, kindness, goodness——these are some of the "fruits of the Spirit."

There's no such time as twenty-seven o'clock.

| Rule 9.4 | **Use punctuation to enclose parts of a sentence or a whole sentence. These punctuation marks are usually used in pairs. The six enclosure marks used for this purpose are commas, dashes, quotation marks, single quotation marks, parentheses, and brackets.** |
|---|---|

☞**EXAMPLES:**

The school librarian, Miss Andrews, is a very helpful person.

His two top qualifications——the abilities to run fast and to jump high——made him a valuable member of the track team.

"Walt Whitman's poem, 'O Captain, My Captain,' was written about Abraham Lincoln," our teacher said.

The First Amendment (to the U.S. Constitution [adopted in 1791]) provides for essential freedoms.

# LESSON 41: USING THE PERIOD AND THE ELLIPSIS

The period ( **.** ) is usually an ending mark, but it also has special uses in abbreviations, in outlines, and as a mark of separation.

| Rule 9.5 | Use a period at the end of a declarative sentence. |
| --- | --- |

☞**EXAMPLES:**

She enjoys reading Christian novels.

The light bulb is burned out and needs replacing.

| Rule 9.6 | Use a period at the end of a mild imperative sentence. |
| --- | --- |

☞**EXAMPLES:**

Please accept my apology.

Don't forget to call me when you arrive at home.

| Rule 9.7 | Use a period at the end of a sentence containing an indirect question. |
| --- | --- |

☞**EXAMPLES:**

He asked me when I could help him with his homework.

She wanted to know where to buy a computer.

| Rule 9.8 | Use a period after a standard abbreviation. |
| --- | --- |

☞**EXAMPLES:**

Mr.  Mrs.  Dr.  Ph.D.  St.  Blvd.  A.D.  B.C.  a.m.  p.m.  Co.  Inc.

Periods are **not** generally used in abbreviations of organizations, agencies, systems, etc. or in acronyms.

NATO  UN  CIA  FBI  AP  UPI  MADD  ASCII  HHS

| Rule 9.9 | Use periods following numerals in an outline. |
| --- | --- |

☞**EXAMPLE:**

I. Main outline point

A. Outline subpoint

1. *Outline subsubpoint*

A period usually is *not* placed at the end of lines in a topical outline. It *is* used at the end of sentences in a sentence or paragraph outline.

| Rule 9.10 | **Use a period to write decimals, to separate dollars and cents, and to precede cents written alone with a dollar sign.** |
|---|---|

☞**EXAMPLES:**

5.5 percent    1.5 million    $5.25    $.25 ($0.25)    (no period in 25¢)

| Rule 9.11 | **If a declarative or mild imperative sentence ends with an abbreviation, only one period is needed at the end.** |
|---|---|

☞**EXAMPLE:**

He bought 400 shares of stock in Acme Corp.

| Rule 9.12 | **If an interrogative or exclamatory sentence ends with an abbreviation, a question mark or exclamation point is needed.** |
|---|---|

Inside a sentence, an abbreviation's period may be followed by any necessary punctuation in the same way as if the period were not present.

☞**EXAMPLES:**

Is her address 346 Elm St.?

Don't ever telephone me at 3 a.m.!

Despite the efforts of people like Martin Luther King, Jr., race relations have not improved much in this country.

| Rule 9.13 | **Use three ellipsis periods ( ... ) to indicate intentional omission of material from a quotation or sentence.** |
|---|---|

☞**EXAMPLE:**

"Four score and seven years ago, our fathers brought forth ... a new nation."

| Rule 9.14 | When ellipsis periods come at the end of a sentence, ADD a fourth ending period, a question mark, or exclamation mark. |
|---|---|

☞**EXAMPLES:**

"For, in the first place, no man can survey himself without forthwith turning his thoughts toward the God in whom he lives and moves...." (John Calvin)

"Oh, the unutterable guilt involved even in one moment's unbelief...!" (Horatius Bonar)

"May not, therefore, the law be proclaimed to men of all faiths; and may it not, if it is so proclaimed, serve as a restraint against the most blatant forms of evil through the common grace of God...?" (J. Gresham Machen)

| Rule 9.15 | Do NOT use a period at the end of a title or subheading in a manuscript. |
|---|---|

☞**EXAMPLE:**

**HOW TO BUILD A BIRDHOUSE**

Getting Ready

xxx xx xxxxxx xxxxxxx xxxx xxxxxx xxx xxx
xxxxx xx xxx xxx xxxxxxx xxxx xxxx xx xxxxx

| Rule 9.16 | Do NOT use a period after a quotation mark that is preceded by a period. |
|---|---|

☞**EXAMPLES:**

WRONG:     Mother said, "Please wash up for dinner.".

CORRECT:   Mother said, "Please wash up for dinner."

✎ **EXERCISE A** Punctuate the following correctly.

1.  Ronald Turner, M.D., is one of the doctors in The Family Practice Medical Group, Inc.

2.  Do Mr and Mrs Henry live at 2541 Pacific Blvd

3.  Be careful when you cross the street

4.  She told me, "Turn left at the next intersection "

5.  My father has a Ph D  in physics and works as a researcher for Beckman Engineering Co

6.  Did that war occur in A D  70 or 70 B C

7.  Meet me at the corner of 12th St and Beach Ave at 7 p m

8.  One item cost under $2 ($1 98 to be exact) and the other item was just under $1 ($ 95)

9.  The decimal equivalent of the fraction $^1/_4$ is 0 25

---

✎ **EXERCISE B** *Abbreviate* the following, punctuating each item correctly.

1.   one million, 500 thousand          _____*1.5 million*_____

2.   twenty-five dollars, 14 cents       _____

3.   thirteen and seven-tenths percent   _____

4.   September 7                          _____

5.   Mister Gunderson                     _____

6.   et cetera                            _____

7.   Doctor Beecham                       _____

8.   bachelor of arts degree              _____

9.   Micronix Corporation                 _____

10.  7:30 (in the morning)                _____

11.  16 feet, 4 inches                    _____

---

# LESSON 42: USING QUESTION MARKS AND EXCLAMATION POINTS

The **question mark** ( **?** ) is used to mark the end of a question (*interrogative* sentence or phrase). The **exclamation point** ( **!** ) is used to mark the end of an *exclamatory* sentence, phrase, or word. Both marks also have special, limited uses within sentences.

---

| Rule 9.17 | **Use a question mark at the end of a direct question.** |

☞**EXAMPLES:**

What is the meaning of this word?

Do you really want this shirt?

| Rule 9.18 | **If an interrogative sentence ends with an internal question, only one question mark is needed at the end.** |

☞**EXAMPLES:**

Which psalm asks, "What is man that thou art mindful of him?"

Who said, "Why are we here?"

| Rule 9.19 | **Do NOT use a question mark after an indirect question.** |

☞**EXAMPLES:**

**WRONG:**   I asked myself whether I really understood the meaning of love?

**CORRECT:**   I asked myself whether I really understood the meaning of love.

| Rule 9.20 | **Use question marks in a series of questions within one sentence.** |

☞**EXAMPLES:**

Does the organization accept Asians? African-Americans? Jews? Hispanics?

Have you met all of your uncles? aunts? cousins? second cousins?

| Rule 9.21 | **Use a question mark in parentheses within a sentence to express doubt or uncertainty.** |

☞**EXAMPLES:**

I think he was born on June 27 (?), 1955.

The creation of the world took place about 6,000 B.C. (?), some creationists say.

| Rule 9.22 | On limited occasions, you may use an exclamation point in parentheses to express irony or humorous meaning. |
|-----------|---------------------------------------------------------------------------------------------------------------|

It is considered weak and undesirable to use a question mark for such purposes. Creative wording and context, however, are better ways than the use of punctuation marks to express irony or humor.

☞**UNDESIRABLE:**

The brazen young woman pranced around in her modest (?) attire.

A balmy (?) breeze sent shivers through the parade spectators.

☞**ACCEPTABLE:**

The brazen young woman pranced around in her modest (!) attire.

A balmy (!) breeze sent shivers through the parade spectators.

| Rule 9.23 | Use an exclamation point at the end of an exclamatory sentence or strong imperative sentence. |
|-----------|-----------------------------------------------------------------------------------------------|

☞**EXAMPLES:**

You are a fantastic pianist!

Get out and stay out!

| Rule 9.24 | Use an exclamation point to terminate a strong interjection or emphatic phrase. |
|-----------|----------------------------------------------------------------------------------|

☞**EXAMPLES:**

Ouch!  Help!  What a lie!  Phooey!   Never again!  Good job!

| Rule 9.25 | Do NOT overuse the exclamation point. Too frequent use may cause this mark to lose its effectiveness. |
|-----------|-------------------------------------------------------------------------------------------------------|

☞**EXAMPLES:**

Do NOT (!) overuse (!) the exclamation point!!! Too frequent use (!) may cause this mark to lose (!) its effectiveness! Do you understand?!!!!

---

✎ **EXERCISE** Punctuate the following sentences correctly.

1.   Ouch! That hurts!

2.   When will dinner be ready

3.   Jerry asked Jill whether she liked classical music

4.   If only I could relive my childhood How differently I would have done things

5.   A fine friend ( ) you turned out to be

6.   Is this the way to Bretonville

7.   Bah Humbug What good is Christmas

8.   Come back here at once

9.   Help Help I can't swim

10.  Where is the main office

11.  I have often wondered why I was chosen by God to receive His grace

12.  Who used my toothbrush

13.  These seem to be genuine leather ( ) shoes

14.  Have you ever doubted her sincerity

15.  Try to keep your conversations down to a gentle ( ) roar

16.  Is your father coming your mother your brother your sister

17.  When are we going to study something more interesting

18.  Perhaps everyone asks himself at one time or another why he was born

19.  How should we dress for the occasion

# LESSON 43: USING THE COMMA

The *comma* ( **,** ) is one of the most widely used—and troublesome—punctuation marks. It is used to *introduce,* to *separate,* or (in pairs) to *enclose* parts of a sentence. Whereas the **period** indicates a full pause in speech and the **semicolon** a nearly full pause, the **comma** indicates only a brief pause. It is always used *inside* sentences, never as an ending mark. While there are some standard rules regarding commas, their use is somewhat flexible, allowing writers to use them in special ways to enhance the effectiveness or clarity of their expressions. Modern usage tends to use commas more sparingly than writers in the past used them.

| | |
|---|---|
| **Rule 9.26** | **Use a comma to separate independent clauses joined by a simple conjunction (and, but, or, nor, neither, yet) in a compound sentence, unless the clauses are very short and closely related in meaning.** |

☞**EXAMPLES:**

The computer is an important tool in many modern endeavors, and you would do well to master its use.

I tried to understand his reasoning, but his line of argument was too obscure.

| | |
|---|---|
| **Rule 9.27** | **Do NOT use a comma to separate compound predicates in a simple sentence.** |

☞**EXAMPLES:**

**WRONG:**     She read the letter, and quietly began to cry.

**CORRECT:**    She read the letter and quietly began to cry.

| | |
|---|---|
| **Rule 9.28** | **Use a comma to separate introductory modifying clauses or phrases from the rest of the sentence.** |

☞**EXAMPLES:**

When I was a child, I thought as a child.

By the time you reach London, we will be sleeping.

Carefully considering his answer, John impressed his questioners with his knowledge.

| | |
|---|---|
| **Rule 9.29** | **Do NOT use a comma to separate an introductory clause or phrase used as the subject of a sentence.** |

☞**EXAMPLES:**

What you have said is certainly wise.

Where you go is your own business.

| | |
|---|---|
| **Rule 9.30** | **Use commas to separate items in a series.** |

☞**EXAMPLES:**

The teacher selected Jenny, Kathy, Megan, Mike, and Derek.

They searched in the house, in the garage, in the attic, and in the yard.

*Journalistic usage*, however, generally eliminates the comma before the conjunction preceding the last item in a series:

The candidates included Benjamin Smith, Timothy Jones and Harry Brown.

The convention platform was decorated with red, white and blue bunting.

| | |
|---|---|
| **Rule 9.31** | **Use commas to separate two or more adjectives that equally modify the same noun. Do not place a comma between the last adjective and the noun.** |

☞**EXAMPLES:**

A tall, stately tree stands next to the Capitol.

The old, rusty car was sold for junk.

| | |
|---|---|
| **Rule 9.32** | **When the adjectives are *not equal*, commas are NOT used to separate them.** |

☞**EXAMPLES:**

A tall oak tree stands next to the Capitol.

The antique spinning wheel had not been used in years.

The new television season does not have many good shows.

It is sometimes difficult to tell whether a series of adjectives modifying the same noun are equal or not. Try these **two tests:**

■ **Insert the word "and" between the adjectives. If it sounds awkward, the adjectives are likely not equal.**

A tall, (and) stately tree stands … (equal)

A tall (and) oak tree stands … (awkward, unequal)

■ **Reverse the order of the adjectives. If the result does not make good sense, the adjectives are likely not equal.**

The antique spinning wheel … (makes good sense)

The spinning antique wheel … (confuses meaning)

| | |
|---|---|
| **Rule 9.33** | **Use a comma to separate contrasted, coordinate items.** |

☞**EXAMPLES:**

"Psychology" starts with a "p," not an "s."

Her parents were loving, yet stern.

The pesticide was effective, but environmentally safe.

Next are two distinct sentence arrangements, both of which contain two contrasting clauses:

■ **Use a comma to punctuate a sentence containing two contrasting dependent clauses.**

There is a unique sentence structure consisting of *two contrasting <u>dependent</u> clauses*. Neither clause is complete in itself, but together they make a meaningful sentence. Use a *comma* to separate the clauses in such sentences.

The higher the altitude is, the thinner the air becomes.

The harder we tried, the more mistakes we made.

The less she practiced her piano lessons, the poorer she performed.

■ **Use a comma to punctuate a sentence containing two contrasting independent clauses.**

Another special sentence arrangement consists of *two contrasting <u>independent</u> clauses*, the first being a *declarative* statement and the second an *interrogative*. Use a *comma* to separate the clauses in such sentences.

You do like chocolate cake, don't you?

He is eligible for a raise in pay next month, isn't he?

We are invited, aren't we?

| | |
|---|---|
| **Rule 9.34** | **Use a comma to separate sentence elements that might otherwise be misread.** |

☞**MISLEADING:**

The year after the war was brought to a close.

Inside the car was in good condition.

In May 1995 450 people were killed in auto accidents here.

☞**BETTER:**

The year after, the war was brought to a close.

Inside, the car was in good condition.

In May 1995, 450 people were killed in auto accidents here.

| | |
|---|---|
| **Rule 9.35** | **To prevent misreading, use a comma before the conjunction "for" when it means "because."** |

☞**MISLEADING:**

The students had to study for a test would be given the next day.

I cannot attend the men's conference for women are not invited.

☞**BETTER:**

The students had to study, for a test would be given the next day.

I cannot attend the men's conference, for women are not invited.

| Rule 9.36 | **Use commas to separate thousands, millions, billions, etc. in numerals with four or more digits.** |
|---|---|

☞**EXAMPLES:**

When will the population of the earth reach 1,000,000,000,000?

More than 36,500 people attended the game.

They paid $750,300 for their new house.

| Rule 9.37 | **Do NOT use commas in numerals representing years, telephone numbers, addresses (such as house numbers, street numbers, and postal code numbers), catalogue numbers, or part numbers.** |
|---|---|

☞**EXAMPLES:**

In 1978, the college had only 1,978 students.

Their telephone number is 555-3456.

Send your contribution to: 5432 Avonlea Blvd., Newtown, CA 95371.

Please send replacement part No. A578923.

My book club numbershipnumber is 76085890.

| Rule 9.38 | **Use a comma to separate a short quotation from the speaker to whom it is attributed.** |
|---|---|

☞**EXAMPLES:**

Persius observed, "We consume our tomorrows fretting about our yesterdays."

"No army can withstand the strength of an idea whose time has come," Victor Hugo once said.

"The battle for the Lord must begin within ourselves," Abraham Kuyper declared, "only then can it kindle outward and be sincerely waged with equal fervor against enemies all around."

| Rule 9.39 | Do NOT use a comma when there is no specific attribution (i.e., speaker) with the quotation. |
|---|---|

☞**EXAMPLES:**

His response of "No Comment" was not unexpected.

"This life will soon be past, only what is done for the Lord will last" is a good motto to adopt.

| Rule 9.40 | Use a comma after the salutation (greeting) of a friendly or social letter. |
|---|---|

☞**EXAMPLES:**

Dear Mom,    Dear Mrs. Greene,   Dear Aunt Gloria,   Dear Jim,

| Rule 9.41 | Use a comma to enclose words, phrases, or clauses that are parenthetical. |
|---|---|

☞**EXAMPLES:**

They do, *however,* require proper identification.

We shall, *in that case,* return to port.

He did offer, *on the other hand,* one good suggestion.

The network, *if you can believe it,* is going to broadcast some pro-Christian programs.

*Parenthetical elements* vary in their **intensity**. *Weak* parenthetical elements may **not** require commas. *Stronger* ones (those representing clear breaks in thought or those expressing emphasis) should be enclosed with commas.

☞**WEAK PARENTHETICAL ELEMENTS:**

We *also* have heard the news.

I was *indeed* pleased to hear from you.

He *too* wished to be considered with the others.

Why *then* did you lie?

☞**STRONGER PARENTHETICAL ELEMENTS:**

*Indeed*, that is a difficult question.

I have never, *as you well know,* made such insulting remarks.

Then, *too,* you should always remember to pray.

How important, *then,* is my participation?

---

| **Rule 9.42** | **Use commas to enclose "transposed" sentence elements (those out of their natural order).** |
| --- | --- |

☞**NORMAL:**

I believe the time has come to speak out.

It seems there is an inconsistency here.

☞**TRANSPOSED:**

The time has come, *I believe,* to speak out.

There is, *it seems,* an inconsistency here.

---

| **Rule 9.43** | **Use commas to enclose "suspending" sentence elements (those which interrupt the flow of the sentence and thus cause key thoughts to be delayed until the end of the sentence).** |
| --- | --- |

☞**EXAMPLES:**

We must do this, *not just because it is convenient,* but because it is right.

We should never forget, *and this is the most important point,* that many have died to maintain our freedoms.

---

| **Rule 9.44** | **Use commas to enclose appositives (words or phrases identifying a preceding noun or pronoun).** |
| --- | --- |

☞**EXAMPLES:**

My grandfather, *a World War II veteran,* fought in France in 1944.

Your job, *to check tickets as the patrons arrive,* is an easy one.

There are two instances where **commas** are NOT needed to enclose appositives.

■ **Commas are not needed if the appositive is preceded by the introductory words "such as," even though it is a parenthetical element.**

Large cities *such as* New York and Los Angeles have large crime problems.

■ **Commas are also not needed if the appositive is a proper name, closely related to the preceding word, or a noun clause.**

My brother *John* is ill.

Alexander *the Great* was a mighty conqueror.

The fact *that she is my cousin* did not influence my decision.

Words that introduce *some appositives*, such as "namely," "for example," "for instance," or "i.e.," are enclosed with *commas* because they are parenthetical elements.

Large cities, *for example,* New York and Los Angeles, have large crime problems.

Two of the Reformers, *namely,* Ulrich Zwingli and Martin Luther, disagreed on the meaning of the Lord's Supper.

All of the major news networks, *i.e.,* NBC, ABC, CBS, and CNN, carried the news conference.

| Rule 9.45 | Use commas to enclose words used in direct address. |
|---|---|

☞EXAMPLES:

And now, *ladies and gentlemen,* I would like to introduce our special guest.

*Father*, can you help me with my math?

Which of these dresses do you prefer, *madam?*

No, *Virginia,* there is not a Santa Claus.

| Rule 9.46 | Use commas to enclose numbers representing years in full dates. |
|---|---|

☞EXAMPLES:

He died on May 31, 1917, at the age of seventy-two.

NO *comma* is needed to enclose a number representing a year when no day of the month is mentioned.

He died in May 1917 at the age of seventy-two.

| Rule 9.47 | Use commas to enclose the name of a state or province (and country) following the name of a city. |
|---|---|

☞EXAMPLES:

He lived in Nashville, Tennessee, all his life.

The company's headquarters is located in Winnipeg, Manitoba, Canada.

Here is the way to punctuate a *complete address*:

John Smith, 390 Elm St., Douglas, WA 98765, U.S.A.

Mapleleaf Corporation, P.O. Box 7050, Burlington, ON L7R 3Y8, Canada

Bushman Safaris, Box 85, Nairobi 4356, Kenya

Martin Johnson, Nypongatan 10, 565 00 Mullsjö, Sweden

| Rule 9.48 | Use commas to enclose initials or titles following a person's name. |
|---|---|

☞**EXAMPLES:**

Adams, J.Q., fifth president of the United States

John Norman, M.D., will perform the operation.

Robert J. Willson, Jr., is the author.

| Rule 9.49 | Use commas to enclose non-restrictive (nonessential) clauses. Do NOT use commas to enclose restrictive (essential) clauses. |
|---|---|

☞**EXAMPLES:**

NONRESTRICTIVE:     The magazine, which costs $2.50, is published monthly.

RESTRICTIVE:     All people who rely on Christ for salvation are Christians.

| Rule 9.50 | Do NOT use a comma to separate a subject from its predicate or to separate a verb from its object or a complement. |
|---|---|

This is usually not a problem, except when the subject or object is a phrase or clause. This should not be used.

☞**WRONG:**

What you ask, is impossible. *(noun clause as subject)*

To do my best, is my goal. *(infinitive phrase as subject)*

She asked, what the commotion was all about. *(noun clause as object)*

The problem is, that we do not have enough money. *(noun clause as predicate nominative)*

| Rule 9.51 | Do NOT use a comma to replace an omitted word. |
|---|---|

This mistake is sometimes made when the signal word "that" is omitted from a noun clause or the relative pronouns "who," "whom," "which," or "that" are omitted from adjective clauses.

☞**WRONG:**

Mark said, he would call me this evening.

The woman, you saw was my mother.

The car, they bought was made in Japan.

She realized, she was in the wrong room.

---

> **Rule 9.52**    **Do NOT use a comma AFTER a simple coordinating conjunction unless parenthetical material immediately follows the conjunction.**

---

☞**WRONG:**

I was wrong, but, I have learned my lesson.

The item was broken, and, you should refund my money.

☞**OKAY:**

I was wrong, but, as a result of my mistakes, I have learned my lesson.

The item was broken, and, it seems to me, you should refund my money.

---

✎ **EXERCISE** Place commas where they are needed in the following sentences. If the sentence needs no commas, leave it as it is.

1.   There is one part of me that always aches after I have been skiing**,** my thighs.

2.   "They should be coming out soon" she said.

3.   She said she was the girl I was asking to see.

4.   The polite response would be a simple "Thank you."

5.   I have not seen him lately nor do I want to see him.

6.   The teacher gave me an A on my composition and that makes me happy.

7.   We had toast eggs pancakes and potatoes for breakfast.

8.   The boy rushed into the room and hurried out again.

9.   The boy rushed into the room looked around and hurried out again.

10.  We did not expect you but here you are.

11.  I love you Lord for you first loved me.

12.  If you find my jacket give me a call.

13.  What she said is not true.

14. After an hour of discussion a vote was taken.

15. By all accounts the experiment was a success.

16. Walking through the fallen leaves I recalled the happy autumn days of my childhood.

17. Walking through the fallen leaves reminded me of the happy autumn days of my childhood.

18. In order to get good grades in school you must study your lessons daily.

19. For my birthday she sent me only a greeting card not a gift.

20. The vegetables were covered with a rich creamy sauce.

21. "Give me a great big bear hug" Grandmother said to Timmy.

22. It seems to me and I know this sounds strange that the faster I work the greater my backlog of unfinished business grows.

23. You did make your bed didn't you?

24. Instead of the expected 500 guests 600 people attended.

25. The budget for the project totaled $2356789340.

26. The disabled aircraft which normally carries 450 passengers returned to the airport.

27. Will all those who wish to participate in this experiment raise their hands?

28. Yes this is a good choice. We do not however want that one.

29. The budget deficit is very high and according to experts it will continue to grow.

30. Thank you dear friends for your wonderful gift.

# LESSON 44: USING SEMICOLONS AND COLONS

## *THE SEMICOLON*

The *semicolon* ( **;** ) has only one purpose—to *separate*. It is a stronger mark of separation than the comma; that is, it signifies a greater "break" or "pause" between elements in a sentence. However, it is a weaker break mark than a period; therefore it cannot be used as an end-of-sentence mark. Elements separated by a semicolon must be equal and coordinate.

| | |
|---|---|
| **Rule 9.53** | **Use a semicolon to separate independent clauses that are NOT joined by a simple coordinating conjunction (and, but, or, nor, neither, yet).** |

☞**EXAMPLES:**

I think you will enjoy this book; it deals with your favorite subject.

She volunteered for the job; no one else would do it.

| | |
|---|---|
| **Rule 9.54** | **Use a semicolon to separate independent clauses that ARE joined by a simple coordinating conjunction if the independent clauses have internal commas or if the clauses are long.** |

☞**EXAMPLES:**

It is currently said that hope goes with youth, and lends to youth its wings of a butterfly; but I fancy that hope is the last gift given to man, and the only gift not given to youth. Youth is preeminently the period in which a man can be lyric, fantastical, poetic; but youth is the period in which a man can be hopeless. *(G.K. Chesterton)*

| | |
|---|---|
| **Rule 9.55** | **Use a semicolon to separate independent clauses that are joined by a conjunctive adverb (see Lesson 3).** |

If the conjunctive adverb has two or more syllables, place a **comma** after it in addition to the *semicolon* before it. If the conjunctive adverb has only one syllable, no comma is needed.

☞**EXAMPLES:**

Don't drink too much milk; otherwise, we won't have enough for breakfast.

He is not a very deep thinker; still he comes up with good ideas occasionally.

| | |
|---|---|
| **Rule 9.56** | **Use semicolons to separate items in a series when the items themselves have internal commas.** |

☞**EXAMPLES:**

Four of the largest cities in the United States are New York, New York; Los Angeles, California; Chicago, Illinois; and Philadelphia, Pennsylvania.

> **Rule 9.57**  **Do NOT use a semicolon to set off a dependent clause or a phrase.**

A *semicolon* represents the end of a *complete thought*; it might be thought of as a "weak period." Therefore, it should NOT be used to set off *incomplete thoughts*.

☞**WRONG:**

Since Mary had the greater experience; she was given the job.

Bowing his head in shame; Jason confessed he had done wrong.

We can eat; as soon as the potatoes are cooked.

## THE COLON

The *colon* ( **:** ) is used primarily as a *mark of introduction*. It is often used to introduce series, lists, and quotations. Occasionally, it is used as a *mark of separation*.

> **Rule 9.58**  **Use a colon to introduce a series or list.**

☞**EXAMPLES:**

The three greatest virtues are these: love, hope, and faith.

I enjoy the following sports: golf, bowling, volleyball, and skiing.

> **Rule 9.59**  **Use a colon to introduce a word, phrase, or clause for special emphasis.**

☞**EXAMPLES:**

We should strive for one thing above all: a loving and obedient heart.

The question is this: where do we go from here?

He sought one thing in life: fame.

> **Rule 9.60**  **Do NOT use a colon to introduce such elements when there is not a clear break between the introductory words and the series, list, or emphasized material that follows.**

Among the indicators of a clear break are words such as "the following" or "as follows" or "these." NEVER use a colon after the expression "such as" (see the preceding sentence, for example).

☞**WRONG:**

I read: books, newspapers, magazines, and newsletters.

You can gain weight from eating foods such as: candy, cake, and cookies.

In our area, snow usually falls only in: December, January, and February.

☞**CORRECT:**

These are what I read: newspapers, magazines, and newsletters.

You can gain weight from eating foods such as candy, cake, and cookies.

In our area, snow usually falls only in the following months: December, January, and February.

| **Rule 9.61** | **Use a colon to introduce a clause that gives an example of, summarizes, or adds to the thought of a preceding clause.** |
|---|---|

☞**EXAMPLES:**

Many Christians have stood firm in their convictions, even in the face of severe threat: Martin Luther was such a man.

Education is not only to help you get a good job: it is to make you a well-rounded person.

You should eat your vegetables for two reasons: first, because I told you to eat them, and, second, because they are good for you.

| **Rule 9.62** | **Use a colon to introduce a formal or long quotation or a quotation that is placed in a separate paragraph.** |
|---|---|

☞**EXAMPLES:**

Booker T. Washington once said: "The longer I live the more I am convinced that the one thing worth living for and dying for is the privilege of making someone more happy and more useful. No man who ever does anything to lift his fellows ever makes a sacrifice."

William Law has described gratitude this way:

The greatest saint in the world is not he who prays most or fasts most; it is not he who gives most alms, or is most eminent for temperance, chastity, or justice. It is he who is most thankful to God, and who has a heart always ready to praise God. This is the perfection of all virtues. Joy in God and thankfulness to God is the highest perfection of a divine and holy life.

| Rule 9.63 | Use a colon following the salutation (greeting) of a formal or business letter. |
|---|---|

☞**EXAMPLES:**

Dear Sir:    Dear Dr. Smith:    Gentlemen:    To whom it may concern:

| Rule 9.64 | Use a colon as a mark of separation to: 1) separate hours and minutes in time figures: 2) separate a book title from a subtitle: 3) separate chapter and verse in a Bible citation: and 4.) separate act and scene numbers in reference to a play: |
|---|---|

☞**EXAMPLES:**

The service begins at 10:30 a.m.

Ronald H. Nash is the author of *The Closing of the American Heart: What's Really Wrong With America's Schools.*

My favorite Bible passage is John 3:16.

We were asked to memorize a passage from *MacBeth, III:ii.*

✎ **EXERCISE** Some of the following sentences make proper use of commas, semicolons, or colons; and some do not. Rewrite incorrectly punctuated sentences, correcting any mistakes by adding the necessary mark, replacing any incorrectly used mark with the correct mark, or removing any mark which should not be in the sentence. If the sentence is correct as written, do not rewrite it.

1.  Our curriculum includes such basic subjects as: history, English, math, and science.

    *Our curriculum includes such basic subjects as history, English, math, and science.*

2.  In John 1,1 Jesus is called "The Word."

    _____

3.  My dentist appointment is at 2;45 p.m. but I am not eager to go.

    _____

    _____

4.  The conference schedule consists of: an opening prayer; a general session; small group discussions; lunch; another general session and closing activities.

    _____

    _____

5.  I am not feeling well, however I must fulfill my duties.

    _____

    _____

6.  Paid holidays include the following, New Year's Day, Memorial Day, Independence Day, Labor Day, Thanksgiving Day, and Christmas.

    _____

    _____

7.  We have lived in: Sherman, Tex., Charleston, W.Va., Salt Lake City, Utah, and Helena, Mont., and we hope we do not have to move again.

    _____

    _____

8.  My favorite dessert is this; homemade ice cream with peaches.

    _____

    _____

9.  Although she is young; she has a remarkable understanding of: the subject.

    _____

    _____

10. The weather forecast is uncertain; therefore, you should be prepared for anything.

    _____

    _____

11. The weather forecast is uncertain, thus, you should be prepared for anything.

_____

_____

# LESSON 45: USING OTHER PUNCTUATION MARKS

## *THE LONG DASH*

The *long dash* ( ——— ) is used as a *mark of introduction, separation,* or *enclosure*. It signifies a break in thought or shift in direction of thought. In some cases, it serves the same purpose as a comma, except that the dash signifies a stronger break or shift in thought.

| Rule 9.65 | Use a dash to introduce an emphasized word, phrase, or clause. |
|---|---|

☞**EXAMPLES:**

The Bible teaches the opposite—that natural man is capable only of rejecting God.

Ancient paganism had its own cultural norm—"the community of mankind."

Scrooge thought of only one thing—money.

| Rule 9.66 | Use a dash to separate a final clause that summarizes a series of preceding ideas. |
|---|---|

☞**EXAMPLES:**

Faith, hope, and love—these are gifts from God.

The "poor in spirit," the "peacemakers," "the meek," "the merciful," "the pure in heart"— Jesus calls such persons blessed.

Do NOT use a colon for this purpose. A *colon introduces a series* that follows it; a *dash follows a series* that precedes it.

☞**WRONG:**

Faith, hope, and love: these are gifts from God.

These are gifts from God—faith, hope, and love.

| Rule 9.67 | Use dashes in pairs to enclose parenthetical information you wish to emphasize or isolate. |
|---|---|

☞**EXAMPLES:**

Let it never be forgotten—either by today's church or its enemies—that the ancient church was the foundation of a magnificent civilization.

My advice—if I may offer it—is to form a committee to consider the project.

If the parenthetical material requires an exclamation point or question mark, place it BEFORE the second dash.

The sponsor notified us—could it really be true?—that we had won the contest.

It was true—hallelujah!—that God heard our prayers.

| Rule 9.68 | Use a dash to indicate a major turn, shift, or break in thought. |
|---|---|

☞**EXAMPLES:**

Can we—should we—even think of such a major undertaking?

May I suggest that you could—but, no, that would be a bad idea.

He seemed unaware—but surely he had to know—that his actions were foolish.

## THE HYPHEN

The **hyphen** ( - ) can be considered either a *mark of separation* or a *mark of unification*. It is a mark of separation in the sense that it comes between two or more parts of a compound word or at a syllable break at the end of a line. It is a mark of unification in the sense that it joins these word parts together. Because it always comes *within* a word, it is really more of a *mark of spelling* than a mark of punctuation.

Do NOT confuse the **hyphen**, which is a short horizontal line ( - ), with a **dash**, which is a longer horizontal line ( — ). The dash as used in typography is called the EM dash, because it is as wide as the uppercase letter 'M.' This character is made by using a special code on a computer. However, when typing documents on a standard typewriter or with an electronic word processor which does not have a dash character on the keyboard, a **dash** may be created by typing *two hyphens* ( - - ).

| Rule 9.69 | Use a dictionary to determine whether certain word combinations are hyphenated, written as a single word, or written as separate words. |
|---|---|

How certain **word combinations** are written varies from generation to generation, from writer to writer, and from dictionary to dictionary. Often when two or more words begin to be used together to form a single meaning, they are written as *separate words*. As this combination comes more and more into use, the words may be *hyphenated* in common usage. Later, in many cases, the words are joined into a *single word*. If you were to trace the history of words such as "baseball," and "railroad," for example, you might find that they were originally written as "base ball" and "rail road" and later as "base-ball" and "rail-road." Similarly, the word "today" was once commonly written "to-day." Currently, you may see the commonly used farewell greeting written either as "good-bye" or "goodbye." Its original form had four separate words—"God be with ye."

| Rule 9.70 | Hyphens are generally used when two or more words are combined in any of the following ways to form an *adjective*: |
|---|---|

■ **Use a hyphen to combine an adjective or noun with a participle.**

able-bodied man, absent-minded professor, wind-blown alleys,

funny-looking clown, star-shaped design

■ **Use a hyphen to combine two adjectives, an adjective and a noun, or a noun and an adjective.**

African-American literature, ten-foot pole, two-bedroom apartment, sky-blue water

■ **Use a hyphen to combine a prefix attached to a capitalized word.**

un-American, anti-Christian, pre-Columbian, trans-Atlantic

■ **Use a hyphen to combine an adverb (other than an -ly adverb) and a participle.**

fast-moving train, above-mentioned persons

☞**EXCEPTION:**

rapidly boiling water

| Rule 9.71 | Hyphens are generally used between parts of a compound word in the following situations: |
|---|---|

■ **Use hyphens to combine nouns consisting of three or more words.**

brother-in-law, jack-of-all-trades, will-o'-the-wisp, attorney-at-law, mother-of-pearl

■ **Use hyphens to combine words with an adverb or a preposition as the second element.**

a leveling-off, a go-between, hangers-on, a goof-off, first runner-up

■ **Use hyphens to combine compounds having "fellow," "father," "mother," "sister," "brother," "daughter," or similar words as the first part. (There are many exceptions.)**

my fellow-Americans, our sister-school, her mother-country, our church's daughter-congregation, a mother-city, his brother-monks.

☞**EXCEPTIONS:**

fatherland, father figure, mother lode, mother tongue, mother church, fellowman, fellow traveler, fellow servant

> **Rule 9.72**    Hyphens are generally used in compound words using "self," "ex," "half," or "quarter" as the first element.

☞**EXAMPLES:**

self-respect, self-control, ex-wife, ex-president, half-truth, half-crazy, quarter-share, quarter-tone

> **Rule 9.73**    Hyphens are generally used between a single capital letter joined to a noun or participle.

☞**EXAMPLES:**

S-curve, U-turn, B-flat, A-sharp, T-square, I-beam, C-clamp, D-ring

> **Rule 9.74**    Hyphens are generally used in improvised compounds.

☞**EXAMPLES:**

never-say-die, devil-may-care, make-believe, know-it-all, top-of-the-line

> **Rule 9.75**    Hyphens are generally used in compound numerals (from 21 to 99).

☞**EXAMPLES:**

twenty-two, sixty-five, one hundred forty-three, two thousand thirty-six

> **Rule 9.76**    Hyphens are generally used between the numerator and the denominator of a fraction.

☞**EXAMPLES:**

two-thirds, four-fifths, two-sixteenths, one-hundredth

Omit the hyphen between a numerator and denominator if either the numerator or the denominator itself is hyphenated:

four thirty-seconds, sixty-six hundred-thousandths

> **Rule 9.77**    Use a hyphen to indicate a syllable division when a word comes at the end of a line.

☞**EXAMPLE:**

> "The fountain of cleansing is not sealed by any demands in the gospel requiring you to prepare yourself for it before you come."
> — *Spurgeon*

## THE APOSTROPHE

The **apostrophe** ( ' ) is a *mark of separation* and a *mark of omission*. It is used to show possession in nouns and indefinite pronouns, and the plural form of letters and numbers. It is used in contractions and other words to indicate omitted letters.

| | |
|---|---|
| Rule 9.78 | **Use an apostrophe and an "s" to form the possessive of all nouns NOT ending in "s."** |

☞**EXAMPLES:**

Dr. Smith's office, the man's coat, the women's club, the children's bedtime

| | |
|---|---|
| Rule 9.79 | **To form the possessive of most *singular* nouns ending in "s" or an "s" or "z" sound, first write the singular form and then add an apostrophe and an "s."** |

☞**EXAMPLES:**

the class's project, Robert Burns's poetry, Karl Marx's ideas, a lynx's ears, Horace's name, Buzz's reputation, Hertz's rental agency

☞**EXCEPTIONS:**

■ Certain *ancient names* with more than one syllable and ending in "s":

Socrates' death, Hippocrates' oath, Jesus' birth, Moses' voice

■ Certain *expressions* such as the following:

for righteousness' sake, for conscience' sake, for old acquaintance' sake

| | |
|---|---|
| Rule 9.80 | **Use an apostrophe alone to form the possessive of a *plural* noun ending in "s."** |

☞**EXAMPLES:**

the boys' restroom, the Smiths' house, the students' willingness, our churches' policies

| Rule 9.81 | Use an apostrophe and an "s" to form the possessive of compound nouns and pronouns. Put the 's after the element closest to the thing possessed. |

☞**EXAMPLES:**

my mother-in-law's recipe; John Smith, Jr.'s nickname; someone else's problem

| Rule 9.82 | Use an apostrophe and an "s" after only the LAST word in an expression showing JOINT possession. |

☞**EXAMPLES:**

Brown & Williamson's policies, Bob and Mary's daughter

☞**EXCEPTION:**

If the last element in the expression is a *possessive pronoun*, use an apostrophe and an "s" after the first word.

Gary's and his science project (NOT Gary and his science project)

| Rule 9.83 | Use an apostrophe and an "s" after EACH word in an expression showing INDIVIDUAL possession. |

☞**EXAMPLES:**

Davy Crockett's and Daniel Boone's fur hats were probably much alike.

Darwin's and Marx's ideas had much in common.

| Rule 9.84 | Use an apostrophe and an "s" to form the possessive of indefinite pronouns. |

☞**EXAMPLES:**

everyone's privilege, anybody's guess, neither's fault, both's room

| Rule 9.85 | Use an apostrophe in contractions to indicate omitted letters. |

☞**EXAMPLES:**

can't, wouldn't, isn't, aren't, won't, you're, I'm, he's, they're, she'll

Bob's eating his sandwich.

| Rule 9.86 | Use an apostrophe to indicate other omissions as well. |
|---|---|

☞**EXAMPLES:**

He lost his fortune in the stock market crash of '29.

He was a member of the Class of '86.

The ol' man was sawin' logs.

| Rule 9.87 | Use an apostrophe to form the plural of letters, numbers, signs, and words used as words. |
|---|---|

☞**EXAMPLES:**

Watch your P's and Q's.

In Europe, many people write their 7's differently than we do.

Change all the &'s in this paragraph to "and's."

Use +'s and —'s in your checkbook entries.

I will accept no *if's, and's,* or *but's* from you.

| Rule 9.88 | Do NOT use an apostrophe to form the possessive case of personal or relative pronouns. |
|---|---|

**Note:** Be especially careful not to confuse the contraction "it's" (meaning: it is) for the possessive pronoun "its." This is a common mistake which you should avoid.

| WRONG: | CORRECT: |
|---|---|
| our's | ours |
| your's | yours |
| yours' | yours |
| his' | his |
| hers' | hers |
| it's | its |
| their's | theirs |
| theirs' | theirs |
| who's | whose |

| Rule 9.89 | Do NOT use an apostrophe to form the plural of nouns. |
|---|---|

☞**WRONG:**

The Jones' live next door.

He has taken two year's of Latin.

There are fewer boy's in our class than girl's.

## PARENTHESES AND BRACKETS

*Parentheses* **( )** and *brackets* **[ ]** are *marks of enclosure*. Whereas dashes are used to *emphasize* the material they enclose, parentheses and brackets are designed to *de-emphasize* the enclosed material. Usually, material within parentheses and brackets is less closely related to the main statement than material enclosed with dashes.

| Rule 9.90 | Use parentheses to enclose material remotely related to a main statement. |
|---|---|

☞**EXAMPLES:**

Alexander Hamilton and James Madison (two of our Founding Fathers) wrote *The Federalist Papers.*

Sometime last spring (I think it was in April) I received a lovely gift.

The worldwide computer network known as the Internet uses hypertext markup language (HTML).

| Rule 9.91 | Use parentheses to enclose references, directions, citations, and similar material. In all these cases, place the ending period *after the final parenthesis.* |
|---|---|

☞**EXAMPLES:**

Jesus told a visitor he must be "born again" (John 3).

"The LORD is my Shepherd, I shall not want" (Psalm 23:1).

Study the material about noun clauses (see Lesson 14, page 40).

Former Supreme Court Justice Felix Frankfurter once said that judgments must reflect the "feelings of our society" (*Haley v. Ohio, 332 U.S. 596, 603 [1948]*).

| Rule 9.92 | On rare occasions, use parentheses to enclose figures repeated or expanded for accuracy. |
|---|---|

☞**EXAMPLES:**

She paid twenty dollars ($20.00) for that necklace.

There are more than four hundred (435) members of the House of Representatives.

---

**Note:** Use this device *sparingly*. It is almost never used in formal writing but is sometimes used in **commercial** or **technical** writing to ensure precision.

---

| **Rule 9.93** | **Use parentheses to enclose numbering figures used within written text.** |
|---|---|

☞**EXAMPLES:**

Verbals include the following: (1) present participles, (2) past participles, (3) gerunds, and (4) infinitives.

| **Rule 9.94** | **Use brackets to enclose parenthetical material inserted within other parenthetical material.** |
|---|---|

☞**EXAMPLES:**

The comic strip was drawn by cartoonist Bill Holbrook (*On the Fastrack* [published in 1995]).

| **Rule 9.95** | **Use brackets to enclose your own comments, explanations, or corrections inserted within a quotation.** |
|---|---|

☞**EXAMPLES:**

"During his first year in office [1985], the chairman met strong opposition," the report said.

"I'm not ashaimed [*sic]* for the world to know it was me," he wrote.

## QUOTATION MARKS

*Quotation marks* are *marks of enclosure*. They are always used in pairs, opening and closing quoted material, special-use material, and titles. There are two types of quotation marks: *double* ( " ... " ) and *single* ( ' ... ' ).

| **Rule 9.96** | **Use quotation marks to enclose direct quotations—including complete quotations, partial quotations, and each part of an interrupted quotation.** |
|---|---|

☞**EXAMPLES:**

"A good book is the best of friends, the same today and forever," Martin Tupper said.

According to Andrew Jackson, "one man with courage" is as strong as a majority.

"Your bedtime," Mother reminded him, "is 9:30 p.m."

Use a *separate paragraph* for every change of speaker when writing dialogue:

☞**EXAMPLE:**

> "Can I help you?" the clerk asked.
>
> "Yes," Cybil replied. "I'm looking for some bed linens."
>
> "We have several new items in that department," the clerk answered.

| Rule 9.97 | **If a direct quotation extends for more than one paragraph, place opening quotation marks at the beginning of each paragraph but closing quotation marks at the end of only the LAST paragraph of quotation. Otherwise, always use quotation marks in pairs.** |
|---|---|

☞**EXAMPLE:**

"Now, just as the Gates were opened to let in the men, I looked in after them; and behold the City shone like the Sun, the streets also were paved with Gold, and in them walked many men with crowns on their heads, Palms in their hands, and Golden Harps to sing praises withal.

"...And after that, they shut up the Gates: which when I had seen, I wished myself among them."

—From *The Pilgrim's Progress,* by John Bunyan

| Rule 9.98 | **Use quotation marks to enclose words with unusual, specific, or limited usages, such as illiteracies, slang, technical words, or common words use in irregular or emphasized ways.** |
|---|---|

☞**EXAMPLES:**

This thing that we call "failure" is not the falling down, but the *staying* down.

—*Mary Pickford*

I hope that when I am old, no one thinks of me as a "stuffed shirt."

His mind always seemed to be haunted by several "bogeymen" of his own making.

Some people do not like "longhair" music.

This "always-on-top" utility lets you "see" what your internal modem is doing by supplying the missing status lights. "Smart-sense" port detection logic makes setting up this modem simple. —CompuServe magazine

| Rule 9.99 | Use quotation marks to enclose chapter headings of books and titles of short stories, poems, songs, and similar short literary works when used in a body of prose. |
|---|---|

☞**EXAMPLES:**

She read Longfellow's poem "Hiawatha" to the class.

My grandmother's favorite hymn is "What a Friend We Have in Jesus."

The manual's "Maintenance and Troubleshooting" chapter may help you.

| Rule 9.100 | Do NOT put quotation marks around a *title* when it is placed in the *title position* at the beginning of a theme paper, essay, report, or other composition. |
|---|---|

☞**EXAMPLES:**

WRONG:

"THE PROBLEM OF EVIL"

One of life's many problems, one of the most commonly voiced is the problem of evil. The main

CORRECT:

THE PROBLEM OF EVIL

One of life's many problems, one of the most commonly voiced is the problem of evil. The main

The only exception to this rule is when a quotation is used as a title of a composition.

| Rule 9.101 | Use single quotation marks to enclose quotations, titles, etc. within a quotation. |
|---|---|

☞**EXAMPLES:**

"I want you to read 'Hiawatha' before Tuesday," the teacher told the class.

"When you said, 'That was funny,' did you mean 'humorous' or 'strange'?" he asked.

| Rule 9.102 | Do not put quotation marks around an indirect quotation. |
|---|---|

In the third correct example sentence below, notice that a **partial quotation** (which is enclosed by quotation marks) may be combined with an **indirect quotation** (which is *not* enclosed).

☞**EXAMPLES:**

WRONG:        She said that "I should clean up my room or face the consequences."

CORRECT:      She said that I should clean up my room or face the consequences.

              She said, "Clean up your room or face the consequences."

              She said that I should clean up my room or "face the consequences."

---

**Rule 9.103**    **Do NOT word an *indirect quotation* in such a way that it appears to be a *direct quotation*.**

---

☞**EXAMPLES:**

INDIRECT:    He asked me what color I wanted.

DIRECT:      He asked me, "What color do you want?"

*CONFUSED:*  He asked me what color did I want.

---

**Rule 9.104**    **Place quotation marks correctly in relation to other punctuation marks.**

---

■ **Commas and periods go *inside* the quotation marks, even when only the last word before the comma or period is enclosed.**

☞**EXAMPLES:**

"Merry Christmas," she said, "and a Happy New Year."

He called the script "mediocre," but he said the acting was "excellent."

■ **Place question marks, exclamation points, and dashes *outside* the quotation marks unless these punctuation marks are part of the quotation.**

☞**EXAMPLES:**

Did he say, "The battery is dead"?

Jamie asked, "When shall we eat?"

Don't ever again call me "stupid"!

"What a wonderful idea!" she exclaimed.

When a quoted question comes at the end of a sentence which is also a question, only one ending question mark is needed. Similarly, if a quoted declaratory statement comes at the end of an interrogative sentence, only a final question mark is needed.

However, an interrogative sentence ending with a quoted exclamation would require two ending marks. Similarly, if an exclamatory sentence ends with a quoted question, two marks are needed.

☞**EXAMPLES:**

    WRONG:    Did she really ask, "What are you doing here?"?

                    Did she really say, "You are welcome here."?

    CORRECT:    Did she really ask, "What are you doing here?"

                      Did she really say, "You are welcome here"?

    CORRECT:    Did I hear him shout, "Halt!"?

                      I've told you a thousand times to stop asking me, "What time is it?"!

■ Semicolons and colons always come *outside* the quotation marks.

☞**EXAMPLES:**

I memorized the "Gettysburg Address"; it is certainly a stirring document.

Take the following "essentials": food, water, clean clothes, and toiletries.

## *SPECIAL MARKS AND FOREIGN LANGUAGE SYMBOLS*

There are a wide variety of marks and symbols used in written communications. Among these are marks used in English and others used with such foreign languages as Spanish, German, and French. Note the following marks:

| SYMBOL | MEANING | SYMBOL | MEANING |
|---|---|---|---|
| { } | Braces | * | Asterisk, denotes a reference |
| / | Forward slash or virgule | \ | Backslash or reverse virgule |
| % | Percent | ‰ | Percent thousand |
| ¶ | Paragraph Marker | § | Section Marker |
| † | Dagger | ‡ | Double dagger |
| & | Ampersand | @ | at, about |
| © | Copyright | ® | Registered |
| TM | Trademark | \| | Bar |
| ° | Degree symbol | # | Pound or number sign |
| $ | Dollar, US currency | • | Bullet |
| £ | Pound, English currency | ❏ | Ballot box |
| ¥ | Yen, Japanese currency | ÷ | Divide |
| > | Greater than | < | Less than |
| ∞ | Infinity | + | Plus |
| ≠ | Not equal | ± | Plus or minus |

| SYMBOL | MEANING | SYMBOL | MEANING |
|---|---|---|---|
| = | Equals | ≈ | Approxamately equal |
| π | Pi | √ | Radical |
| ∑ | Summation | Δ | Delta |
| ~ | Tilde or similar | ^ | Caret or curcumflex |
| ` | Grave | ´ | Acute |
| ¯ | Macron, indicates a long vowel | ¨ | Umlaut or dieresis |
| ˘ | Breve, indicates a short vowel | ° | Ring |
| ¸ | Cedilla | ˇ | Caron |
| « | Guillemet left | » | Guillemet right |
| Œ œ | Oe | Æ æ | Ae |

| | |
|---|---|
| **Rule 9.105** | **Use a caret ( ∧ ) to insert an omitted letter or expression. Place the caret *below* the line and write the inserted material above the line.** |

☞**EXAMPLE:**

*only*
This is the time to apply.
                   ∧

| | |
|---|---|
| **Rule 9.106** | **Use a dieresis ( ¨ ) or umlaut in certain foreign words. This mark may also be used in English words to show that the second of two adjacent vowels should also be pronounced.** |

☞**EXAMPLE:**

Our German teacher asked, "Wo sind Ihre Bücher?" (Where are your books?)

In modern English usage, words formerly written with a dieresis, such as *zoölogy* and *coöperate*, are now usually written without the mark. However, other words, such as *naïve*, still require it to prevent mispronunciation.

| | |
|---|---|
| **Rule 9.107** | **Use accent or other marks in words with foreign origins where the spelling requires them. Consult a dictionary as a guide.** |

☞**EXAMPLE:**

| | |
|---|---|
| Acute accent: | passé, résumé |
| Grave accent: | à la mode |
| Circumflex accent: | hôtel de ville |
| Cedilla mark: | façade |
| Tilde mark: | piñata |

| | |
|---|---|
| Rule 9.108 | **When writing a question in Spanish, use *Spanish question marks*: ¿ at the beginning of the question and ? at the end.** |

✎ **EXERCISE A** Place the correct punctuation mark in each of the boxes in the following sentences. Add the correct ending punctuation in the last box.

1. Three ☐-☐ fourths of Mrs. Spencer ☐'☐ s class was absent due to illness ☐.☐

2. I have learned ☐ praise God ☐ to be content in most situations ☐

3. The program was designed for Mexican ☐ American students ☐

4. ☐ What have you done with my book ☐ ☐ Gina asked Nancy ☐

5. ☐ In the beginning was the Word... ☐ ☐ John 1:1 ☐ ☐

6. When did Pontius Pilate ask Jesus ☐ ☐ Are you a king ☐ ☐

7. Mercy ☐ justice ☐ and a humble walk with God ☐ these are the things that the Lord requires of us ☐ Micah 6:8 ☐ ☐

✎ **EXERCISE B** Use apostrophes correctly in the following. In the blanks, write the correct **possessive** (or, in No. 10, the plural form) for the words or letters in parentheses.

1.  (He) _His_ (cousin) _cousin's_ name is Elizabeth.

2.  You seem to think this is (everyone else) _____ fault except (you) _____.

3.  He refrained from participating for (conscience) _____ sake.

4.  A (fox) _____ tail is bushy.

5.  Samson tied several (foxes) _____ tails together and set them on fire.

6.  (John Adams and Abigail Adams) _____ son was the sixth president of the United States.

7.  (Jesus and Moses) _____ view of the law of God was different, some theologians argue.

8.  The (girls) _____ track and field events will be held on Friday.

9.  (Frank Sanders) _____ dog is a German shepherd.

10. Don't forget to cross (you) _____ ( t ) _____ and dot (you) _____ ( i ) _____.

# LESSON 46: UNIT REVIEW

✎ **EXERCISE:** Fill in the blanks below:

1.  What is punctuation?

    _____

    _____

2.  The marks of punctuation reflect _____ and _____ in our spoken communications.

3.  The four main purposes of punctuation are the following:

    a.  _____

    _____

b. _____

_____

c. _____

_____

d. _____

_____

4.  The period is usually an _____ mark, but it also has special uses in

_____, in _____, and as a mark of _____.

5.  Periods are used to mark the end of _____ or _____ sentences.

6.  The question mark is used to mark the end of a _____.

7.  How many question marks are used at the end of an interrogative sentence which ends with a

quoted question? _____

8.  An exclamation point is used to mark the end of _____ or _____

_____ sentences.

9.  Commas are used to _____, to _____, or to _____.

10. A _____ is used after the salutation of a friendly or social letter; a _____ is used

after the salutation of a formal or business letter.

11. The semicolon has one purpose—to _____.

12. The period represents a _____ break or pause in speech; the semicolon represents a

_____ break; a comma represents a _____ break.

13. The colon is used primarily as a mark of _____.

14. A colon _____ a series that follows it; a dash _____ a series that pre-

cedes it.

15. _____ de-emphasize parenthetical material which they enclose;

_____ emphasize parenthetical material which they enclose.

16. A _____ is used to connect parts of a compound word.

17. An _____ is used in the formation of the possessive of nouns; this mark is

not used in the formation of the possessive of _____ or

_____ pronouns.

18. Use _____ to enclose your own comments, explanations, or corrections in-

serted with a quotation.

19. Quotation marks are always used in pairs except when _____

_____

20. Place question marks, exclamation points, and dashes outside quotation marks unless these

punctuation marks

_____

# Unit 10
# Good Composition

In your present school career, in high school, and in college you will often be required to write compositions. These may range from simple paragraphs and short themes to complex research papers and essays. Your academic writing is to prepare you for the writing you will do in your adult life. Even if you do not become a professional writer, you will be called upon many times to use your writing skills, whether it be for home and family matters, in church life, or in your career and occupational activities. Everyone must write letters, papers, reports, proposals, or other compositions to fulfill social obligations or professional requirements.

The foundation of good writing is the knowledge of the rules of grammar. But that is only the foundation. Good writing has many other facets which are more personal and stylistic. In this unit, you will learn some guidelines which will help you build good writing skills upon the foundation of the grammatical studies you have made so far in this workbook.

## LESSON 47: APPROPRIATENESS IN WRITING

When we consider the *appropriateness* of writing, we usually classify writing as either *formal* or *informal*. You may notice that these terms have often been applied also to clothing. Some clothes we wear are considered "informal" or "casual," and certain types of activities are associated with these styles. Or we might say that informal clothes are "appropriate" for informal, casual, or leisure activities. Other types of dress are considered formal and are appropriate for dignified occasions. Similarly, there are certain styles of writing that are appropriate for certain types of activities or situations.

| Rule 10.1 | **Use words that are in keeping with the subject of your composition, the occasion for which you are writing, and the type of readers you expect to have.** |
|---|---|

## FORMAL WRITING

Formal writing is serious writing, the kind that is done in serious books and magazines, in business settings, in academic and scholarly papers, in most school compositions, for formal social occasions, and the like. **Contractions** are NOT usually used in formal writing.

INAPPROPRIATE:      The Bible teaches that God ***got history off to a bang*** when He created all things.

APPROPRIATE:      The Bible teaches that God ***originated history*** when He created all things.

| INAPPROPRIATE: | *Shoot me a memo* with your *brainstorm ASAP* (as soon as possible). |
|---|---|
| APPROPRIATE: | Please *send me a memorandum* outlining your ideas *at your earliest convenience.* |

## ■ *Avoid Slang*

Do NOT use *slang* inappropriately in serious writing. A serious writer may, however, employ *acceptable* slang in a way that shows his intention to create a special effect. (Using quotation marks around words that are somewhat "out of place" in their setting is sometimes a good way to show your intentions.)

| INAPPROPRIATE: | The senator's remarks were *baloney.* |
|---|---|
| APPROPRIATE: | The senator's remarks were *pretentious nonsense.* |
| ACCEPTABLE: | The senator's remarks were *what is commonly called "baloney."* |

## ■ *Avoid Stuffy Language*

Avoiding informal language in formal writing does *not* mean that you should use "pompous," "stuffy," or "bookish" language when simpler words will serve. Whether your writing is formal or informal, the clear and effective expression of your ideas is the primary goal.

| STUFFY AND INEFFECTIVE: | The quaesitum of advantageous inscribing is to eschew conceptual obfuscation. |
|---|---|
| APPROPRIATE AND CLEAR: | The goal of good writing is to express thoughts clearly. |

## *INFORMAL WRITING*

Informal writing is the kind we use for common, ordinary communications in the social and casual areas of life. It has a *conversational* tone to it. Use of *contractions* is more common. Letters and notes to friends or loved ones and routine notes or memos to fellow workers in the daily affairs of an office are examples of situations in which informal writing would be appropriate. In such situations, it may be inappropriate to choose words that are formal or dignified even if such words are clear and otherwise acceptable.

| INAPPROPRIATE: | I hope you are enjoying your week at camp and are *realizing your potential for personal development.* |
|---|---|
| | *Report to my office* for a *colloquy* about your proposal. |
| APPROPRIATE: | I hope you are enjoying your week at camp and are *making the most of it.* |
| | *Come on in. Let's talk about* your idea. |

---

✎  **EXERCISE A** Write a more **formal** version of the following expressions. In some cases, substituting more formal words for those in *italics* will be sufficient. In other cases, it may be necessary to rewrite the entire sentence.

1.  The minority-party senators decided to **back down** on their demands.

     *The minority-party senators decided to compromise on their demands.*

2.  **He's** always trying to **cut others down.**

    _____

3.  **How come?**

    _____

4.  She asked me to **stick around** for a few days.

    _____

    _____

5.  If you **buy that line**, you are **really a sucker**.

    _____

    _____

6.  **Don't let out** what I told you.

    _____

7.  Jerry's **boss** gave him his **walking papers**.

    _____

    _____

8.  Our team tried to **go** the other team **one better.**

    _____

    _____

9.  When **you're** interviewed for a job, always **put your best foot forward**.

    _____

    _____

10. You must **face up to** your sins.

_____

11. The burglar **made off with** the valuable painting.

_____

_____

12. Your teacher **isn't going to put up with** your misbehavior much longer.

_____

_____

✎ **EXERCISE B** Write a more **informal**, conversational version of the following.

1. (Postcard message): "We are having a **prodigious experience** during our **annual respite**."

   _____*We're having a wonderful time on our vacation.*_____

2. (Bumper sticker): "**Sound your automobile's warning device** if you love Jesus."

   _____*"Honk if you love Jesus."*_____

3. **I am** so hungry I could **consume an equine organism**.

   _____

4. **Not one individual** came to the airport to **bid him farewell**.

   _____

5. After I ran for two miles, my legs **were nearly ready to cease their support function**.

   _____

   _____

6.  When I **instruct** you to do something, **simply accomplish the task.**

_____

_____

7.  My **mother** told me, **"Organize** your **habitat; it is in great disarray."**

_____

_____

8.  When Jason's **father discovered** what Jason had done, he **commenced an angry tirade.**

_____

_____

9.  **Remain silent!**

_____

10. After buying this, **I will** be **without monetary resources.**

_____

_____

# LESSON 48: WRITE WITH CONCRETENESS

In the popular musical play and film, *My Fair Lady,* Eliza Doolittle tells Professor Henry Higgins, "Don't tell me about love, show me." There is good advice for writers hidden in that statement. Good writers have learned that it is much more effective to *dramatize* their ideas and characters than to make general statements about them. Instead of saying that "a certain person" is "stubborn," use concrete words to place "George" before your readers' eyes and show him refusing to agree to "Martha's" request to clean the garage.

| Rule 10.2 | **A concrete word generally has greater effect than an abstract one, a specific word evokes better response than a general one, and a homely word is friendlier than a pretentious one.** |
|---|---|

## ABSTRACT VS. CONCRETE

*Abstract* words relate to ideas and qualities. *Concrete* words are those which appeal to the senses of sight, hearing, smell, taste, and touch.

| ABSTRACT | CONCRETE |
|---|---|
| stamina of animals | worked like a horse |
| misfortune of travel | car was a twisted wreck |
| peacefulness of music | hummed a soft carol |
| boredom | yawned and blinked his eyes |
| childish happiness | giggled, squealed with glee |

## GENERAL VS. SPECIFIC

*General* words deal with broad classes and groups. *Specific* words point to particular objects, qualities, and actions.

| GENERAL | SPECIFIC |
|---|---|
| furniture | rocking chair |
| weapon | stiletto dagger |
| musical composition | violin concerto |
| attitude | snobbishness |
| crime | aggravated assault |

## MODEST VS. PRETENTIOUS

*Modest* or *homely* words are those associated with common, everyday life. *Bookish* or *pretentious* words are those with excessively difficult meanings used by scholars, technicians, and the highly literate. Such words are sometimes called *jargon*.

| PRETENTIOUS | MODEST |
|---|---|
| inebriated | drunk |
| incarcerated | jailed |
| to masticate | to chew |
| palpate | touch |
| personal communication device | telephone |

The advice given at the beginning of this lesson does not mean that there is no place in your writing for abstract, general, or scholarly/technical words. It only states principles which writers who wish to communicate effectively to the largest range of readers may wish to follow.

Notice from the examples below how some famous or successful writers have turned abstract or general impressions into concrete and effective expressions.

# EXAMPLES OF CONCRETE WRITING

■ **"Friendship is a concept filled with meaning and cherished by many people."**

Friend! How sacred the word. Born in the heart of God, and given to man as a treasure from the eternities—no word in the languages so heavily freighted with meaning.

Mother! That dearest name is lost in the sphere of Friendship for I have seen a mother cast off her child, but a friend does not know how to cast off or turn from.

I am a crank on the subject of Friendship. With one friend I would count myself rich; to possess more than one, I were rich beyond comparison. A friend is a priceless gem for the crown of life here and a cherished star in memory forever.

*—Cyrus S. Nusbaum*

Observe the powerful, concrete words and phrases in the above: *sacred, born, heart of God, treasure from the eternities, heavily freighted, sphere of friendship, cast off, crank, priceless gem, crown of life, cherished star.*

■ **"A ship and its crew are much alike, since they are both made up of individual parts working as a whole under a single leader."**

They were one man, not thirty. For as the one ship that held them all; though it was put together of contrasting things—oak, and maple, and pine wood; iron, and pitch, and hemp—yet all these ran into each other in the one concrete hull, which shot on its way, both balanced and directed by the long central keel; even so, all the individualities of the crew, this man's valor, that man's fear; guilt and guiltlessness, all varieties were welded into oneness, and were all directed to that fatal goal which Ahab their one lord and keel did point to.

*—Herman Melville*

■ **"Guy Hawkes was a large boy who would be hard to defeat in a fight. He was strong and taller than I. The winner of the fight would be he who hit hardest and first."**

Guy had big hands. His right hand covered the back of his *First Reader.* And he had powerful arms. The muscles rippled under his clean blue-faded shirt. I measured him as I stood beside him. I knew that if I ever had to fight him, it would be a fight. And I knew that I wasn't going to fight him unless he forced me to fight. He was more powerful physically than I was. And the outcome of our fight might depend on the one who successfully landed the first haymaker to the other's jaw.

*—Jesse Stuart*

Note that the writer not only "tells" how big and strong Guy was, but also "shows" his size and power by comparing the size of his hand to that of a book, by describing his rippling muscles, and by measuring his height in comparison to that of the writer. Notice the concrete words that appeal to the senses: *rippled, clean, blue-faded, landed...haymaker, jaw.* The author has "dramatized" his description of the subject.

✎ **EXERCISE A** Write two examples of **specific words** or **phrases** for each of the general words below.

1.   **to laugh**          _____*to chuckle*_____          _____*to snort in scorn*_____

2.   **animal**           _____          _____

3.   **to speak**         _____          _____

4.   **a fish**           _____          _____

5.   **clothing**         _____          _____

6.   **music**            _____          _____

7.   **beverage**         _____          _____

8.   **colorful**         _____          _____

9.   **a book**           _____          _____

10.  **an outing**        _____          _____

11.  **trees**            _____          _____

12.  **tired**            _____          _____

✎ **EXERCISE B** Write sentences giving **concrete examples** of the abstract ideas implied in each of the following words.

1.   **selflessness**

_____*When Terry noticed that the little girl next to him was shivering,*_____

_____*he removed his jacket and slipped it over her shoulders.*_____

2.   **fear**

_____

_____

3.   **laziness**

_____

_____

4. mercy

_____

_____

5. faith

_____

_____

6. excitement

_____

_____

# LESSON 49: WRITE WITH CONCISENESS

When you write, make sure that every word is carrying a *load*. By that we mean that every word you use should be necessary to convey your meaning. One of the most obvious signs of a lazy or unskilled writer is the use of more words than are needed to accomplish the writer's purposes. This fault is called **wordiness**, and its solution is **conciseness**.

*Conciseness* is not necessarily the same as "shortness." Sometimes it takes many words to express a thought completely and precisely. But the writer should use no more words than *necessary*. "Do-nothing" words only clutter up a composition and make the ideas in it harder to find and follow. Keeping your prose "lean and mean" requires discipline, one of the hardest traits for a writer to learn.

## *MAKE EVERY WORD COUNT*

Notice the difference between the following pairs of sentences. In each case, the first, *wordy* version says little or nothing more than the second, *concise* version.

### ☞WORDY

Abraham Lincoln himself was one of those unique and special presidents of which the United States in the period of its history has had really very few like him or similar to his abilities.

On this particular compact disc, you will find a number of various and sundry selections and samples of music that were written many years ago by the composer Mozart.

### ☞CONCISE

The United States has had few presidents like Abraham Lincoln.

This compact disc contains music by Mozart.

## *HOW TO BE CONCISE*

Here are some ways to achieve *conciseness*:

| Rule 10.3 | Avoid useless repetition of the same word or phrase. |
|---|---|

☞**WORDY:**

He spoke on an *interesting subject* which has been the *longtime subject* of great *interest* among his peers for a *long time.*

☞**BETTER:**

He spoke on a subject which has interested his peers for a long time.

| Rule 10.4 | Avoid useless repetition of words with the same meaning. |
|---|---|

☞**WORDY:**

The concert was *thoroughly* and *completely* enjoyable.

The *one* and *only single* factor to be *considered* or *thought about* is the price.

☞**BETTER:**

The concert was *thoroughly* enjoyable.

The *only* factor to be considered is the price.

| Rule 10.5 | Avoid useless repetition of the word "that" before an interrupted noun clause. |
|---|---|

☞**WORDY:**

I was happy *that* after you called *that* I no longer had to worry about you.

☞**BETTER:**

I was happy *that* after you called I no longer had to worry about you.

| Rule 10.6 | Avoid roundabout expressions. |
|---|---|

☞**WORDY:**

The *explanation* for *why* I was late was *because* I could not find my coat.

☞**BETTER:**

I was late *because* I could not find my coat.

| Rule 10.7 | **Avoid the excessive use of intensifiers and other modifiers.** |
|---|---|

☞**WORDY:**

We *certainly* were *really very much* pleased to hear from you.

☞**BETTER:**

We were *pleased* to hear from you.

| Rule 10.8 | **Avoid the use of "officialese"—that official-sounding language which is almost always wordy.** |
|---|---|

☞**OFFICIALESE:**

The manufacturer of this product warrants, to the original buyer only, that the product shall be free of defects in materials and workmanship under normal use and service for a period of thirty (30) days from the date of purchase. With respect to the product and the accompanying written materials, the manufacturer and its suppliers, if any, disclaim all warranties, other than the enclosed warranty by the manufacturer, either express or implied, including but not limited to implied warranties of merchantability and fitness for a particular purpose. The manufacturer does not warrant that the product will meet your requirements or that the operation of the product will be uninterrupted or error free. This limited warranty gives you specific legal rights; you may have others, which vary from state to state.

☞**BETTER:**

As the makers of this product, we can guarantee to you, the original buyer, that it was manufactured in perfect condition. If you use it normally, we can stand by this guarantee for 30 days, starting with the day you bought it. We cannot honor any other guarantees which anyone else may have made or implied. We cannot guarantee that the product will perfectly meet all your requirements, despite the fact that, physically speaking, it was made defect-free. You have specific legal rights under this pledge of ours. In addition, the laws of your state may give you other legal rights.

> **Rule 10.9**     **Avoid "purple prose"—flowery, artificial, overly colorful writing.**

Consider the following four accounts of a fire by three members of the Sloan family and a local news reporter. All of the accounts are grammatically correct. Susan Sloan's report, though childish, is **simple and concise**. The account by George Sloan is typical of "**purple prose**," the mark of an inexperienced writer who is trying too hard to be creative. Mrs. Sloan's account is an effective example of an **informal, conversational** style that is easy to read and understand. Jack Wheeling's account is an example of a more **formal and factually informative** style. Three of the accounts do an appropriate, concrete, and concise job of telling the story of the fire. Only George's is ineffective. It is a good example of what to avoid.

■ **Susan Sloan, 3rd Grader, Class Report**

I saw a fire. It was a big fire as red as a beet. It burned up a store where I buy candy. I got smoke in my eyes. It made me cough. A whole lot of people were there. Some men put water on the fire, and it went out. Then my father took me home, and I went to bed.

■ **George Sloan, 9th Grader, English Composition**

It was a fearful sight to behold. Scarlet-tinged tongues of flame, resembling those emitted by satellite rockets, arose to the heavens as the devouring element licked greedily at the doomed structure. The heroic firemen risked their all to quench the devastating conflagration and, at long last, conquered the holocaust to the plaudits of the admiring multitude.

■ **Mrs. Sloan, Housewife, Letter to a Friend**

We had quite a serious fire last evening in one of our neighborhood stores. We all went over for a while to see it. Several fire engines were called, and it was very interesting to watch them. The fire was finally extinguished, but it probably will cost the people who own the premises a good deal of money.

■ **Jack Wheeling, Reporter, News Report**

A stubborn two-alarm fire caused by a leaking oil burner partly destroyed the Shop-and-Save Supermarket at 932 Oak St. last night.

Four fire companies brought the blaze under control at 11 p.m. No one was injured. R.M. Gregg, the owner, estimated the damage at $10,000. The market, he said, will be rebuilt at once.

—Adapted from Carl Warren, *Modern News Reporting*, (New York: Harper & Brothers., Publishers), 1959, pp. 57-58.

✎ **EXERCISE** Thoroughly rewrite the following sentences to eliminate wordiness. Use only as many words as are necessary. Hint: First rewrite the sentences on a separate paper; then search again for unnecessary words or more direct ways to express the thought before you write a final version in the blanks below.

1.  You really and surely do not actually have to reference or refer to a dictionary for each and every word you write in your composition.

    _____ *You need not look in a dictionary for every word you write.* _____

2.  I have noticed and discovered that after I eat spicy foods that I always get heartburn from spicy foods.

    _____

    _____

3.  You must learn to rid yourself of the problem you have of arrogant pride.

    _____

    _____

4.  Boastful bragging is an evil, sinful trespass.

    _____

    _____

5.  We hope our muscles will grow in strength and grow in might as we repeat our daily exercise repetitions each day.

    _____

    _____

6.  The basic, most fundamental elementary problem we face is a lack of monetary funding to pay for our undertaken project which we have begun.

    _____

    _____

7.  Because the infant Jesus was born as a baby to be our Savior for our salvation is the reason why we celebrate the Christmas holiday nativity event.

_____

_____

# LESSON 50: WRITE WITH BRIGHTNESS

Without falling into the "purple prose" trap mentioned in the last lesson, a good writer should try to use words and phrases that add life, freshness, color, and brightness to his expressions. We have already discussed some of the ways to do that—by using concrete terms and by being concise, for example. In this lesson we will discuss other ways to enliven your writing.

## *DULL VS. INTERESTING*

| Rule 10.10 | **Use specific rather than general nouns.** |
|---|---|

Notice how the brighter versions below give the reader more information for building a better mental image of the subjects mentioned.

☞**DULL**

I heard a bird sing.

My brother bought a vehicle.

A person helped me with my school work.

☞**INTERESTING**

I heard the song of a meadowlark.

My older brother bought a new dune-buggy.

My teacher, Mrs. Blackman, helped me with my mathematics.

| Rule 10.11 | **Use picturesque adjectives and adverbs instead of commonplace ones.** |
|---|---|

☞**DULL**

He is a nice boy.

The air was cold yesterday.

The pastor had a very good sermon today.

☞ **INTERESTING**

He is a kind and considerate boy.

The early morning air was frigid yesterday.

The pastor had an exceptionally inspiring sermon today.

| Rule 10.12 | **Use descriptive, active verbs instead of colorless, dead ones.** |
|---|---|

☞ **DULL**

The cat moved toward the mouse.

The man spoke to the crowd.

The cowboy got on his horse.

☞ **INTERESTING**

The cat edged toward the mouse.

The man harangued the crowd.

The cowboy mounted his horse.

## USE FIGURES OF SPEECH

| Rule 10.13 | **Use figurative language to brighten your style.** |
|---|---|

Here are four *figures of speech* which can add vividness to your writing:

### ■ Similes

A simile is a figure of speech by which one thing is compared to another through the use of words such as "like" or "as."

His countenance was like the countenance of an angel of God (Judges 13:6).

Your eyes shall be opened, and ye shall be as gods (Genesis 3:5).

### ■ Metaphors

A metaphor implies a comparison without the use of words such as "like" or "as."

She was putty in his hands.

My life is a blank page on which God may compose His poetry.

### ■ Hyperbole

Hyperbole uses extreme exaggeration to convey meaning.

When I received the award I felt twenty feet tall.

He always has a thousand excuses for failing to complete his homework.

## ■ *Personification*

Personification is the giving of human characteristics to inanimate objects.

> The winter wind's frosty knuckles rapped on the cabin's window panes.

> The heavens declare the glory of God (Psalm 19:1).

## *AVOID CLICHÉS*

Many metaphors, similes, and other phrases, which were once witty and bright, have been used so often that they have become *trite*. Frequent use of these overused expressions tends to make writing stale and flat. Here is a list of "hackneyed" phrases:

| CLICHÉS AND OVERUSED PHRASES | | |
|---|---|---|
| after all is said and done | easier said than done | none the worse for wear |
| all in all | equal to the occasion | no sooner said than done |
| all work and no play | face the music | playing with fire |
| as luck would have it | familiar landmark | powers that be |
| at a loss for words | favor us with a selection | ripe old age |
| avoid it like the plague | festive occasion | sadder but wiser |
| beat a hasty retreat | few and far between | silence reigned supreme |
| better late than never | fine specimen of humanity | sweat of his brow |
| blissfully ignorant | goes without saying | tempest in a teapot |
| busy as a bee | grim reaper | tired but happy |
| by leaps and bounds | ignorance is bliss | troubled waters |
| caught like rats in a trap | in all its glory | untold wealth |
| clear as crystal | in the last analysis | vale of tears |
| clear as a bell | last but not least | venture a suggestion |
| conspicuously absent | left speechless | water over the dam |
| doomed to disappointment | method in his madness | wee small hours |
| drastic action | more than meets the eye | with a vengeance |
| dull, sickening thud | mother nature | with bated breath |
| dyed in the wool | needless to say | words fail to express |

✎ **EXERCISE A** Rewrite the following sentences. Replace common, uninteresting nouns, verbs, adjectives, or adverbs with brighter, livelier ones. If possible, substitute fresher expressions for any clichés you find, or otherwise eliminate them.

1. The little girl walked into the store to get the new pet she wanted.

   *The excited young lass skipped into the pet store hoping to find the cocker spaniel pup for which she had been longing.*

2.   The man put the cargo into the vehicle by the sweat of his brow.

_____

_____

3.   The official spoke several words of encouragement to the tired-but-happy hikers after their rescue.

_____

_____

4.   We always have a nice meal, with all the trimmings, on the holiday.

_____

_____

5.   The company had a good reputation for making fine products.

_____

_____

✎ **EXERCISE B** Write two sentences giving examples of each of the following figures of speech.

1.   **Simile**

_____

_____

_____

_____

2.   **Metaphor**

_____

_____

_____

_____

3.  **Hyperbole**

_____

_____

_____

_____

4.  **Personification**

_____

_____

_____

_____

✎ **EXERCISE C** Underline phrases which might be considered clichés in the following sentences. Then rewrite the sentences, avoiding the use of the clichés.

1.  The negotiators said they were <u>cautiously optimistic</u> that an agreement could be reached.

    *The negotiators said they believed they could reach an agreement, but certain* ____

    *obstacles remained.* _____

2.  I was startled when the telephone rang during the wee small hours of the morning.

    _____

    _____

3.  If you ignore your parents' instructions, you will likely have to face the music when they return.

    _____

    _____

4.  When we have all reached a ripe old age and face the grim reaper, we hope we will pass from this vale of tears to live blissfully in the great beyond.

    _____

    _____

5.  The powers that be in our school athletic department have chosen this year's new basketball team.

    _____

    _____

6.  The rock climbers returned to their base camp seemingly none the worse for wear.

    _____

    _____

# LESSON 51: PROPER WORD ARRANGEMENT

Unlike some other languages, English often depends on the *arrangement of words* in a sentence to convey the proper meaning. It is normally assumed that words placed near one another in a sentence are logically related. Writers must therefore be careful to place words, phrases, and clauses in a logical order that will meet readers' expectations. The general principle to follow is to place all modifiers as near to the words they modify as possible and to avoid placing them near words to which they are not properly related.

## ■ *Adverb Placement*

| Rule 10.14    Place adverbs logically in formal writing. |
| --- |

In formal writing, avoid making errors with the placement of such adverbs as *only, not, hardly, just, almost, nearly, merely,* and *scarcely.* Be sure to place the adverb as close as possible to the word it modifies to avoid confusing the meaning.

☞**COMMON IN SPEECH:**

She *only* sang one song.

Everyone is *not* happy with the test results.

Our team *hardly* made any touchdowns.

He *just* ate one cookie.

The rampaging river *almost* flooded the whole town.

☞**MORE LOGICAL: pinpoints which word is being modified by the adverb**

She sang *only* one song.

*Not* everyone is happy with the test results.

Our team made *hardly* any touchdowns.

He ate *just* one cookie.

The rampaging river flooded *almost* the whole town.

## ■ *Phrase Placement*

| Rule 10.15 | Avoid confusing placement of phrases. |
| --- | --- |

In some sentences, a certain phrase may appear related to any of several other words. Avoid placing such phrases near words to which they are not intended to relate.

☞**CONFUSING:**

He suspected what was wrong with the car *at the beginning of the trip.*

(Did he suspect at the beginning, or was there something wrong at the beginning?)

She had practiced and was ready and waiting to give her piano recital *for three hours.*

(Had she practiced for three hours, or was she ready and waiting for three hours? Or was the recital to last for three hours?)

☞**BETTER:**

He suspected *at the beginning of the trip* what was wrong with the car.

She had practiced *for three hours* and was ready and waiting to give her piano recital.

## ■ *Modifier Placement*

| Rule 10.16 | Avoid "dangling" and misplaced modifiers. |
| --- | --- |

*Dangling* modifiers are those which have no word in the sentence to logically modify. *Misplaced* modifiers are those which are placed in such a way as to make them appear to be modifying the wrong word. Dangling and misplaced constructions often produce silly or humorous results, but they should be avoided because they confuse meaning.

### Avoid dangling or misplaced participial phrases.

**DANGLING PARTICIPIAL PHRASE:**

*Walking through the fog,* the buildings could barely be seen.

**MISPLACED PARTICIPIAL PHRASE:**

*Walking through the fog,* the buildings could barely be seen by us.

**IMPROVED:**

Walking through the fog, we could barely see the buildings.

## Avoid dangling or misplaced gerundial and elliptical phrases.

**DANGLING GERUNDIAL & ELLIPTICAL PHRASES:**

*By turning on your lamp*, your eyes will not be strained while reading.

**MISPLACED GERUNDIAL PHRASE:**

*By turning on your lamp*, your eyes will not be strained while you are reading.

**IMPROVED:**

By turning on your lamp, you will not strain your eyes while reading.

## Avoid dangling infinitive phrases.

**DANGLING INFINITIVE PHRASE:**

*To achieve success in school,* homework must always be complete.

**IMPROVED:**

To achieve success in school, you must always complete your homework.

## Avoid misplaced adjective or adverb phrases.

**MISPLACED ADJECTIVE PHRASE:**

A truck was stopped along the road *with a flat tire.*

**MISPLACED ADVERB PHRASES:**

A truck was stopped *with a flat tire along the road.*

**IMPROVED:**

A truck with a flat tire was stopped along the road.

There are three ways to correct dangling phrases:

■ 1. **Change the phrase into a clause.**

■ 2. **Provide a noun or pronoun for the phrase to logically modify.**

■ 3. **Rewrite the sentence to avoid the possibility of misreading.**

# ■ *Participial Phrases*

Certain *participial phrases* may stand alone without a word to modify. Usually these phrases employ participles such as *concerning, considering, judging, providing, regarding,* or *speaking.*

☞**EXAMPLES:**

*Generally speaking,* Christians are law-abiding citizens.

*Considering the weather,* the picnic was a success.

*Regarding your proposal,* I believe we should have a meeting next week to iron out our differences.

*Judging from his attitude,* he should be regarded with some skepticism.

## ■ *Absolute Phrases*

*Absolute phrases* also stand alone without dangling. In an absolute phrase, the participle modifies a word within the phrase itself. (Refer back to the chart in Lesson 6.)

☞**EXAMPLES:**

> *All team members being assembled*, the afternoon practice session began.

> *The game being over*, the stadium was quickly emptied.

## ■ *Infinitive Phrases*

| | |
|---|---|
| Rule 10.17 | **In most cases keep the infinitive phrase together. "Split" an infinitive only to avoid awkwardness or ambiguity.** |

A split infinitive is one with other words placed between the signal word "to" and the infinitive verb.

☞**EXAMPLES:**

| | |
|---|---|
| UNNECESSARY: | I want *to* always *be* your friend. |
| AMBIGUOUS: | I want always *to be* your friend. |
| AWKWARD: | I want *to be* always your friend. |
| BETTER: | I want *to be* your friend always. |
| AMBIGUOUS: | She tried quietly *to leave* the room. |
| AWKWARD: | She tried *to leave* quietly the room. |
| ACCEPTABLE: | She tried *to* quietly *leave* the room. |
| BETTER: | She tried *to leave* the room quietly. |

## ■ *Clarity vs. Confusion*

| | |
|---|---|
| Rule 10.18 | **Avoid any unnecessary or awkward interruption of words that naturally belong together in a sentence.** |

☞**AWKWARD:**

> Jenny, after hearing about her friend's tragic accident, cried.

> "A rose by any other name would smell," she said, "as sweet."

> We finally found, after an hour of diligent searching, the keys.

☞ **BETTER:**

Jenny cried after hearing about her friend's tragic accident.

After hearing about her friend's tragic accident, Jenny cried.

"A rose by any other name would smell as sweet," she said.

We finally found the keys after an hour of diligent searching.

Finally, after an hour of diligent searching, we found the keys.

After an hour of diligent searching, we finally found the keys.

| | |
|---|---|
| Rule 10.19 | **Avoid the misplacement of any phrase, appositive, or expression that might make the sentence misleading, awkward, or confusing.** |

Correct the problem by repositioning the misplaced expression, changing phrases to clauses as needed, or supplying any words necessary to make the meaning clear and accurate.

☞ **POOR:**

In these examples, it is not clear what the phrase at the beginning of the sentence is referring to.

An excellent amateur writer, his works were read by many people.
*(Were his **works** an excellent amateur writer?)*

After living in New York, life in a small town was relaxing for her.
*(Did **life** live in New York?)*

While sitting on the park bench, an acorn fell into my lap.
*(Was the **acorn** sitting on the bench?)*

A former mayor of our city, the speech was given by Henry Yost.
*(Is the **speech** a former mayor?)*

☞ **BETTER:**

An excellent amateur writer, *he has produced works read by many people.*

After living in New York, *she found life in a small town relaxing.*

While *I was sitting on the park bench,* an acorn fell into my lap.

The speech was given by Henry Yost, *a former mayor of our city.*

---

✎ **EXERCISE** Rewrite the following sentences, correcting flaws in arrangement.

1. To get the full effect, the story should be read in one sitting.

   *To get the full effect, you should read the story in one sitting.*

2.  One of the classical period's most beloved composers, the symphony was by Mozart.

    _____

    _____

3.  While watching television last evening, the telephone rang six times.

    _____

    _____

4.  A famous artist of the time, the pope commissioned a work by the painter Raphael.

    _____

    _____

5.  I only needed one new battery, not two.

    _____

6.  She put the food into the refrigerator which the guests had not eaten.

    _____

    _____

7.  The boy who entered the classroom quietly opened his books.

    _____

    _____

8.  He just saw one hawk during his outing.

    _____

    _____

9.  I put the money into my pocket that I intended to use for your gift.

    _____

    _____

10. Having soaked into the carpet, I had difficulty removing the ink.

   _____

   _____


11. It is honoring to God to even pray for the smallest need.

   _____

   _____


12. We want to first consider the cost.

   _____


13. President Lincoln, after being carried from Ford's Theater to a boarding house across the street where he rested until the next day, died.

   _____

   _____


14. To get a good photograph, enough light must be shining on the subject.

   _____

   _____


15. It only takes a spark to get a fire going.

   _____


16. While walking to school yesterday, a startling event took me by surprise.

   _____

   _____

# LESSON 52: SHIFTS IN POINT OF VIEW

Your writing will be more effective and pleasing to the reader if you avoid various unnecessary shifts in the point of view of your composition. Try to maintain a consistent point of view unless there is a good reason to change it.

| Rule 10.20 | **Avoid unnecessary shifts between active and passive in the voice of verbs.** |
|---|---|

☞**POOR:**

His family *cared* about his health and well-being, so his doctor bills *were paid* by them. **(active shifts to passive)**

We first *placed* the Christmas tree into its stand, and then it *was decorated.* **(active shifts to passive)**

☞**BETTER:**

His family *cared* about his health and well-being, so they *paid* his doctor bills. **(both clauses are active)**

We first *placed* the Christmas tree into its stand, and then we *decorated* it.

☞**ACCEPTABLE SHIFT:**

The motorcade *was escorted* by four policemen who *traveled* on motorcycles before and behind it.

| Rule 10.21 | **Avoid unnecessary shifts in verb tense.** |
|---|---|

☞**POOR:**

He *goes* right up to the man and *introduced* himself. **(present shifts to past)**

I *watched* the fight to see what *will happen* next **(past shifts to future)**

After *suggesting* the idea, she *did* not *expect* anyone to accept it. **(present shifts to past)**

☞**BETTER:**

He *went* right up to the man and *introduced* himself. **(both past)**

I *watched* the fight to see what *might happen* next. **(both past)**

*Having suggested* the idea, she *did* not expect anyone to accept it. **(both past)**

☞**ACCEPTABLE SHIFT:**

God *has* always *helped* me before, and He *will help* me again—of this I am sure.

| Rule 10.22 | Avoid unnecessary shifts in person. |

☞**POOR:**

If *one* wishes to avoid illness, try to eat healthy food. **(3rd person shifts to 2nd)**

*No one* knew what he would do next; *you* would have been surprised if I had told *you*.

*One* would suppose this test to be difficult, so *you* should study the subject matter well.

☞**BETTER:**

If *you* wish to avoid illness, try to eat healthy food. **(2nd person)**

If *one* wishes to avoid illness, *he (or she)* should try to eat healthy food. **(3rd person)**

*No one* knew what he would do next; *they* would have been surprised if I had told *them*. **(3rd person)**

*One* would suppose this test to be difficult, so *one* should study the subject matter well.

☞**ACCEPTABLE SHIFT:**

*We* do not know who did it, and *you* probably do not know either.

| Rule 10.23 | Avoid "mixed constructions." |

A *"mixed construction"* is an arrangement which places two distinctly different grammatical constructions into one sentence. Mixed constructions usually result when a writer starts a sentence in one grammatical vein and ends it in another grammatical vein without checking to see if the sentence parts flow logically together.

☞**MIXED:**

In my opinion, this is a good car which I have been trying to tell you.

He explained the idea in what seemed to me somewhat vaguely.

He was unqualified was the reason he was not hired.

☞**FIXED:**

In my opinion, this is a good car, as I have been trying to tell you.

He explained the idea in what seemed to me to be somewhat vague terms.

He was unqualified, and that was the reason he was not hired.

---

| **Rule 10.24** | **Avoid mixed metaphors.** |
|---|---|

One form of mixed expression is the so-called *mixed metaphor*. This writing flaw involves putting incompatible figures of speech together.

☞**MIXED:**

He turned a deaf ear to his victim's thirst for mercy.

Their teacher tried to water the small spark of interest the students were finally showing.

The politician sought vainly to ride out the waves of the firestorm which his remarks ignited.

☞**FIXED:**

He turned a deaf ear to his victim's cries for mercy.

Their teacher tried to fan the small spark of interest the students were finally showing.

The politician sought vainly to shield himself against the firestorm which his remarks ignited.

---

✎ **EXERCISE** Rewrite the following confused sentences, correcting unnecessary shifts in point of view.

1.  You can approach this problem as an obstacle or as a person seeking opportunities.

    _____*You can approach this problem as an obstacle or as an opportunity.*_____

2.  My fellow committee members held a meeting which they forget to ask me to come.

    _____

    _____

3.  Vermeer's paintings are infused with light and objects of admiration for many generations.

    _____

    _____

4.  His fans loved his music that he was the best guitarist they had ever heard.

    _____

    _____

5.  They advocated a thoroughly Christian education which everyone should have an opportunity despite the cost.

    _____

    _____

6.  He walked the little traveled path of individuality through a sea of conformity.

    _____

    _____

7.  He comes to me and said he will be happy to help.

    _____

    _____

8.  One should be aware of their own abilities and limitations.

    _____

    _____

9.  John Kennedy's war record is well known, but we remember his assassination better.

    _____

    _____

10. The fishermen first pack their catch in ice; it is then shipped to market.

    _____

    _____

11. Before entering the race, he had thought he will win easily.

    _____

    _____

12. Before a person says something in anger, you should count to ten.

_____

_____

13. The future of our company's sales record was clearly in a slump.

_____

_____

14. He hovered at death's door.

_____

_____

# LESSON 53: UNIT REVIEW

It is now time to put into practice what you have learned about writing. Choose a subject of interest to you and write a paragraph of approximately 150-200 words (the number of words is not as important as *how well* you do) for each of the following exercises. Use separate sheets of paper for your first draft and your final version for each paragraph.

After you select well-focused subjects and before you start writing, consider which type of writing will best communicate your ideas: **story telling** *(narrative)*; **explaining how** *(expository)*; **describing or "painting a picture"** *(descriptive)*; or **influencing, reasoning, or giving opinions** *(argumentative)*. Consider which facts, quotations, examples, illustrations, arguments, or other supporting information you will need for each of these types of writing. Of course, compositions will sometimes be a combination of these approaches; but your subjects will likely require you to take one main approach.

After writing your first draft for each exercise, read it over with the following concepts in mind:

## ■ *Meaning*

Have you carefully chosen precise and appropriate words and phrases? Are your main ideas clearly stated in the topic sentence? Is the meaning made clear with appropriate details in the body of the paragraph? Is there logical order in the presentation of your ideas?

## ■ *Sentence structure*

Is there variety or are all of your sentences pretty much alike? Are your sentences grammatically correct? Have you used transitional devices to create unity, progress, and smoothness?

# ■ *Mechanics*

Is your punctuation correct? Have you spelled your words correctly? Did you capitalize the first word of every sentence? Do verbs and subjects agree? Do pronouns have antecedents and do they agree? Are modifiers used and placed correctly?

After writing and reviewing your first draft for each exercise, make corrections and write a second version. Keep reviewing and rewriting until you are satisfied that your paragraph is as good as it can be. It will be acceptable when it is *correct, clear, effective,* and *appropriate.*

✎ **EXERCISE A** Write a 150-word paragraph on one of the following topics. The topics are broad; you may wish to narrow your chosen topic to a specific aspect of the subject.

| | | |
|---|---|---|
| 1. Christian Friendship | 5. Patriotism | 9. Freedom from sin |
| 2. Contentment | 6. Tithing | 10. Faith in Christ |
| 3. Courage | 7. Gratitude | 11. The Christian home |
| 4. Facing Death | 8. Sportsmanship | 12. Physical handicaps |

✎ **EXERCISE B** Write a 200-word paragraph on one of the following topics or a subject of your own choice. Since these topics are also broad, you should narrow your chosen topic to a specific aspect of the subject.

| | |
|---|---|
| 1.  The Bible and Politics | 11.  The Protestant Reformation |
| 2.  The Goal of Christian Education | 12.  Francis Schaeffer and L'Abri Fellowship |
| 3.  The Great Awakening | 13.  Charles Dickens |
| 4.  Wisdom in the Bible | 14.  Puritanism in New England |
| 5.  Creation versus Evolution | 15.  The Internet and homeschooling |
| 6.  Art and the Bible | 16.  The Work of a Missionary |
| 7.  The Idols of Secular Humanism | 17.  The Gold Standard |
| 8.  The Huguenots | 18.  Patrick Henry and Liberty |
| 9.  The Sabbath | 19.  Albrecht Dürer the Artist |
| 10. King Charlemagne | 20.  Handel's *Messiah* |

# Glossary

**Absolutes**
Adjectives and adverbs that are logically incapable of comparison because their meanings are absolute. Such words include: *unique, perfect, perpendicular, horizontal, parallel, excellent, accurate, absolute, round, square, final, fatal, impossible, correct, current, normal, original, average.* Comparison may be achieved only by the addition of qualifying adverbs, such as *nearly, more/most nearly, almost.*

**Active voice**
The form of an action verb which tells that the subject is the doer of the action.

EXAMPLE:

George *mowed* his lawn.

**Adjective**
A part of speech that modifies or limits the meaning of a noun or pronoun. They usually answer one of the following questions about the noun or pronoun they modify: *which one? what kind? how much? how many?* Simple adjectives are generally located immediately before the word they modify. Predicate adjectives are usually located after a linking verb and modify the subject of that verb.

EXAMPLES:

the *happy* people (simple adjective)

The eggs are *rotten.* (predicate adjective)

**Adjective clause**
A dependent clause used to modify a noun or pronoun.

EXAMPLE:

The car *which you rented* must be returned tomorrow.

**Adverb**
A part of speech that modifies a verb, adjective, or another adverb. Adverbs used as transitional devices in sentences may modify the entire thought of the sentence.

EXAMPLE:

We are, *however,* planning to visit you shortly.

**Adverb (adverbial) clause**
A dependent clause that modifies a verb, adjective, or adverb.

EXAMPLES:

Mary quit her job *because she preferred her role as a mother.* (Modifies verb)

The test was harder *than most others were.* (Modifies adjective)

I think more sharply *after a good night's rest.* (Modifies adverb)

**Agreement**
Sameness in number, gender, and person. Agreement in number is required between a subject and predicate. Pronouns must agree with their antecedents in person, number, and gender.

**Antecedent**
The substantive (noun or pronoun) to which a pronoun refers.

**Antonyms**
Pairs of words that have the opposite or negative meanings.

**Appositive**
A noun or noun clause added to (usually following) another noun or pronoun to further identify or explain it. The appositive signifies the same thing as the noun or pronoun it seeks to identify or explain.

EXAMPLES:

One economic system, *socialism,* is a proven failure. A basic socialist premise, *that all people deserve an equal share of the world's material substance,* is a false assumption.

**Auxiliary verb**
Also called a **helping verb.** A verb used to "help" another verb in forming voices, tenses, and other grammatical ideas. The most common are forms of *be, have, do, can, could, may, might, shall, should, will, would, must, ought, let, dare, need,* and *used.*

**Case**
The forms that nouns or pronouns have (nominative, objective, possessive) signifying their relationship to other words in a sentence.

EXAMPLES:

The *car* was new. (Nominative)

The subject of the *speech* was crime. (Objective)

The *children's* story hour was always popular. (Possessive)

**Clause**
A group of words including a subject and a predicate and forming a part of a sentence. All words in a sentence must be part of a clause. Clauses are classified as to their *use* (adjective, adverb, noun), their *character* (dependent, independent, elliptical), and their *necessity* (essential [restrictive], non-essential [non-restrictive]).

## Comparative degree

The form of an adjective or adverb used when comparing two entities. The comparative form is created by adding -er to one-syllable and some two-syllable adjectives and adverbs or by preceding adjectives and adverbs of two or more syllables with the word *more*.

EXAMPLES:

That painting is *prettier* than the other one.

Robert seems to learn *more easily* than Sally. *(See also Absolutes.)*

## Comparison, degrees of

A change in the form of adjectives and adverbs signifying greater or smaller degrees of quantity, quality, or manner. The three degrees of comparison are: *positive, comparative,* and *superlative.*

EXAMPLES:

*small, smaller, smallest; beautiful, more beautiful, most beautiful.*

## Complement

A word or expression used to *complete* the action or idea indicated by a verb. Predicate *complements* include predicate nominatives (noun or pronoun) and predicate adjectives following linking verbs and describing, identifying, or modifying the subject.

## Complex sentence

A sentence consisting of one independent clause and one or more dependent clauses.

EXAMPLE:

When Jesus came, He preached a message of salvation to all who would believe.

## Compound sentence

A sentence consisting of two or more independent clauses.

EXAMPLE:

The battle was won, but the war was lost.

## Compound-complex sentence

A sentence consisting of two or more independent clauses and one or more dependent clauses.

EXAMPLE:

Since Mike was artistic, he designed the brochure; but Jennifer, who was a better writer, wrote the text.

## Compound pronoun

A pronoun with the suffix -self. There are two types: reflexive and intensive. (See entries for *reflexive pronoun* and *intensive pronoun*.)

## Conjugation

Changes in the form and use of a verb to signify *tense, voice, number, person,* and *mood.*

## Conjunction

A part of speech used to connect words or groups of words such as phrases and clauses. Conjunctions are classified as *coordinating* when they link equal elements or *subordinating* when they link unequal elements.

EXAMPLES:

I like apples *and* bananas. (Coordinating conjunction linking two direct objects)

My hair is brown, *whereas* Mary's is blonde. (Subordinating conjunction linking an independent clause with a dependent clause)

(See also *Conjunctive adverb*.)

## Conjunctive adverb

An adverb used as a coordinating conjunction connecting two independent clauses.

EXAMPLE:

The picnic was cancelled; *nevertheless,* we had a pleasant afternoon in the park.

## Coordinating conjunction

A conjunction linking words, phrases, or clauses of equal grammatical rank, importance, or value.

EXAMPLE:

Do your duty, *or* turn in your badge.

## Correlative conjunction

Coordinating conjunctions used in pairs. Each member of the pair must be followed by words of equal grammatical value. The most common are: *either...or, neither...nor, both...and,* and *not only...but also.*

EXAMPLE:

*Neither* my grandfather *nor* my grandmother was born in America.

## Declarative sentence

A sentence that states a fact, possibility, or condition.

## Demonstrative pronoun

A pronoun pointing to, pointing out, identifying, or calling attention to: *this, that, these, those, such.*

## Dependent (or subordinate) clause

A clause that does not express a complete thought in itself but which depends for its full meaning upon an independent clause in the same sentence. The three use-related classifications of dependent clauses are: *adjective, adverb,* and *noun.*

## Direct quotation

Stating the exact words (all or part) of a writer or speaker.

## Exclamatory sentence

A sentence or sentence fragment expressing strong feeling or surprise.

**Future perfect tense**
The time of a verb's action beginning in the present and reaching completion sometime in the future.

EXAMPLE:

He *will have finished* his work by this time tomorrow.

**Future tense**
The time of a verb expressing action or state of being after the present time.

EXAMPLE:

She *will be* ten years old next Tuesday.

**Gender**
The classification of nouns or pronouns indicating sex: *masculine, feminine, neuter,* or *common.*

**Gerund**
A verb form used as a *noun.* Like nouns, gerunds can be used as *subjects, direct objects, objects of prepositions, predicate nominatives,* and *appositives.* The gerund ends in *-ing* most often. Sometimes gerunds end with *-ed.*

EXAMPLES:

*Walking* is now a popular sport.
(Gerund used as a subject)

She enjoys *teaching.*
(Gerund used as a direct object)

Wisdom comes from *meditating* on God's Word.

(Gerund used as an object of a preposition)

Their greatest battle involved *fighting* Satan with the Word of God.
(Gerund used as a predicate nominative)

Her struggle, *overcoming* fear, ended when she claimed God's promises.
(Gerund used as an appositive)

Jesus healed the *cripped.*
(Past gerund used as a direct object)

**Homographs**
Two or more words that are spelled alike but which have different meanings and may have different pronunciations.

**Homonyms**
Pairs of words that sound alike but are spelled differently and have different meanings.

**Imperative sentence**
A sentence expressing a command or declaring a request.

**Indefinite pronoun**
A pronoun with an implied antecedent but referring to no specific person, place, or thing: *one, someone, everyone, somebody, everybody, each, none, no one, nobody, everything, nothing,* etc.

**Independent clause**
A clause that expresses a complete thought in its context and could, if necessary, stand alone as a complete sentence.

EXAMPLE:

If she is chosen next Friday night, *Kim will be the first Chinese homecoming queen in the school's history.*

**Indirect object**
A noun or pronoun preceding a direct object of a verb and indicating a recipient of the object of the verb. An indirect object usually could have the prepositions *to* or *for* placed before them.

EXAMPLE:

I sent *Mother* a birthday card. (I sent (to) *Mother* a birthday card.)

**Infinitive**
A verb form which is the first principal part of a verb, equivalent to the first person present tense. The infinitive has the function of a verb (as part of the predicate) but is also a verbal or in a verbal phrase, commonly used as a noun, adjective, or adverb. As a verbal it is preceded by an introductory *to,* either expressed or implied. The infinitive may also serve as the predicate of an infinitive "clause."

**Intensive pronoun**
A pronoun ending with *-self,* usually non-essential to the sentence but added for emphasis or intensification of its antecedent.

EXAMPLE:

I will make the announcement *myself.*

**Interjection**
An exclamatory word expressing strong feeling or surprise and having little or no grammatical connection with other words in a sentence.

EXAMPLES:

*Ouch!* That hurts. *Oh,* what a lovely day!

**Interrogative pronoun**
A pronoun used in a question: *who, which, what, whoever, whatever.*

**Interrogative sentence**
A sentence asking a question. A question mark is used as its closing punctuation.

**Irregular verb**
A verb whose past and past participle forms are different in spelling from the present (infinitive) form and do not follow the regular pattern of having the last two principal parts formed by the addition of the letters *-d, -t,* or *-ed.*

EXAMPLES:

*see, seeing, saw, seen; drive, driving, drove, driven; lose, losing, lost, lost; set, setting, set, set.*

## Linking verb

A non-action verb that expresses a state of being or fixed condition. It "links" a subject to a noun or adjective (or equivalent phrase or clause) in the predicate. The most common linking verbs are forms of *be, look, seem, appear, feel, smell, sound, become, grow, remain, stand, turn, prove.*

EXAMPLES:

She *is* small. His theory *proved* correct. You *look* better today. That dog *smells* bad. The Word of the Lord *stands* secure.

## Modify (Modifier)

To describe or limit. Adjectives and adverbs *modify* other words.

EXAMPLES:

sang *happily* (describes); the *only* child (limits).

## Nominative case

The *case* of nouns or pronouns used as subjects or predicate complements.

EXAMPLE:

*He* is Lord. This is *he.*

## Non-restrictive or non-essential

A modifier, usually a phrase or clause, that does not limit but describes or adds information.

## Noun

A part of speech that names a person, place, thing, idea, action, or quality.

EXAMPLES:

*John, sky, table, capitalism, eating, ugliness.*

## Number

The form of a noun or pronoun showing whether one or more than one is indicated. Nouns and pronouns are either *singular* (one) in number or *plural* (two or more) in number. Verbs have singular or plural forms corresponding to the number of the nouns or pronouns that perform their action or state of being.

EXAMPLES:

The *boy sings.* (Singular noun and verb)

The *children sing.* (Plural noun and verb)

## Object

The noun, pronoun, or noun clause following a transitive verb or preposition.

EXAMPLES:

Larry ate the *cake.*
(Noun as object of a transitive verb)

Put the cake on the *table.*
(Noun as object of a preposition)

She gave him *what he wanted.*
(Noun clause as object of a transitive verb)

## Objective case

The *case* of nouns or pronouns used as objects of prepositions or as direct or indirect objects of verbs.

EXAMPLE:

I gave *him* some advice. Tell your problems to *me.* She loves *us* very much.

## Participle

A verb form functioning either as a verb in a predicate or as an adjective. Participles have three forms: *present participle, past participle,* and *perfect participle.*

EXAMPLES:

I am *enjoying* my lunch.
(Present participle in a predicate)

I have *finished* my lunch.
(Past participle in a predicate)

A *steaming* bowl of soup would make a good lunch.
(Present participle as adjective)

*Having finished* my lunch, I returned to work.
(Perfect participle used as adjective)

## Part of speech

A classification for every word in a language. In English, the primary parts of speech are: *noun, pronoun, adjective, verb, adverb, preposition, conjunction,* and *interjection.*

## Passive voice

The form of a verb telling that the subject is not the doer of the action but the entity which is acted upon.

EXAMPLE:

The song *was performed* by the choir.

## Past participle

The fourth principal part of a verb used as part of a predicate or an adjective.

EXAMPLE:

I have *eaten* my breakfast. (Fourth form of the verb *eat, eating, ate, eaten*)

## Past perfect tense

The time of a verb beginning at a point in the past and ending at a later point in the past.

EXAMPLE:

She *had said* the same thing before.

## Past tense

The time of a verb before now. The third principal part of a verb.

EXAMPLE:

She *baked* a cake.

(Third form of the verb: *bake, baking, baked,* [have/had] *baked*)

### Perfect infinitive
Formed by the auxiliary *to have* and the past participle.

EXAMPLE:

*to have loved.*

### Perfect participle
Formed by the auxiliary *having* and the past participle.

EXAMPLE:

having loved

### Person
The form of a pronoun (and corresponding form of a verb) indicating whether the "person" or "thing" represented by the pronoun is the one speaking or writing (*first person*: I/we worship), the one spoken or written to (*second person*: you worship), or one spoken or written about (*third person*: he/she/it/they worship).

### Personal pronoun
A pronoun referring to the speaker or writer, the person spoken or written to, or the person spoken or written about.

EXAMPLES:

I, you, he, she, it, we, they, me,
him, her, she, us, them

### Phrase
A group of related words not containing a subject and predicate.

EXAMPLE:

The sound *of the old church bell* brought back many memories.

### Plural
The classification of nouns, pronouns, subjects, and predicates indicating a number of two or more.

EXAMPLES:

*cows, they,*
The *animals graze.*

### Positive degree
The simple form of an adjective or adverb expressing no comparison.

EXAMPLES:

The *blue* sky. The *old* woman. The *beautiful* words of the psalm.

### Predicate
The verb or verb phrase in a sentence that makes a statement about the subject. A *simple predicate* is the verb or verb phrase alone. A *complete predicate* is the verb or verb phrase plus its object(s), indirect object(s), and all of their modifiers. A *compound predicate* consists of two or more verbs or verb phrases in a single sentence.

EXAMPLES:

She *wrote the letter yesterday.*
(*Wrote* is the simple predicate. *Wrote the letter yesterday* is the complete predicate.)
She *sealed* the envelope and *stamped* it.
(Compound predicate)

### Predicate adjective
An adjective placed in a predicate after a linking verb and used to modify the subject of a sentence or clause.

EXAMPLES:

Children are *happiest* when they know that they are *loved.*

### Predicate nominative
A noun, pronoun or equivalent clause used in a predicate after a linking verb to identify the subject.

EXAMPLES:

God is our *Father.* This is not *what it seems to be.*

### Preposition
A part of speech "positioned before" a noun or pronoun showing the relationship of that noun or pronoun (object) to some other word in the sentence.

EXAMPLES:

*at* school, *under* the couch, *behind* the house, *across* the ocean

### Prepositional phrase
A preposition plus its object and related words. The preposition usually precedes, but sometimes follows, its object in the phrase.

EXAMPLES:

They crawled {*through the dark and damp tunnel*} {*to the other side*} {*of the cave*}.
*What* is the world coming to?

### Present participle
The second principal part of a verb. The present participle is the *-ing* form of a verb and is used as part of a predicate or as an adjective.

EXAMPLES:

He is *working* at a local factory.
(Part of predicate)
This is the *working* part of the engine.
(Adjective)

### Present perfect tense
The time of a verb beginning in the past and ending just now or still in progress in the present.

EXAMPLE:

I *have been studying* all morning.

### Present tense
The time of a verb showing action or state of being now.

EXAMPLE:

God *loves* me.

### Principal parts

The four primary forms of verbs — *present (infinitive), present participle, past, past participle* — from which all other forms and uses (tense, mood, tone, voice) of verbs are created.

EXAMPLES:

*(to) love, loving, loved, (have/had) loved; (to) burst, bursting, burst, (have/had) burst; (to) swim, swimming, swam, (have/had) swum.*

(See also *Irregular verbs* and *Regular verbs*.)

### Progressive (tense) tone

A verb form, sometimes referred to as *progressive tense* and sometimes referred to as *progressive tone*, expressing on-going action or state of being. The progressive tense or tone consists of an appropriate form of the auxiliary verb *to be* plus the present participle.

EXAMPLES:

Jody *is going* to the store. Bill *was playing* golf this morning.

Darlene *will be helping* her mother clean the house.

### Pronoun

A part of speech used to replace a noun, often to prevent undue repetition of a noun.

Pronouns include:
*I, me, you, he, him, she, her, it, they, them, who, whom, which, that, etc.*

Pronouns are classified as:
*personal* (he),
*relative* (which),
*reflexive* (she gave *herself*),
*interrogative* (Who?),
*demonstrative* (these),
*intensive* (he *himself*),
*indefinite* (all),
*reciprocal* (each other)

### Reciprocal pronoun

A pronoun indicating interchange. English has only two: *each other* (interchange between two) and *one another* (interchange among more than two).

### Reflexive pronoun

A pronoun ending in *-self* and referring back to the subject. It usually comes after the verb and is essential to the meaning of the sentence.

EXAMPLE:

She told *herself* not to be afraid.

### Regular verb

The most common type of verb in English, which forms its past and past participle forms by adding *-d, -t,* or *-ed* to the present form.

EXAMPLES:

move, moved, (have/had) moved; mean, meant, (have/had) meant;

laugh, laughed, (have/had) laughed

### Relative pronoun

A pronoun connecting or *relating* an adjective clause to its antecedent. They include *who, whom, which,* and *that*.

### Restrictive or essential

A modifier, usually a phrase or clause, that limits or identifies the word modified.

### Simple sentence

A sentence containing one subject (simple or compound) and one predicate (simple or compound); tantamount to one independent clause.

EXAMPLES:

The weather was ideal for working outdoors.
(One simple subject and one simple predicate)

Rock music is loved by some people but hated by others.
(One simple subject and one compound predicate)

### Singular

The number classification of nouns, pronouns, verbs, subjects, and predicates indicating a quantity of *one*.

EXAMPLES:

a *girl*, the *cowboy*, a *truck*
One *game* of tennis *makes* me tired.

### Subject

The noun, pronoun, noun phrase, or noun clause about which a sentence or clause makes a statement. A *simple subject* is the noun or pronoun alone. A *complete subject* consists of a simple subject and all its modifiers. A *compound subject* consists of two or more subjects in a single sentence.

EXAMPLE:

The *president* of the United States spoke on television. (Simple subject)

*The president of the United States* spoke on television. (Complete subject)

*George Washington* and *Abraham Lincoln* are two well-known presidents. (Compound subject)

### Subordinating conjunction

A conjunction connecting a dependent clause to an independent clause.

EXAMPLES:

*because, that, since, if, although*
I have been lonely *since* you left.

## Superlative degree

The form of an adjective or adverb comparing three or more entities. It is formed by adding *-est* to one-syllable and some two-syllable adjectives or adverbs, or by preceding an adjective or adverb of two or more syllables with the word *most*.

EXAMPLES:

*sharpest, loudest, heaviest, most peculiar, most unpredictable.*

## Synonyms

Words that have the same or similar meanings.

## Tense

The time of action or state of being expressed in a verb: *present, past, future* (simple tenses), *present perfect, past perfect, future perfect* (perfect tenses). The *progressive* form of a verb is sometimes called a *tense* and sometimes a *tone* within some of the other six primary tenses.

## Tone

A characteristic of verb tenses indicating *progress, emphasis,* or *simple* time.

EXAMPLES:

*am eating* (progressive tone), *did eat* (emphatic tone), *eat* (simple tone)

## Topic sentence

A sentence which expresses the central idea in a paragraph.

## Transitional sentence

A sentence which serves as a link between one paragraph and another. It connects what has already been expressed with what will follow.

## Verb

A part of speech expressing *action* or *state of being*, or *helping* another verb complete its meaning.

EXAMPLES:

*construct* (action verb), *is* (state of being or linking verb), *have* built (helping verb)

## Verb phrase

A group of words consisting of a verb and its helpers.

EXAMPLES:

has spoken, did speak, will have been spoken

## Verbal

A verb form used as another part of speech: *participles, gerunds,* and *infinitives.*

## Voice

The form or use of a transitive verb indicating whether its subject is the doer (*active* voice) or receiver (*passive* voice) of the verb's action.

EXAMPLES:

The buck *stops* here.
(Active voice)

The book *was written* in the 19th century.
(Passive voice)

# *Index*